THAI POLITICS IN TRANSLATION

NIAS – Nordic Institute of Asian Studies

ASIA INSIGHTS

A series aimed at increasing an understanding of contemporary Asia among policymakers, NGOs, businesses, journalists and other members of the general public as well as scholars and students.

NIAS Press is the autonomous publishing arm of the Nordic Institute of Asian Studies (NIAS), a research institute located at the University of Copenhagen. NIAS is partially funded by the governments of Denmark, Finland, Iceland, Norway and Sweden via the Nordic Council of Ministers, and works to encourage and support Asian studies in the Nordic countries. In so doing, NIAS has been publishing books since 1969, with more than two hundred titles produced in the past few years.

UNIVERSITY OF COPENHAGEN

Nordic Council of Ministers

THAI POLITICS IN TRANSLATION

Monarchy, Democracy and the Supra-constitution

Edited by

Michael K. Connors

&

Ukrist Pathmanand

 niasPRESS

Thai Politics in Translation
Monarchy, Democracy and the Supra-constitution
Edited by Michael K. Connors and Ukrist Pathmanand

Nordic Institute of Asian Studies
NIAS Asian Insights, no. 10

First published in 2021 by NIAS Press
NIAS – Nordic Institute of Asian Studies
Øster Farimagsgade 5, 1353 Copenhagen K, Denmark
Tel: +45 3532 9503 • Fax: +45 3532 9549
E-mail: books@nias.ku.dk • Online: www. niaspress. dk

A CIP catalogue record for this book is available from the British Library

ISBN: 978-87-7694-284-7 (Hbk)
ISBN: 978-87-7694-285-4 (Pbk)
ISBN: 978-87-7694-720-0 (Epub)

Typeset in 11.5 pt Arno Pro by Don Wagner
Printed and bound in Thailand
Cover design: NIAS Press

Cover illustration: Old parliament compound and Ananda
throne hall, the adjacent plaque commemorating constitutionalism from a royalist perspective (photo: Duncan McCargo)

Contents

Acknowledgements and Translation Note

We must begin with our gratitude to the authors of the original works contained in this volume. We were fortunate to conduct interviews with several of them. The authors, mostly, wrote these pieces under different political circumstances and when they were younger. Their later works may not reflect the positions presented here. Even so, they generously granted permission to translate or reproduce them. We could not interview the late political scientist (*nakratthasat*) Professor Kramol Thongthammachart, who was ill when the project commenced and passed away before its completion. Kramol was an influential thinker among peers and national policymakers. We hope his inclusion in this volume might spark greater interest in the ideological work he and other *nakratthasat* (literally, scientists of the state) undertook in the name of state and nation-building from the 1970s onwards.

We must also thank the translation team, which wishes to remain anonymous. The editors commissioned the translations and worked through the first drafts to produce the penultimate draft. The translation lead checked the final versions, which were then subject to final editing. Translation necessarily involves cuts to redundancies, repetition, or curious tangents that seem incidental to a work's gist. Sometimes we mark cuts by an ellipsis. And as every translator knows, there are times when a choice simply must be made that seems right, but only just. A creative approach to syntax – putting intended meaning ahead of the formal equivalence of word choice or structure – marks this translation. We shared the translations with as many of the original authors as possible; they provided valuable and supportive feedback.

On the transliteration of names, words or phrases, we have followed conventional usage for regularly used names or words. In some cases, such transliterations will appear archaic. We also found spelling variations in the Thai sources, and transliterations will reflect this. In several of the chapters, royally conferred names are used. If these are not well known and the author does not provide the conventional name, we do so parenthetically. In the Footnotes and the Bibliography, names appear in romanised script with the title of the work provided in Thai script followed by an English translation. Chapter 6 originally appeared in English and its original transliterations remain, creating some inconsistencies with usage in other chapters. One particular and critical Thai noun *kharachakan* has been translated variously in the chapters that follow for ease of prose and variation. Perhaps best translated as 'crown servant', the Thai word *kharachakan* covers all so designated employees of the state, regardless of service or sector. For example, civil servants are *kharachakanphonlaruen,* while military personnel are *kharachakanthahan.* We may refer to state bureaucracy (*rabobkharachakan*) or state officials (*kharachakan*) when the service sector is not specified in the text. In legislation, elected politicians who serve as ministers are also political crown servants (*kharachakankanmueang*). Still, conventional usage when referring to the state bureaucracy as a corporate class does not typically extend to such politicians despite their formal status.

Financial support for this project is gratefully acknowledged. The Institute of Asian Studies at Chulalongkorn University provided support for the first round of translations. The Department of International Studies at Xi'an Jiaotong-Liverpool University (XJTLU) funded the final translation check. Monash University Malaysia supported indexing costs.

Finally, we would like to thank the NIAS Press team for taking on this project and seeing it through despite difficult circumstances. In particular, we thank Gerald Jackson, whose cheery prods and encouragement kept the project going, and Leena Höskuldsson and David Stuligross for careful editing and suggestions. Anonymous peer reviewers helped us rethink the introduction and context chapter.

Translation opens up conversations on better terms. In appreciation of that possibility, we dedicate this work to the frontline translation team of this volume.

Introduction: Debating the Bhumibol Era

Michael K. Connors and Ukrist Pathmanand

Since a movement arose in 2005 to overthrow Thaksin Shinawatra, the populist Thai prime minister from 2001 to 2006, the Thai peoples have struggled through a prolonged and debilitating crisis that continues into the present. For over a decade, Thai politics has regularly catapulted to the front of global news bulletins. Incredulous audiences watched as tanks rolled onto the streets of Bangkok to consolidate the 2006 coup that deposed Thaksin. They marvelled at the almost decade long drama of tit-for-tat protest encampments in the middle of Bangkok occupied by yellow-shirted anti-Thaksin and red-shirted pro-Thaksin forces. In April and May 2014, opposing camps faced off across Bangkok when the Constitutional Court removed Prime Minister Yingluck Shinawatra from office. Then, in late May, the military launched a coup that aimed at decisively ending the Thaksin legacy. The coup group and their civilian backers launched a programme of extensive repression. Under these conditions, a new constitution was drafted and finally promulgated in 2017. It explicitly mandated a statist authoritarian political system that included enhanced royal prerogatives for the king and, for a five year transition period, a senate handpicked by the military.[1] Under the constitution's provisions the 2014 coup leader, General Prayuth Chan-ocha, continued as prime minister after highly controlled elections in 2019.

---

1   King Vajiralongkorn returned the draft constitution to the government with several key changes, including to Article 16. He is now able to live abroad without appointing a regent. His change to Article 5 removed reference to the formation of a crisis management council and instead re-inserted a clause from the 1997 and 2007 constitutions: 'Whenever no provision under this Constitution is applicable to any case, it shall be decided in accordance with the constitutional convention in the democratic regime of government with the King as Head of the State.' This clause is open to an interpretation that gives the king great prerogative. See Mongkol Bangprapa, 'Six Changes in the Constitution', *Bangkok Post*, 6 April 2017.

As we write in 2020, the crisis has transformed. A new generation of students and activists have joined an older cadre, calling for a democratic constitution. Most remarkably, some elements of that movement now explicitly criticise the economic and political aspects of the monarchy. Activists issued a ten-point manifesto for reform of the monarchy at mass rallies attended by tens of thousands of idealistic youths. Some of the protestors' adolescence had coincided with rising criticism of the monarchy on dissident social media sites since the coup of 2014. They have now taken that criticism onto the streets of Bangkok and elsewhere. Unencumbered by old habits and dispositions, they have challenged the monarchy's image, national purpose, and alignment with democracy. The manifesto's conclusion calls for a symbolic constitutional monarchy within a democracy:

> These demands are not a proposal to topple the monarchy. They are a good-faith proposal made for the monarchy to be able to continue to be esteemed by the people within a democracy.
>
> Therefore, for the monarchy to be secure in the present-day world, it must not hold power related to politics. It should be able to be controlled, audited, and criticised and it should not be a burden on the people. Then it will be able to be held as the monarchy that is dignified in line with a universal meaning of democracy.[2]

Such demands challenge the historical weight of Thai conservative notions of an activist monarchy and its role in the nation and democracy. This book offers insights into these notions.

This introduction does three things. It first summarises the volume's contribution to understanding conservatism. Then, for readers unfamiliar with Thai history, there follows a brief excursion into the monarchy's tribulations from the 1930s to the 1970s. The final section considers how scholars have characterised King Bhumibol's remarkable late reign (the 1980s to 2016).

ASPECTS OF THAI CONSERVATISM

The texts appearing in this volume were originally published between 1983 to 2016, roughly bookending the rise and decline of what Kasian Tejapira called the 'Bhumibol Consensus'. King Bhumibol Adulyadej reigned from 1946 to

---

2   See the full manifesto here: https://prachatai.com/english/node/8709.

2016. Arguably, it was only in the late Bhumibol era (the 1980s–2000s) that there existed an enduring elite strategic consensus on the king's role as an active force in the context of competing pressures of political liberalisation and state retrenchment. It was also the period in which a hybrid modern-traditional politics of 'Democracy with the King as Head of State' congealed into a national ideology.[3]

The history of the king's role and its impact has scarcely been written. In 2006, Paul M. Handley described his iconoclastic book *The King Never Smiles: A Biography of Thailand's Bhumibol Adulyadej* as 'an initial perspective' from which further research might grow.[4] Writing in 2020, we are no closer to a definitive version of the reign. Perhaps, as Handley noted, that 'awaits the day internal palace and government records regarding the monarchy are open to scrutiny.'[5] Nevertheless, there is no doubt that hagiographers and iconoclasts want to write that history.[6]

For a good twenty-five years from the 1980s, the dominant appraisal of King Bhumibol was at once ecstatic and fatefully hubristic: the celebrated soul of the nation, genius of the arts and sciences, benevolent father of the people, presiding over a liberalising regime as the super ombudsman keeping political conflict in check and governments on course.[7] Even though the king had declared himself human and open to criticism, outraged ultra-roy-

---

3 Kasian Tejapira, 'รัฐพันลึก, the First Chinese Coup และ the Bhumibol Consensus' [The Deep State, the First Chinese Coup และ the Bhumibol Consensus], *Prachatai*, 4 July 2018 prachatai.com/journal/2018/07/77684. A translation of this phrase that is increasingly favoured is 'The democratic regime with the king as head of state'.

4 P. M. Handley, *The King Never Smiles: A Biography of Thailand's Bhumibol Adulyadej*, New Haven: Yale University Press, 2006, x.

5 *Ibid.*

6 On the hagiographical side one may consult Pichai Chuensuksawadi, *King Bhumibol Adulyadej: Thailand's Guiding Light*, Bangkok: Post Publishing, 1996 and Anonymous, *King Bhumibol: Strength of the Land*, Bangkok: National Identity Office Bangkok. Prime among the iconoclastic treatments, although sympathetic, is Handley, *The King Never Smiles*. Notably that book draws attention to Christine Gray's 'Thailand: The Soteriological State in the 1970s', Ph.D. dissertation, University of Chicago, 1986. This remains unparalleled for its interpretative brilliance of royal ritual gained by insider observations of palace activities. See also Christine Gray, 'Hegemonic Images: Language and Silence in the Royal Thai Polity', *Man* (n.s.) 26, 1, 1991.

7 Notably the power regulation function of the monarchy in an emerging constitutionalism was anticipated by the CIA in 1974, which described the king's role as analogous to a national ombudsman. See www.cia.gov/library/readingroom/docs/DOC_0005379411.pdf.

alists were horrified when encountering disapproval of their beloved king.[8] When royalist protestors formed in 2005 and grew into a mass movement, the People's Alliance for Democracy, they questioned then prime minister Thaksin Shinawatra's loyalty to the crown. Unwittingly, they set in motion a colour-coded political polarisation that led to unprecedented criticism of the monarchy. By making the struggle about the king they made him a target. They called on Thaksin to resign and for power to be returned to the king so a new political settlement could emerge. Thaksin, armed with an electoral mandate, resisted. In September 2006 the military overthrew his government. Subsequent judicial and military interventions blocked his influence and that of his supporters. In response, a mass movement of red-shirt protestors and activists, primarily organised through the United Front for Democracy against Dictatorship, began to question the palace's role in the coup and politics more generally.[9] Such criticism, either by cautious implication (attacking members of the Privy Council or using dysphemisms) or made explicitly, recast Bhumibol's celebrated reign in dimmer light. The response of governments and state agencies to such profanity was the excessive application of a seldom-used but draconian *lèse majesté* law and military-led repression and surveillance of red-shirts.[10]

Censorship and repression only confirmed the revisionist reappraisal of the Bhumibol era and focused the will of those newly scrutinising Thailand's political system. It is to that endeavour that this book speaks by offering reflections on conservatism. However, we do not seek to press the chapters that follow into the service of a singular argument, preferring instead that readers engage them in their own right. Significantly, the authors do not dismiss ideas about monarchy or tradition or even the military's political ideology as mere rationalisations of venal interests with little intrinsic quality. Instead, the chapters help observers move away from such reduc-

---

8 For an overview of the rise of criticism see M. K. Connors, 'When the Walls Come Crumbling Down: Monarchy and Thai-style Democracy', *Journal of Contemporary Asia*, 41, 4, 2011; S. Ivarsson and L. Isager (eds), *Saying the Unsayable: Monarchy and Democracy in Thailand*, Copenhagen: NIAS Press, 2010.

9 Naruemon Thabchumpon, 'Contending Political Networks: A Study of the "Yellow Shirts" and "Red Shirts" in Thailand's Politics', *Southeast Asian Studies*, 5, 1, 2016.

10 For an outstanding discussion of *lèse majesté* and the wider politics of truth, see D. Streckfuss, *Truth on Trial in Thailand: Defamation, Treason, and Lèse-Majesté*, New York: Routledge, 2011. On military surveillance, see Pinkaew Laungaramsri, 'Mass surveillance and the militarization of cyberspace in post-coup Thailand', *ASEAS – Austrian Journal of South-East Asian Studies*, 9, 2, 2016.

tionism and invite engagement with a conservative worldview. Some do so sympathetically, some critically.

Conservatism in the practical sense may best be understood as valuing the conservation of the things that purportedly work in holding society together and trusting these to steer societal and political evolution. Conservatism also entrusts in a transcendent authority the work of shaping moral behaviour.[11] The chapters that follow enable us to grasp something of this structure of thinking in Thai conservatism. For the conservatively minded, the monarchy provides a foundation from which to address the challenges of changing political order. Its presence symbolises the supposed organic unity of the primordial nation that since 1932 has constantly fragmented under the pressures of domestic conflict, inequalities and transnational disruptions. The monarchy can extraordinarily conjure historical and cultural resources to forge unity during crises. It may do this because by standing above commoners the monarchy solicits awe and respect. Indeed, acceptance of a dynasty presupposes its superior socialisation or possession of a biological and historical genealogical wisdom that may guide others. This supra-human condition requires a constant policing of the border between profane and the sacral in language, ritual and embodiment such that even the most rational of persons may feel awed in monarchy's transcendent presence. Over a seventy-year reign, Bhumibol was able to rise to these expectations by nurturing transcendence and publicly performing the role of a Buddhist *Dhammaraja*, a righteous king karmically possessing the ten virtues of kingship, or kingly *barami*.[12] Bhumibol also ably achieved transcendence through courtly Brahman ritual.[13]

Conservatism's attachment to tradition and transcendence is not only a form of political reaction. It is future-oriented in its use of the past to promote a tempered modern condition. It seeks to constrain the secular and

11 M. Freeden, *Ideologies and Political Theory: A Conceptual Approach*, Oxford: Oxford University Press, 1996, 332–5.

12 The Ten Virtues (ทศพิธราชธรรม) that allow perfection and enlightenment for a king who is considered a Buddha-in-waiting are almsgiving, morality, liberality, rectitude, gentleness, self-restriction, non-anger, non-violence, forbearance and non-obstruction. See Prince Dhani Nivat, 'The Old Siamese Concept of the Monarchy', in *Selected Articles from the Siamese Society Journal*, 1929–53, Bangkok: Siam Society, 1954, 162–4. See also Patrick Jory, *Thailand's Theory of Monarchy: The Vessantara Jakata and the Idea of the Perfect Man*, Albany: SUNY Press, 2016. E-book edition.

13 Gray, *Thailand: The Soteriological State in the 1970s*.

rationalist designs of authoritarians and democratic social reformers alike who may – in the eyes of conservatives – transact with the masses, sometimes demagogically, to pursue dangerously secularly conceived projects of modernisation that may trash institutions and norms that have supposedly secured social peace. Such modernist projects do indeed undermine the institutions of tradition and transcendence and portend the great levelling, both material and moral, that defies conservative's inherent hierarchism.

In Thailand, the alignment of the monarchy to these features of conservatism was historically structured and earned. It was not inevitable that social forces would elevate the monarchy to the heights Bhumibol scaled – that depended very much on the perceived performance of the monarchy's role. Indeed, the achievements of Bhumibol's reign are highly personal ones. They centre on the claimed unique merit or perfection of virtues he possessed, notwithstanding that state agencies were required to endlessly illustrate this. That being so, this is a book about an era that has passed. King Vajiralongkorn, Bhumibol's successor, and his fledgling institutions are unlikely to develop soon the structural, agential and ideological power that the Bhumibol palace and its more comprehensive strategic network achieved. Indeed, as we write, Vajiralongkorn faces unprecedented opposition from a new generation of Thais. They have taken up the marginal critiques produced during the Bhumibol era and made them a political movement against the new king. The contrasting fortunes of the two kings only underscore Bhumibol's remarkable feat in securing relatively unchallenged legitimacy and royal prerogative across a quarter of a century.

Collectively, the texts in this volume offer an opportunity to understand better the monarchy's conservative power of attraction in the face of nation-state building challenges. They reveal how the military, the state bureaucracy and the liberally inclined middle class advanced their interests and security through conservative royalism.[14]

Chapters 2–5 provide broad overviews of constitutional history, political discourse and the historical basis of military thinking. Chapter 2 features Somchai Preechasilpakul's discussion of how Thai conservative authoritarianism rests on monarchical claims to found the state and exercise sovereignty. This ethos he names the 'supra-constitution', an unwritten norm that some-

---

14 S. Ünaldi, 'Working Towards the Monarchy and its Discontents: Anti-royal Graffiti in Downtown Bangkok', *Journal of Contemporary Asia*, 44, 3, 2014.

times menacingly swoops and gobbles up written constitutions (Thailand has had 20 since 1932). The supra-constitution, evolving since 1932 to adapt to the constant breakdown of constitutional power (and contributing to the latter), assumes that sovereign power lies with the monarchy when a political vacuum arises. Consequently, it legitimates coups d'état as a refounding of political order and circumscribes the character of constitutional framing that follows that refounding. Chapter 3, Nakharin Mektrairat's 'Political Discourse on Thai Democracy', provides readers with an unparalleled overview of the historical narratives and concepts conservatives have used since 1932 to combat rationalist and abstract ideologies of the left and liberalism. His mapping of Thai conservative thought remains indispensable for contemporary interpretations of Thai politics. Chapter 4, Kramol Thongthammachart's 'National Ideology and Development of the Thai Nation', is a seminal document from the early 1980s. As a state ideologist working with security agencies, Kramol explores the elemental requirements for a hybrid national ideology that could heal a wounded nation after the violence of the 1970s. Its publication was part of a broader conservative ideology project launched by state agencies that aimed at royalist rehabilitation by articulating affective and material interests to the official constitutional description of Thailand as a Democracy with the King as Head of State. Chapter 5 is an extended excerpt from Chalermkiat Phiu-nuan's *Political Thought of the Thai Military*. It is a brilliant critique of the underlying conservative cosmology of the Thai military and its self-conception as guarantor of national security. Chalermkiat reveals the self-rationalising logics of Thailand's frequent coups d'état by conceptual analysis of security as an organising principle of the military and how this colours the concepts of social justice, freedom, and equality.

Chapters 6–8 move into the more recent past. Chapter 6, Pasuk Phongpaichit's 'Civilising the State', the only text to have appeared in English, focuses on the challenges faced by Thailand's conservative state apparatuses in the late 1990s. She recounts how state agencies, assailed by the rise of an active civil society and parliamentary democracy, resorted to archaic Cold War rhetoric in response to villagers resource demands. In turn, she tells how Thai citizens, despite rapid political opening during the 1990s, ironically experienced diminished capacity to assert their interest as bureaucratic and political poles of power began to merge. Chapter 7, Pramuan Rujanaseri's 'Royal Power', is an excerpt from his wildly popular book of the same name that became the focus of mobilisation against Thaksin. Here the reader plunges into the extended logics of a publicly avowed royal conservatism in a text that recounts royal powers as central to good governance and liberty – ideas used to counter Thaksin's perceived authoritarian populism. Finally, in Chapter 8, 'Historical Legacy and the Emergence of Judicialisation in the Thai State', the intellectual historian Saichon Sattayanurak explores the urban Sino-Thai middle class's willingness to align with the exceptional, though restraining, power of the monarchy – mediated by the judiciary – to combat Thaksin's authoritarianism. This alignment, she argues, was determined by the middle class's longstanding fear of its outsider status as Sino-Thai, and its resulting vulnerability to rapacious extraction or political demonisation by political forces.

What emerges in these accounts is the different ways in which monarchy and nationalism articulate to various social forces emotionally. Such articulation is not about rigid doctrine but reflects an emotional investment in specific symbolic expressions of values and institutions that may defy strict ideological delineation – what sociologists call a social imaginary. We return to a fuller discussion and contextualisation of the chapters in the next chapter. In the following pages, we first offer a brief historical overview of political contestation from 1932 through to the 1970s, when the monarchy's position was subject to competing forces. This stands in contrast to the period of the Bhumibol Consensus, from the 1980s to the early 2000s, when, defying legalistic understandings of constitutional monarchy, the king became central to political life and enjoyed broad legitimacy.

FROM THE MARGINS TO THE CENTRE: THE MODERN MONARCHY'S REVIVAL

After the People's Party overthrew the absolute monarchy in 1932 until the early 1980s, the monarchy's position was subject to different degrees of peril and marginality: dissensus, not consensus, characterised its position.

The crushing of an attempted rebellion by old regime loyalists in 1933 placed the monarchy in peril. And after the 1935 abdication of King Prajadhipok, the monarchy played either a dependently passive or partisan role concerning the military rulers that governed Thailand from the late 1930s to the 1970s. From 1938 to 1944 and 1948 to 1957, General Phibun Songkram – an original member of the People's Party – led Thailand as prime minister. During this period, the monarchy and its allies gradually built up pockets of wealth and ideological capital but primarily took a position of submission to the government until the mid-1950s. Phibun, an authoritarian nationalist, largely viewed the monarchy with suspicion and hemmed it in.[15] Moments of attempted revival with a reformist flourish were experienced, such as the passing of the 1949 constitution against the military's wishes, that declared Thailand a 'Democracy with the King as Head of State'. In this system, the constitutional monarchy was conceived as a mechanism by which the division of judicial, executive and legislative powers in a parliamentary democracy would be maintained and authoritarianism thwarted.[16] That constitution and the reformist royalist forces that produced it were a spent force by the early 1950s.

In the 1950s, as part of its Cold War state-building strategies, the United States delivered favour and aid to competing Thai cliques in the military, police and bureaucracy and moved to support a consolidated military dictatorship in the late 1950s. The post-1932 monarchy emerged as a relatively independent force in the mid-to-late 1950s as it gradually positioned itself in the struggle against Phibun. That struggle led to dictatorship after 1957 when General Sarit Thanarat overthrew Phibun in a military coup d'état. Under Sarit and his successors, the monarchy and military formed a stable symbiotic relationship that held until 1973. The monarchy became a partisan mobiliser in the Thai state's partnership with the US during the Cold War. King Bhumibol supported Sarit's regime and its strategies against an incipient communist movement and residual regionalist politics. Freed of restrictions imposed by Phibun, the king regularly toured the countryside preaching development, ethics and articulating a national security discourse.[17]

Across this Cold War period and into the divided 1970s, the monarchy did not enjoy broad legitimacy. Indeed, it struggled for its place and identity amidst political polarisation and simultaneously courted reactionaries, conservatives and liberals. When, in 1973, the military government led by Sarit's successors faced mass student protests for a democratic constitution, soldiers reacted by shooting students. In response, the monarchy demon-

---

15 The fragile position of the monarchy during the Phibun period is covered in Handley, *The King Never Smiles*, 81–138.

16 M. K. Connors, 'Towards a History of Conservative Liberalism after the Siamese Revolution: An Ideological Analysis,' *Asian Studies Review*, forthcoming; Handley, *The King Never Smiles*, 81–99.

17 Handley, *The King Never Smiles*, 139–193.

strated strategic public distance by opening palace grounds as a refuge to students. Following the collapse of the military regime, the king appointed a National Forum from which selected members would sit in a National Assembly and approve a new constitution. Among the members of the Forum were liberal politicians and intellectuals. The king had built up a respectful constituency among public intellectuals and students who used royalist speeches and imagery in their attempts to thwart praetorianism and promote cautious liberalism.[18]

Nevertheless, the palace also engaged in mass anti-communist mobilisation of villagers across the nation and used ritualistic performance to foster irrational allegiance and submission to the triadic ideology of nation, religion and monarchy.[19] The split identity of a Cold War warrior rallying paramilitary forces and the enabler of moderate liberal politics codified in the 1974 constitution was unsustainable. Moreover, the palace faced existential threats, including domestic communist insurgency, the radicalisation of farmers, workers and student movements and external communist advances in Indochina, the latter dramatically highlighted by the 1975 abolition of monarchy in neighbouring Laos. On 6 October 1976, after royalist paramilitary forces massacred protesting students at Thammasat University in Bangkok, the palace endorsed the coup launched that evening, ending Thailand's 1973–76 experiment with open democratic politics.

The king's appointee for prime minister, the judge Thanin Kraivichien, supported a guardian democracy of highly restricted rights that gradually opened to fully democratic elections. The government widely circulated Thanin's book *The Democratic Regime*. It characterised the desirable political system as a Democracy with the King as Head of State.[20] Unlike the original 1949 conception of this system, which entailed a parliamentary democracy and protected rights under a constitutional monarchy, Thanin envisaged a graduated twelve-year plan to introduce full democracy and explicitly described the monarchy as a political institution of last resort, a safety valve

---

18 On this period see David Morell and Chai-Anan Samudavanija, *Political Conflict in Thailand, Reform, Reaction, Revolution*, Cambridge: Oelgeschlager, Gunn and Hain, 1981.

19 See Katherine Bowie's extraordinary study of ritual as a form of collective indoctrination and infantilization, *Rituals of National Loyalty: An Anthropology of the State and the Village Scout Movement in Thailand*, New York: Columbia University Press, 1997.

20 Thanin Kraivichien, ระบอบประชาธิปไตย [Democracy], Bangkok: Ministry of Education, 4th ed., 1977. Please note that this text translates ระบอบประชาธิปไตย economically as 'democracy'. Others prefer 'democratic regime'.

that could moderate polarised politics and which was essential to the defeat of communism. However, Thanin proved too draconian even to the military, and his rule ended with a coup in 1977. If the king's preferred prime minister did not last long, Thanin's popularised notion of the monarchy as a safety valve would be the key to the monarchy's political rehabilitation among different political currents.

By the 1980s, the left and right either moderated their political positions or found themselves diminished by international circumstances. The military shifted from suppression to political warfare against leftists. Students who had fled after the October 1976 massacre to the jungle to find refuge with the insurgent Communist Party of Thailand began to return to cities under the protection of an amnesty. Disenchanted by communist dogma and austere discipline, they were willing to embrace a more limited politics of rights and reform. By the mid-1980s, the military was on the defensive against renewed political liberalisation driven by civic groups campaigning for constitutional reform and political parties in parliament seeking to push the bureaucratic state from its perch. At this time Thirayut Bunmi, the former 1970s student leader and jungle returnee, gave expression to a new sentiment. He criticised military and bureaucratic forces for aggrandising the aura of the monarchy to maintain power. He argued for a more encompassing ideology of 'Liberal Democracy with the King as Head of State': a national monarchy rather than a bastion of the Right.[21] Like many of his generation, as Kanokrat notes, Thirayut made peace with Bhumibol's ascendance.[22]

This moment takes us to what is properly the rise of the Bhumibol Consensus when seemingly the monarchy began to stand above the fray, able to command broad respect and affect the distribution of power in a semi-regularised way. It had become the safety valve, even the super ombudsman as royalists would have it. The Bhumibol Consensus was in the making.

---

21 Thirayut Bunmi, ทางสองแพร่งของประชาธิปไตยไทยในทัศนะสังคมวิทยาการเมือง [Thai Democracy at the Crossroads: a Politico-sociological Perspective], วารสารสังคมศาสตร์ [Social Science Review], 24, 1, 1987, 16–17.

22 Kanokrat Lertchoosakul, *The Rise of the Octoberists in Contemporary Thailand*, New Haven, CT: Yale Southeast Asia Studies, 2016.

CONCEPTUALISING THE LATE REIGN

If strategic consensus on the king's role unevenly emerged in the later period of the reign from the mid-1980s onward and reached its zenith in the early 2000s, precisely what was the consensus? The consensual elements of this politics were not about common goals – despite the mantra of unity professed by the palace. Rather, 'consensus' generously describes the acceptance of boundaries for allowable conflict under the king's watchful eye.

Like any developing country's modus operandi, the Bhumibol Consensus was contested and strained by dissenting military and capitalist fractions that in turn rebuffed the king's presumed regulatory role or sought to diminish or even supplant it. There were two coup attempts in the 1980s against the Prem administration (1980–88) favoured by the king. Strains between elected governments and the palace and military from the late 1980s onwards led to coups in 1991 and 2006.[23] Clearly, observers should not idealise the modus operandi as a uniquely practical and integrating consensus. Indeed, given the lack of ideological and organisational unity in the Thai state – despite the discourse of official national ideology – the system urgently required the lubricant of informal networks. Arguably, the Bhumibol Consensus was partly sustained by what Duncan McCargo labelled the 'network monarchy'.[24]

McCargo's network monarchy concept was a pioneering and prescient critique of the then obscure or at least unnamed nature of political power in Thailand. McCargo brought to light the informal network by which the king and royalist political notables shaped political and economic outcomes in Thailand. More precisely, McCargo identified what Prime Minister Thaksin was challenging when he used his networks to advance his ambitious capitalist development and governance goals.[25] In an example of life following social science, during Thaksin's struggle to return to power after the 2006 coup, the concept of network monarchy was translated into Thai and used as an explanatory framework for what was at stake: palace networks that fanned out across governmental and civil society institutions versus a democratically elected government empowered by its networks.

---

23 Pasuk Phongpaichit and Chris Baker, *Thailand, Economy and Politics*, Oxford: Oxford University Press, 1996, 323–66.

24 D. McCargo, 'Network Monarchy and Legitimacy Crises in Thailand', *The Pacific Review*, 18, 4, 2005.

25 D. McCargo and Ukrist Pathmanand, *The Thaksinization of Thailand*, Copenhagen: NIAS Press, 2004, p. 131.

Networks are, of course, the lubricant of many polities, but few can claim to have had a network monarchy in the late 20th century.

The system was thus: the palace networked with a range of bureaucratic, civilian and military figures to give character to the state. It shaped debates, decisions and outcomes within the same system that it was constitutionally mandated to safeguard 'above politics' by serving as the source of national legitimacy and arbitration during crises. It was, to McCargo, in effect a semi-monarchical mode of governance laid across formal democratic structures. The king did not shy away from this reality.[26] He explained his incumbency to a journalist in 1989:

> You can do just what the law says. That is, if you say something, the prime minister or a minister must countersign, and if he is not there to countersign, we cannot speak. That is one way to do it: do nothing, just nothing at all. The other way is to do too much, use the influence we have to do anything. That doesn't work, either. We must be in the middle and working in every field.[27]

Being in the middle required some degree of independence. A precondition of the Bhumibol Consensus was the king's and his advisors' adaptive sagacity in carving out an increasingly independent space for the palace through ritual, financial and political means.[28] Survival instincts enabled this. A once threatened dynasty won favour by association with authoritarian politics and military leaders during the Cold War. Similarly, adapting to political liberalisation from the 1980s onwards put the king in the middle, even if his natural inclinations were profoundly conservative.[29]

Another source of consensus is hinted at in the above: various networks sought to sometimes advance political agendas by feeding off monarchical prestige. By 'working towards the monarchy', as Serhat Ünaldi memorably put it, different forces enhanced the overall status of the institution they sought to utilise.[30] Underpinning the authority to forge consensus on its central importance was state-backed ideological propagation. Indeed, ideas on

---

26 *Ibid.*, 500–1.

27 *Ibid.*, 502.

28 Christine E. Gray, 'Royal Words and Their Unroyal Consequences.' *Cultural Anthropology*, 7, 4, 1992, pp. 448–463.

29 K.Hewison, 'The Monarchy and Democratization', in K. Hewison (ed.), *Political Change in Thailand: Democracy and Participation*, London: Routledge, 1997, pp. 58–74.

30 S. Ünaldi, 'Working Towards the Monarchy'.

Buddhist kingship as embodying and upholding the laws of Dhamma that were once hardly considered even worthy of casual genuflection to urbanites in the 1950s, were by the 1990s nationally celebrated and woven into an increasing rotation of dynastic celebrations and milestones, including the bicentennial of the Chakri dynasty in 1982 and various royal birthdays.

For those who perceived the king as a virtue-embodying semi-deity, the monarchy was naturally expected to wield moral and instructive influence in the profane realm of politics. These sacral developments were not specific to Thailand, for they were part of what Peter Jackson has described as a broader process of the global re-enchantment of modernity against the expected rise of secularism.[31] Moreover, it may be noted that the Buddhist and animist elements of popular culture, empowered by mass markets and communications, fuelled expectations that the monarchy was more than a constitutional mechanism that merely symbolically unified the separation of legislative, executive and judicial powers, as Thailand's various constitutions stipulated. Rather, the monarchy was disposed to be an active moral power in the people's interest, exemplified in the king's occasional offering of compassionate judgements in cases where he sat as presiding judge and his lecturing of crown servants on the value and integrity of public service. The image promoted by the place was that the monarchy and its agents were compassionate actors whom the people could petition to rectify an injustice. The king cultivated this perception and extended it to the judiciary, who worked 'in the name of the king'. He told judges, 'if you act immorally, the king becomes an immoral person … and if I am in trouble, the people will be in trouble as well, since they will not receive justice.'[32]

Regardless of the king's preferences, the multiple ways of interpreting the monarchy as a public good enabled it to be positively perceived, by some of those building a relatively open political system, as an 'indispensable para-political institution' existing parallel to formal political institutions.[33]

31 P. A. Jackson, 'Re-interpreting the Traiphuum Phra Ruang: Political Functions of Buddhist Symbolism in Contemporary Thailand', in T. Ling (ed.) *Buddhist Trends in Southeast Asia*, Singapore: ISEAS, 1993; P. A. Jackson, 'Markets, Media, Magic: Thailand's Monarch as a Virtual Deity', *Inter-Asia Cultural Studies*, 10, 3, 2009.

32 On the relationship between the monarchy and courts, see D. McCargo, *Fighting for Virtue: Justice and Politics in Thailand*, Ithaca and London: Cornell University Press, 2019, especially the chapter, 'Bench and Thone'. The quotation appears on p. 62.

33 M. K. Connors, *Democracy and National Identity in Thailand*, Copenhagen: NIAS Press, 2007 (originally Routledge, 2003), 131.

In such an interpretation, the monarchy sometimes functioned to break deadlocks within those institutions, shaping them and providing a stabilising force for the gradual development of democracy by exemplifying the requisite civic virtues needed for the public good.

But such a central place for the monarchy had a perverse outcome. Each of these consensus-building factors coincided and reinforced each other to create what Thongchai Winichakul called hyper-royalism: an excessive presence of the monarchy in the everyday aural and visual life of people (broadcasts and posters, for example); the rise of the exaltation of royal capacities; and an aura of religiosity surrounding royals.[34] These characteristics were not simply a product of monolithic propagation. Instead, they emerged from multiple sites and were advanced by social forces identifying with the monarchy and a mass public engaged in royal spectatorship.[35]

Christine Gray speaking of the revival of ritual performance in the 1960s around the figure of the king as a Righteous Ruler notes, '[t]hese ideologies and royal practices (plus a strict law forbidding insult to the Crown) create a magic circle of silence around the present king.'[36] By the 1990s, hyper-royalism formed a garrison protecting the king's authority. It put on notice the subordinate status of all other political actors. Without it, the king would have been just one more node in a network.

McCargo seized on the notion of network monarchy just as Thaksin challenged its capacities. Kasian introduced the idea of the Bhumibol Consensus in a 2018 seminar when both the king and the consensus were dead. His speech was not a retrospective on the Bhumibol era. He did not venture how the king's broadly accepted networked regulation of competing interests might have provided relief or disruption to an emerging constitutional system. Instead, he was interested in what happened after the consensus ended. Ironically, Kasian averred that with the end of the Bhumibol Consensus people were now free to long for a politics informed by nostalgia for dictatorship or absolute monarchy.[37]

---

34 See Thongchai Winichakul, *Thailand's Hyper-royalism: Its Past Success and Present Predicament*, Singapore: ISEAS, 2016.

35 Sarun Krittikarn, 'Entertainment Nationalism: The Royal Gaze and the Gaze of the Royals', in Ivarsson and Isager (eds), *Saying the Unsayable*.

36 Gray, 'Royal Words and Their Unroyal Consequences', p. 452.

37 Kasian, รัฐพันลึก, 'The First Chinese Coup'.

This brings us to the reduction of the late Bhumibol era as the politics of the 'deep state' – a theory that tends towards conspiracy by its very nature. Critical of the claimed narrowness of the concept of 'network monarchy', Eugénie Mérieau, in perhaps the most influential article in English to emerge from Thailand's political crisis, saw a broader and systemic form to anti-democratic politics in Thailand. She described flanks of reactionaries, organised in support of royalism and authoritarianism, from the highest office to the lowest functionary working in unison as a 'Deep State', working to block democratic institutions and the popular will.[38] In a polemical critique of the judicialisation of Thai politics that served the establishment, Mérieau noted how the courts removed pro-Thaksin prime ministers, invalidated elections won by pro-Thaksin parties and disbanded the latter. She argued that such outcomes possessed logic. The 'Deep State' was fearful of its position after the Bhumibol reign, and so 'the Deep State organised for the Constitutional Court to take on the "king's role" as defined by McCargo.'[39] Although there is no formal or practical equivalence between the role of the network monarchy and the judiciary, the 'Deep State' idea led to several university seminars. Thailand's intellectual luminaries spoke of its utility, for it seemed to explain the judicial tribulations of Thaksin and his proxies, as well as the challenges faced by the red-shirt movement that emerged to support his return to power after the 2006 coup. Indeed, that struggle had already led to the revival of ideas of shadowy forces dictating or manipulating official governments in protest literature, but Mérieau's was by far the most provocative and expansive.[40] For many, the idea of a Deep State cast a condemning retrospective light on modern politics – a politics of oligarchic preservation made visible by judicial, military and state repression of pro-Thaksin forces. The political crisis, the argument went, had seemingly revealed what was always there – a conspiring Deep State. Any sense of intra-elite conflict around different political projects in the anti-Thaksin camp was lost.

The brutal politics of the last fifteen years has fuelled a view that tends to see the period of Bhumibol Consensus as no longer one of political opening

---

38 Eugénie Mérieau, 'Thailand's Deep State: Royal Power and the Constitutional Court (1997–2015)', *Journal of Contemporary Asia*, 46, 3, 2016.

39 Ibid., 447.

40 See for example Jakraphop Penkair,'รัฐบาลภายในรัฐบาล' [Government within a Government], ไทยเรดนิวส์ [Thai Red News], September 18–24, 2009.

and liberalisation but one dominated by a strategy of maintaining oligarchy. This oligarchy has now revealed how far it would go to hold onto power.[41] Of course, such views of Thai politics predate the crisis, but the state's reaction to the Thaksin challenge and the challenge of democracy more broadly has given such ideas an expanded constituency. While capturing essential insights, this view under-appreciates the monarchy's polyvocality and sometimes slides into Manichean if not Machiavellian interpretations and speculations. It tends to view history from 1932 to the present as one recurring pre-existing condition – the struggle between the people and the monarchy. We consider the Bhumibol reign to have been marked by multiple transformations of national identity and competing political projects supported by different social bases in the context of a fluid politics when no force, even the monarchy, was fully able to stamp onto the Thai 'ambivalent state' its preference.[42] Rather than serving a monolithic purpose, different political actors recruited the monarchy to different political projects. This book contributes to an undoing of some of the easy assumptions about monarchy and reaction in Thailand by paying attention to conservatism in context.

---

41 See, for variations on this theme, Kasian Tejapira, 'The Irony of Democratization and the Decline of Royal Hegemony in Thailand', *Southeast Asian Studies*, 5, 2016; C. Baker, 'The 2014 Thai Coup and Some Roots of Authoritarianism', *Journal of Contemporary Asia*, 46, 3, 2016; Kengkij Kitirianglarp and K. Hewison, 'Social Movements and Political Opposition in Contemporary Thailand', *The Pacific Review*, 22, 4, 2009; Thongchai Winichakul, 'Toppling Democracy', *Journal of Contemporary Asia*, 38, 1, 2008.

42 Ukrist Pathmanand and M. K. Connors, 'Thailand's Public Secret: Military Wealth and the State', *Journal of Contemporary Asia*, published online 26 July 2019; M. K. Connors, 'Liberalism, Authoritarianism and the Politics of Decisionism in Thailand', *Pacific Review*, 22, 3, 2009, 355–73.

CHAPTER 1

Understanding Thai Conservatism

Michael K. Connors and Ukrist Pathmanand

This chapter offers a brief contextualisation and discussion of each contribution to this book. We pay special attention to Somchai Preechasilpakul's idea of supra-constitution, for we believe it consolidates the insights that the various chapters offer into a general apprehension of Thai conservatism. With this exception, we aim to situate each piece and the author in as economical a fashion as possible.

THE SUPRA-CONSTITUTION

We borrowed and incorporated into the title of this volume the critical concept of Somchai Preechasilpakul's deceptively simple and brilliantly lucid lecture, 'The Thai Supra-Constitution' (อภิรัฐธรรมนูญไทย) delivered in June 2007 at the annual commemoration of Pridi Banomyong, the leader of the 1932 revolution that overthrew the absolute monarchy in the name of the People's Party. We imagine that as a French-educated constitutionalist and broadly rationalist figure, the exiled Pridi, who died in Paris in 1983, may have admired the forensic analysis Somchai brings to the study of moribund constitutions and the manner of their death.

Somchai received a Bachelor of Law from Thammasat University in 1989 and a Master of Law (in Public Law) from the same university in 1998. He is active in social and political movements and regularly offers commentary on legal, political and constitutional affairs. A former Dean of the Faculty of Law, Chiang Mai University, where he currently lectures, Somchai has published on public law and critical legal studies. He has written a pioneering study on the monarchy in Thai constitutions, tracing the recurrent debate about its role and sovereign scope.[1] His participation in a press conference

---

1   Somchai Preechasilpakul, ข้อถกเถียงว่าด้วยสถาบันพระมหากษัตริย์ในองค์กรจัดทำรัฐธรรมนูญของ ไทยตั้งแต่ พ.ศ. 2475–2550 [Debates on the Monarchy in Thai Constitution-Making Organs from 1932–2007]. Chiang Mai: Keant Press, 2017, 16–18.

on freedom of speech in 2015 during the military dictatorship of 2014–19 saw him charged alongside others for disorderly assembly. Serendipitously, his research on legal provisions regarding freedom of peaceful association published in 2014, funded by a Secretariat of the Constitutional Court grant, won him an annual award from the National Research Council of Thailand in 2017.[2]

His written work is weighty with critique and un-bowing to power. He is one of the heirs of a legal tradition that seeks a rule-of-law state governed by the principles of constitutionalism. In his lecture, 'The Thai Supra-Constitution', reproduced in this volume, Somchai set himself the task of bringing order to the chaotic disorder of the many redundant or slain constitutions that litter the Thai political landscape.[3] 'Supra-constitution' (*aphi-ratthathammanun*) may have been translated differently. But in its Latin derivation, 'supra' connotes something privileged, something beyond and above – as does *aphi* in Thai – and so nicely captures the notion of something outside of the written constitutional order that stands in su-perior relation to it.[4] We thus settled on *supra-constitution* to capture the capricious meaning that Somchai reveals in his carefully crafted account of how the supra-constitution functions in the Thai context.

Somchai asked in his lecture if any framework could explain the con-tradiction of a constitution 'being the supreme law at the same time as being frequently torn up.' His answer was yes. In the packed auditorium of the Pridi Banomyong Foundation he proceeded to illuminate, boldly and elegantly, how there stood above the drafting and exercise of written

2   Somchai Preechasilpakul and Team, เสรีภาพในการชุมนุมโดยสงบและปราศจากอาวุธตามบทบัญญัติ ของกฎหมาย [Peaceful Assembly According to Legislated Law], Research supported by the Secretariat of the Constitutional Court, 2014.

3   Somchai Preechasilpakul, อภิรัฐธรรมนูญไทย [The Supra-constitution of Thailand]. Bangkok: Pridi Banomyong Institute.

4   In western legal literature, supra-constitution has been used descriptively to describe the supra-national legal standing of various regional or international organisations. But there is also a limited literature that uses the phrase in ways only broadly analogous to Somchai's usage, connoting a founding norm that must not be transgressed or which being trans-gressed justifies a state of exception. That is, the phrase denotes extra-constitutionality or a more fundamental constitutionality outside the bounds of a written constitution. One can usefully consult discussions on Norway's 'eternity clause' in E. Smith, 'Old and Protected? On the "Supra-Constitutional" Clause in the Constitution of Norway', *Israel Law Review*, 44, 3, 369–88, 2011. As far as we can see, Somchai's usage is *sui generis* for the broader political contexts it engages.

constitutions an evolving unwritten 'supra-constitution' that accounts for the regular demise of ordinary constitutions.

Somchai pointed out that in the seventy five years since the first constitution of June 1932, governments had promulgated 17 constitutions. We can add a further three: the 2007 constitution declared after the coup of 19 September 2006, the 2014 interim coup constitution and the 2017 constitution. Of those promulgated, he identifies three types: 'a parliamentary version, an authoritarian version, and a mixed parliamentary-bureaucratic polity version'. He argued that the authoritarian and mixed constitutions were tools of the elites in their pursuit and maintenance of power and had no regard for justice or social consent. Constitutions thus came and went to serve the interests of the dominant power groups. Democratic hopes were to be invested in the parliamentary constitution. This much is conventional. But Somchai was pointing to something more compelling about the founding of political order.

Since the French Revolution, scholars conventionally understand that those who write constitutions are a constituent power – that is, they are protagonists free of all restraints to decide on or authorise the nature of a constitutional system and design its constituted powers. In his probing exploration of the evolution of a supra-constitution, Somchai excels in uncovering how the military and the monarchy function as constituent powers superior to ordinary constitutions and their framers. He also shows the accretion of norms around this status.

The idea of constituent powers is not a foreign concept in modern Thailand. Thai constitutional framers would also speak in such terms even when appointed by a coup group. One example of this comes from the deliberations of the Constitutional Drafting Assembly that spent nearly eight years drafting the 1968 constitution. An optimistic Detchat Wongkomonchet, an Interior Ministry official steeped in western political theory and constitutionalism, explained to the Assembly that it was a constituent power. This meant that there were no boundaries on its powers to establish a new constitutional order and that it was even possible to discuss the question of whether Thailand should be a 'Democracy with the King as Head of State'. Detchat referred to the new constitutional orders springing up in postcolonial states to indicate the need to have extensive discussions.[5] Another framer,

---

5   Discussed in Connors, 'Towards a History of Conservative Liberalism'.

Kukrit Pramoj – one of the key ideologists of the monarchy – disagreed. He explained that Thailand was not a new country. So rather than rely on academic theory, the constitutional framers should draw on the continuity of king and nation. The only real question to be debated was the extent of monarchical powers.[6] Kukrit prevailed, and the assembly did not debate the question of whether Thailand should maintain Democracy with the King as Head of State, revealing the supra-constitutional nature of monarchy.

The 1968 constitutional debates illustrate the importance of Somchai's idea of the supra-constitution: those committees or assemblies that have written constitutions since the 1947 coup's re-assertion of military and monarchical power are not, in fact, a constituent power but rather a consti-tuted power mandated by presumptive constituent powers – the military and/or the monarchy. As such, the supra-constitution circumscribes what is constitutionally possible when ordinary constitutions are drafted and exercised. The significance of this insight is that it explains the constant tearing up of the 'supreme law'. Of course, many political regimes worldwide settle into constitutional functioning without the constant interruption of constituent powers. However, Somchai describes a situation in which the latent constituent powers of the supra-constitution are never far from the surface – either self-willingly brought into the open when interests and identity are threatened or involuntarily drawn out by intense conflict between competing social forces.

Somchai also recounts the emergence of new and evolving norms around constitutional abrogation and promulgation, which he retells with dripping irony. He speaks of a Thai norm in which the sanctity of constitutions at-taches simply to there being one in force, rather than an actual constitution having such sanctity. Constitutions are expendable. This norm required that when a coup group abrogated a constitution, they must replace it. In this process, the power embedded in the supra-constitution circumscribes what framers write into the replacement. Other evolving norms involve the stylised practices that follow a coup d'état which slays a constitution through revolutionary decree, and there follows the complementary royal command that legitimates an interim constitution before the promulgation of a 'perma-nent constitution'. This becomes an iterative process of refounding political power. Should dissidents or those with grievances legally challenge the new

---

6   *Ibid.*

constitution, the courts legitimate the new constitution by using positivist legal doctrine that force and acceptance of that force create law.[7]

The supra-constitution, and the conventions that evolve around the issuing of constitutions and the power relations they embed, might not be tangible or expressly written. Nevertheless, it is there all the same and coheres and adapts in line with prevailing powers. By speaking of norms and rules that govern the drafting of the constitution, Somchai moves beyond raw power and indicates the emergence of authoritarian cultural thinking that impacts not just the framing of a constitution but the politics that take place under its auspices. Somchai's concept draws attention to how the many interim and permanent charters he observes are subject to a dual movement of monarchical assertation and military guardianship and how these become normative unwritten rules and assumptions that shroud constitutional drafting processes. The supra-constitution acts in many ways as a guiding transcendent spirit, a conservative foundation.

In the preceding elaboration of the concept, we may have given excess meaning to what Somchai intended in his original Thai neologism. And we have certainly not captured the humour that Somchai brings to the topic in his witty subheadings, including *The Constitution is The Highest Law, Temporarily*.

It was noted earlier that Somchai asked if there was a framework that could explain Thailand's constitutional history. He more than amply provides one for that and much more. Indeed, the concept of supra-constitution provides an organising framework for approaching Thai conservatism. While that framework remains skeletal, it is possible to flesh out what this would look like by aligning the concept with the related insights of the works in this book. Indeed, the idea of a supra-constitution is a spectral presence in the remaining chapters. Each of them seeks to understand uncodified power in the context of royal and military ascendancy or the challenge to that ascendancy. This means recognising that the supra-constitution forms the cultural and historical sedimentation against which modern politics has played out. In his lecture's closing moment, Somchai draws connections between the supra-constitution and the idea of 'Democracy with the King as Head of State'. This idea first emerged in the late 1940s as a form of constitutional rule, but by the 1980s it had transformed into something of a contested national ideology with liberal and conservative connotations.

---

7   See Streckfuss, *Truth on Trial on the legality of coups d'état*, 351–2.

CONSERVATIVE ATTRACTIONS AND
DEMOCRATIC DISCOURSE

Ukrist Pathmanand, co-editor of this volume, was present at one of the early seminars in which a then largely unknown intellectual historian, Nakharin Mektrairat, presented some of his early work. He recalls the excitement of the young Nakharin going against the left-wing grain of Thai social history and its archival social history propensity. Such history, to Nakharin, did not sufficiently attend to broader contemporaneous debates among jurists, intellectuals and journalists, for example, and missed how attention to these might enable proper contextualisation of political discourse. Instead, Nakharin was committed to an intellectual history of the immediate period before and after the 1932 revolution. Accordingly, he began to scrutinise texts written by jurists, officials and intellectuals, both Thai and foreign, culminating in a series of brilliant articles written between 1982 and 1990 on the 1932 Siamese Revolution. These were published collectively in 1990 as *Thoughts, Knowledge and Political Power in the Siamese Revolution*. One of them appears here. With a lightly worn Foucauldian inflexion, the young writer's interest in intellectual history went against the trend of both mainstream and critical economic histories of the time.[8] The collection and a monograph, *The 1932 Siamese Revolution*, are widely acclaimed and read by conservatives, liberals, and the left alike, being reissued by the radical press *Faa Diaokan*.[9]

Nakharin had a rather grim perspective on what he labelled the Western School of Thought in Thai history and politics. He regarded left discourse as sterile and heavy with unexamined abstractions. His sympathy for the rhetorical power of tradition and royalism is evident in the work reproduced in this volume. Given these proclivities, it should not surprise anyone that he became a board member of King Prajadhipok's Institute that institutionalises and propagates the monarchical foundations of Thai democracy. In 2006 he published a book extolling the role of the monarchy in Thailand's democrat-

---

8   The latter approach being led by Chattip Natasupa Professor of Economic, Chulalongkorn University, whose Marxism influenced the study of socio-economic transformation in the early Rattanakosin period.

9   Nakharin Mektrairat, ความคิดความอำนาจการเมืองในการปฏิวัติสยาม 2475 [Ideas, Knowledge and Political Power in the Siamese Revolution of 1932], Bangkok: Fa Diaokan, 2003; Nakharin Mektrairat, การปฏิวัติสยาม 2475 [The 1932 Revolution in Siam], Bangkok: Fa Diaokan, 2010.

ic development.[10] Nakharin remains an influential figure in Thailand and is currently serving a second term as a Constitutional Court judge.

Published nearly twenty years before Somchai's lecture, Nakharin's chapter provides readers with an insight into the discursive underpinnings of what Somchai called the supra-constitution and the latter's presumption of monarchical founding of the state. The 1932 revolution inaugurated a long-standing debate on the nature of political sovereignty between two schools. The first is the Traditional School of Thought, which encompasses the first wave of intellectuals in the royal family and courtiers. Traditionalists argued against the progressive ideas of what Nakharin calls the Western School of Thought, including the 1932 revolutionary leader Pridi and others. For the latter, the revolution was a significant step towards wholesale advancement of the Thai people and the emergence of a political community based on people's sovereignty, liberty, equality and fraternity.

In response to the progressive challenge, multiple projects emerged – political, cultural and ideological – to preserve the ideological continuity of the monarchy as the source of sovereign power. Pointedly, the traditional scholars suggested that Thailand already had aspects of democratic rule before 1932 under the notion of 'elective kingship', which emphasises that the Thai king ascends to the throne by unanimous agreement of the political community as the sole ultimate ruler. They averred that the revolution disrupted evolution towards more institutional forms of democratic reform intended by King Prajadhipok. As they saw it, the petulant revolution of 1932 was the source of all subsequent political instability and ushered in an era of dictatorship and corruption. This conservative view draws sustenance from King's Prajadhipok's explanation for his abdication in 1935: 'I am willing to surrender the powers I formerly exercised to the people as a whole, but I am not willing to turn them over to any individual or group of individual to use it in an autocratic manner without heeding the voice of the people.'[11]

In reading Nakharin's work one may be struck by how several of the intellectual figures from the 1970s whom Nakharin placed under the

---

10 Nakharin Mektrairat, พระผู้ทรงปกเกล้าฯประชาธิปไตย: ๖๐ ปีสิริราชสมบัติกับการเมืองการปกครอง ไทย [His Majesty who Protects Democracy: 60 Years of the Reign and Thai Politics], Bangkok: Thammasat University Press, 2006. As Thongchai in 'Toppling Democracy', 24, notes 'The title is a clever design that combines part of the King Rama VII's name in Thai (Pokklao). and the word prachathipatai (democracy) for an official publication to celebrate King Bhumibol as a democratic king'.

11 See Thongchai 'Topping Democracy', 22–3, on the varied uses of this quotation.

Western School and who espoused broadly liberal politics would emerge as significant proponents of Democracy with the King as Head of State. They absorbed elements of traditionalism, seeing the idea of monarchy as beneficial to democratic evolution in the face of military dictatorship, communist insurgency, political corruption and the political crises that accompany rapid modernisation and mobilisation. In the 1980s, such thinkers struggled against statists to liberalise power and institutionalise political competition. This endeavour grew more potent in the political reform movement of the 1990s. Several of these figures are dealt with in Saichon's chapter in this volume, as is their call for royal and military intervention in politics – an instance of political movements conjuring the spirit of the supra-constitution.

TOWARDS RECONSTITUTING NATIONAL IDEOLOGY

In the 1980s the reforming liberalism discussed above was contested by a reforming conservatism. For these reformers, Thailand needed to formulate a new ideological apparatus (ideas and means) that could speak to the rural classes and neither alarm hardened conservatives nor alienate those seeking economic redistribution. This post-1970s crisis re-articulation of ideology that sought to reclaim the mantra of nation, religion and king from the reactionary right came under the significant influence of Kramol Thongthammachart.

Kramol was born three years after the 1932 revolution and died in 2017, receiving a royally sponsored funeral. A former professor at the Faculty of Political Science, Chulalongkorn University, Kramol was an influential figure in shaping state-centred political thought during the Cold War period (the 1960s–1980s) and was central to propagating the village-centred ideology of *phaendin tham phaen din thong* (Land of Justice, Land of Gold) in the 1980s, which aimed at putting into practice some of the elements of national ideology discussed in the translated paper here. He lectured at the Communist Security Operations Command and its successor organisation the Internal Security Operations Command, the Royal Police Cadet Academy and several arms of bureaucracy, particularly in the college of the Ministry of Interior. In addition, he instructed radio broadcasters on the propagation of national ideology. Several generations of Thai bureaucrats who studied political science at Chulalongkorn University were under his intellectual influence. As a prodigious researcher in political development, Kramol shaped the discipline of political science. He was one of the framers of the 'semi-democracy' constitution of 1978 that moved Thailand beyond the crisis of 1976. His influence extended to the high-level National Security Council through which he advocated for the formation of a serviceable national ideology as a basis of political stability. He subsequently served in several high-level positions, including Minister of the Prime Minister's Office (1983–86), Vice President of the Constitutional Drafting Committee (1997) and Constitutional Court judge (2000–05).

Kramol's translated piece reproduced in this volume, 'National Ideology and the Development of the Thai Nation', would better be titled 'In Search of National Ideology'.[12] After the trauma of the 1970s when political polarisation had led to a bloody showdown in October 1976 and the massacre of students by para-state forces at Thammasat University, Kramol, like others, was pre-occupied by the central question of how to incorporate both the urban and rural classes into a developing political system faced with modernisation challenges.

In 1979 he and Sippanon Ketutat presented to the National Security Council a programmatic statement on National Ideology. This may be judged as a formative statement of post-1976 state ideology.[13] They outlined the need for the state to advance an ideology of political, economic and social democracy for the collective good that was sufficiently resilient to defeat opposing ideologies and sustain loyalty to the nation, monarchy and religion. That democracy would be one in which rights and freedoms, under law, would protect the interests of the majority.[14] They called on the government to promote Democracy with King as Head of State according to the constitution and make it a pillar of governing rather than a slogan.[15] By doing so, Kramol and his national security colleagues definitively stamped statist notions on the idea of Democracy with the King as Head of State, assimilating it into a state-led reform project. Subsequently, an entire

---

12 Kramol Thongthammachart อุดมการณ์ของชาติกับการพัฒนาชาติไทย [National Ideology and the Development of the Thai Nation], in Office of the Prime Minister อุดมการณ์ของชาติ [National Ideology], Bangkok: Office of the Prime Minister, 1983.

13 Kramol Thongthammachart and Sippanon Ketutat, 'อุดมการณ์ของชาติแนวความคิดและแนวทางการดำเนินงาน' [National Ideology, Concepts and Operationalisation], in Office of the Prime Minister อุดมการณ์ของชาติ [National Ideology], Bangkok: Office of the Prime Minister, 1983, 11–16.

14 *Ibid.*, 12

15 *Ibid.*, 14.

bureaucratic structure serviced these concerns and involved propagation of national ideology, the training of disseminators and radio techniques for reaching mass audiences, and the facilitation of civic education programmes to produce national sentiment.[16]

Kramol was aware that national ideology could easily fall between the cracks of bureaucratic routine and be nothing but a slogan with little concrete impact. Thus, in 'National Ideology' he makes a case for advancing national ideology by arguing for its importance and sketching the conditions to advance it. First, Kramol observed that the clash between different ideologies could lead to bloodshed and chaos, as seen in Vietnam, Kampuchea and Laos, where people adopted divergent economic and political beliefs. Remarkably, Kramol says nothing of Thai ideological polarisation and violence during the mid-1970s, but the silent analogy is obvious. Societies with such discrepancies need national ideologies to bind people collectively. Then, drawing on the research of Thailand's security agencies that had surveyed the population on aspirations, Kramol proposed lines of national ideological development that persist to this day, with an emphasis on collectivism, moralism, local levels of democracy and leadership of the people by crown servants and political elites.

In Kramol's view, Thailand faced several key challenges: the spread of communism and guerrilla warfare, the lack of ideological commitment of Thai political parties, those parties' inability to offer an attractive alternative to the left, and the cult of personality within them. In contrast, looking at neighbouring Malaysia, Kramol cited the United Malays National Organisation as a successful political party model able to mitigate internal conflicts within a multiracial and multireligious society amidst communist attempts to undermine the nation's stability. Despite its authoritative, total control of power, Kramol regarded UMNO as a political success in unifying and developing Malaysia. He added that leading members of UMNO were upper-class Malays who knew how to bring with them Chinese and Indian elites. This cross-ethnic alliance helped to minimise racial conflicts and led to the continuity of national politics, which contributed to the institutionalisation of political parties. However, Thailand lacked political institutionalisation, and political consensus was scant. Therefore, the answer to how Thailand might move to national unity for Kramol lay first in unity through national ideology.

---

16 On the scope of this, see Connors, *Democracy and National Identity*, 135–47.

To stabilise the three leading institutions of Thailand – the nation, religion and the monarchy – Kramol proposed an expansive ideology that could help Thailand develop, integrate classes, address material grievances, connect individual and national identity, and ease tensions within society. Adherence to a democracy that was secure and appropriate to Thai circumstances was foremost in this project. To read Kramol is to see how conservative ideologists sought to align the triadic ideology of nation, religion and monarchy concretely with people's sense of justice and material wellbeing.

Kramol was not a singular figure. His work represents a broader class of statist intellectuals who tread a similar path and play a role in entwining tradition with political, scientific outlooks. In that sense, Kramol might be considered an archetypal Thai-bureaucratic political scientist who counsels those in power on how to engineer development that simultaneously produces desired change and secures stability. Many political scientists have been central to attempts to engineer political modernisation and maintain stability – all in service to elaborating a national ideology. Political scientists – as civil servants in the Interior Ministry, as senior political advisors and as constitutional judges (others joined Kramol in this capacity) – have played an essential role as engineers of the state and shapers of citizens souls. They reflected on the fragile bonds of national unity and believed the nation to be malleable if made subject to the techniques of political science.

Studies of political culture, political development and institutionalisation in Thailand were not merely academic problems with neat theoretical solutions. Instead, scholars like Kramol prodded them into the service of state and nation. Statist organic intellectuals were servants of what might be called a politico-developmental state. This hyper-conscious state embraces its vanguard role in developing its nascent people, institutions, and economy towards an ideal end by drawing on the techniques and findings of political science in its policy rationalisations. Such scholar-activists as part of that vanguard endlessly planned political development as an entity much like an economy, something that was imaginable in vision statements. If we can think of development economists as shaping economic policy, we can also think of political developmentalists such as Kramol shaping policy on political party and parliamentary institutionalisation towards the teleology of Democracy with the King as Head of State. While there is a temptation to locate the contemporary developmental ideology of the state in a singular figure, it was a legion of political developmentalists who collectively shaped the ideology of Democracy with the King as Head of State. Kramol is one representative figure of those serving the state to advance a line of development through the maze of modernisation.[17]

Finally, we may note that when faced with failure, these political technocrats have ditched plans and even constitutions and started again (and again). Facing pendulum swings of progress and retrogress, they have often leaned on the military, or condoned those who do, to sort out the impending chaos of politics. They, too, conjure the spirit of supra-constitution to reset political order.

This is an under-told story behind Thailand's politics. Yet, without acknowledging its impact, scholars are unlikely to grasp the contradictions and ideological currents of the period.

THE MILITARY'S SACRED MISSION

If the scholars who engaged in planning political development embraced a technocratic and seemingly secular teleology of building a robust democracy with adjunct spiritual cement provided by the monarchy and Buddhism, other state practitioners linked the task to a more soteriological end – a sacred mission of holding the state amid secular and spiritual malaise. Chalermkiat Phiu-nuan, in this volume, explores how the military willingly embraces this mission role.

Chalermkiat was an associate professor in the philosophy department of Thammasat University. A populariser and translator of political and social theory, including Freud's work and author of a text on the political thought of Pridi Banomyong,[18] he is perhaps best known for his work *Political Thought of the Thai Military*. He reputedly hails from a family associated with high-level generals, thought to have been close to the Democratic Soldiers, a clique influential in the early 1980s, and whose politics he discusses sympathetically in the translation included here. More generally, this proximity may in part account for Chalermkiat's non-polemical and empathetic and measured treatment of military thought.

Given his interest in Freud, we might say that Chalermkiat's study offers a unique entry into the ideological psychology of the military. That is,

---

17 *Ibid.*, 10–15, 72, 145, 196–7.

18 Chalermkiat Phiu-nuan, ความคิดทางการเมืองของปรีดีพนมยงค์ [The Political Thought of Pridi Banomyong], Thai Studies Institute, 1984.

Chalermkiat allows us to see the military's superego, or what the military thinks it should do, and its id, or what it cannot help but do. Both are a product of the military's historical development as a central state institution and the anxieties and burden of its power and duty. In service to this idea, Chlaermkiat lays bare the cosmology of Thai military unconscious thought – rooted in the mentalities of the classic Thai Buddhist text, the *Three Worlds Cosmology of Phra Ruang* and its hierarchical view of the cosmos as a model for Thai society. Chalermkiat's work reveals the military as a corporate body taking its place in the great karmic chain of being tasked at the profane level with maintaining stability in a world of impermanence: a necessary but, by definition, impossible task. Writing in the early 1990s, Chalermkiat explained that the sacred mission of the military in this cosmology was principally protection of the state, of which the monarchy was but *one* part.

Chalermkiat's approach opens space for some degree of ideological generalisation and comparison of military coups. While others may see an endless series of military power grabs justified by contentless intellectual gymnastics, Chalermkiat sees a worldview. He concedes that each power grab has its distinction. He notes that generals and their intellectual sidekicks have not shied from writing political tracts and staked a career future on their espoused political ideology. Indeed there is an expectation that leading soldiers would have a coherent view on national development and the protection of sovereignty.[19] Chalermkiat's work references different cliques and personalities, indicating the variety of democratic ideological expressions that have come in the name of Thai-style democracy, from the period which he calls the 'era of the myth of democracy' (1932 to the early 1970s) to the opening of mass politics in the 1970s.

But more central to his contribution, and where it departs from many studies that focus on faction formation or formal aspects of a factions' political outlook, is Chalermkiat's precise dissection of the core concepts of security, freedom and equality used in pragmatic military thought. He outlines the ideational structure of that generation of soldiers that sought to shape the post-1976 landscape, which remains influential today. This is the kind of conceptual work that Nakharin (see above) has argued will better serve those who seek to understand Thai politics. Moreover, indeed

---

19 See Connors, *Democracy and National Identity*, 105–10.

it is precisely because of this conceptual focus that Chalermkiat can avoid a simple description of idiosyncratic political doctrines of the various military figures who have seized power. Instead, his approach discloses the unifying assumptions and fundamental identity of the superficially distinctive policy and doctrines that the military puts forward to rationalise their many power usurpations. Thus, just as Nakharin provides the discursive underpinnings of royalist relationship to the supra-constitution, Chalermkiat provides an accounting of the military's self-justifying role in coups d'état, which are but an episodic moment in the continuity of Thailand's supra-constitution.

Readers do not have to hold that such cosmologies drive all military thinkers as Chalermkiat describes them. However, his analysis of the connotations behind key military concepts should inform our understanding of the military's institutional statism and its willingness to seize power and enact the supra-constitution. This perspective adds both depth and caution to explanations based solely on individual factors such as ambition, ego or acting at the beck and call of the monarchy. His articulation of military utilitarianism in the context of a Buddhist and animist cosmology of impermanence and power is perhaps the most provocative and unexpected analysis of the Thai military ever offered.

BREAKING OUT AND CAGING IN:
POPULAR NEGOTIATIONS OF POWER

The idea of national security being a sacred military mission requiring politics led by the military, or more broadly a politics of statism, appeared by the 1990s to be 'bypassed' as one prominent Thai political scientist Chai-Anan Samudavanija put it.[20] Indeed, the early post-Cold War period of hyper-globalisation generated hyperbole on the state's retreat, but Pasuk Phongpaichit in her 1999 Wertheim Memorial Lecture on 'Civilising the State', reproduced here, sounded a word of caution about what this meant in Thailand.

Pasuk is an award-winning researcher and, with her spouse Chris Baker, recipient of the prestigious Fukuoka Prize in recognition of a remarkable life of joint scholarship and translation. The citation of their 2017 Grand Prize impresses with the range of their achievements and their skill as talented

---

20 See Chai-Anan, 'Old Soldiers Never Die, They Are Just Bypassed: The Military, Bureaucracy and Globalization', in Kevin Hewison (ed.), *Political Change in Thailand: Participation and Democracy*, London: Routledge, 1997.

and brilliant interpreters of social, economic and political changes.[21] Pasuk is a professor, now emeritus, at the Faculty of Economics and held the Political Economic Centre's first chair at Chulalongkorn University. She is a pioneering and fearless researcher on political and bureaucratic corruption and economic inequality, among other things. She continues to provoke and illuminate in recent work on Thailand's political and economic inequality.[22]

The context of Pasuk's 1999 lecture was Thailand's long march from statism to the political reform era of the 1990s. Even as elements of statist machinery and Cold War rhetoric remained in place, the relatively liberal constitutional settlement of 1997 allowed a remarkable re-imagining of the Thai state around different political idioms and practices, informed by a burgeoning civil society sector and the rise of business power.[23] However, rather than celebrate, Pasuk analysed. In 'Civilising the State', she recounted the significant changes that had impacted politics from the 1980s. While Thailand was formally democratising, she noted that politicians, bureaucrats and non-state influential figures were in some senses becoming stronger through patronage networks. Sometimes they collaborated as joint beneficiaries accessing or exploiting state finances, or they united against popular demands.

Pasuk averred that even as the Thai statist system was in retreat and the competitive electoral arena was becoming more critical in gaining national political power, it was not the case that citizens could expect a better future. Rather than a liberal state succeeding a conservative security state, bureaucrats of the old state now aligned with new political patrons, which narrowed the space in which people could play power against power. Ironically, it appeared that formal democratisation might close channels for the pursuit of interests by villagers excluded from national politics.

It was in the activities of civil society, of NGOs and people's organisations, that Pasuk saw the future of democratic deepening in Thailand. To that end, she painted a rich picture of interlocking networks of activists,

---

21 The award citation is available here: fukuoka-prize.org/en/laureates/detail/7ac41fcd-e696-4a6a-80eb-896490b6eaf1.

22 Pasuk Phongpaichit and Chris Baker (eds), *Unequal Thailand: Aspects of Income, Wealth and Power*, Singapore: NUS Press, 2016.

23 On the scope of this change see M.K. Connors, 'Goodbye to the Security State: Thailand and Ideological Change', *Journal of Contemporary Asia*, 33, 4, 2003. Ukrist Pathmanand, 'Globalization and Democratic Development in Thailand: The New Path of the Military, Private Sector, and Civil Society', *Contemporary Southeast Asia*, 23,1, 2001.

journalists, villagers and public intellectuals intent on making real the formal institutional gains of Thailand's democratic transition. Her lecture captures the spirit of the 'people's politics' era, characterised by coalitions of people's organisations and NGOs seeking redress from the state through multiple protests and marches to Bangkok. The kind of political disorder and citizen usurpation detailed in the lecture was anathema to military thinkers of Thai-style democracy described by Chalermkiat. Such developments challenged conservatism's image of unity between the state and the people.

But as is evident, Pasuk was no optimist. Her speech also offered a prophetic observation about the undoing of the 1997 people's constitution by citing Thirayut Bunmi (Boonmee in that chapter's transliteration). The latter recounted that he got no hearing when he went to the countryside to speak with NGOs and activist groups about good governance and the 1997 constitution. He bemoaned that the political possibilities contained in a newly constituted parliamentary democracy with its protection of rights and its support of party representation did not excite those present. Rather, the political discourse remained stuck on the old ground: '[t]he battle was still between the people and the state, the people and paternalist domination, the people and *rabop upatham*, the patronage system which now encompassed not only bureaucrats but elected representatives.'

This emerging fusion of bureaucratic and political power took an un-expected detour with the rise of Thaksin Shinawatra as Thailand's prime minister (2001–06). Thaksin sought to merge party and bureaucracy around his vision of economic development and win popular support through popular redistributive policies and expanded healthcare provision. However, Thaksin's emergence threw up new challenges not just to those associated with network monarchy but to a broader constituency seeking to embed the 1997 constitutional settlement, a challenge that ultimately led to the coup of 2006.

The return of statist politics and a military bent on its sacred mission after 2006, was of course, not Thaksin's responsibility alone, although his increasing authoritarianism was always going to create resistance. The enmity he stirred from those who had made the political reforms of the 1990s possible – the NGOs, intellectuals, scholar-bureaucrats and activists who had sought a constitutional reformation – was channelled into a move-ment against him. Conservative statists were also alarmed at the manner of Thaksin's full-frontal reformation of bureaucracy and his building of a personalistic network in the military.[24] This led to an anti-Thaksin pact among liberal reformers and conservative elements of the security state, which essentially held good through to the coup of 2014.[25] Even those of a liberal persuasion could tragically believe that the monarchy and military might serve to break a political deadlock or deal with an authoritarian figure. This was tragic because what followed such a pact was intensified authoritarianism and para- and actual state violence in 2008 and 2010.

ROYALIST RETURNS AND POLITICAL RUPTURES

The political pact against Thaksin embodied hyper-royalism and a belief in the exceptional abilities of the king to solve problems.[26] Pramuan Rujanaseri's 2005 book *Royal Power* is perceived by many as a hyper-royalist text representing the anti-Thaksin's movement's royalist reaction. It will provide readers with a popular account of the extraordinary role and powers presumed to reside in the monarchy. Pramuan was steeped in the ideological culture of service to the nation and crown. His book may be read as an extension of that service. Pramuan hails from a family with a long lineage in Thailand's powerful Ministry of the Interior, where Pramuan himself was the director of the Local Administration Department. After his retirement, he served as Deputy Minister to the Interior in Thaksin's government.

Although Pramuan was an MP for Thaksin's party, Thai Rak Thai, he was a member of a faction that waged open warfare with Thaksin over the constitutional status of the royally appointed auditor general. As the Auditor-General ramped up investigations into the government's budget irregularities, Thaksin sought to replace her, but the king did not sign or return documents approving her replacement.[27] As this drama played out, in 2004 Pramuan joined the chorus of Thaksin's critics and penned a book, *The Use of Power is Human Nature*.[28] Parliamentary officials obstructed its distribution. Pramuan criticised the semi-presidential nature of the 1997

---

24 See McCargo and Ukrist, *The Thaksinization of Thailand*; Pasuk Phongpaichit and Chris Baker, *Thaksin*, 2nd ed. Chiang Mai: Silkworm. Books, 2009.

25 Ukrist and Connors, 'Thailand's Public Secret'.

26 See Thongchai, *Thailand's Hyper-royalism*.

27 Michael K. Connors, 'Article of Faith: The Failure of Royal Liberalism in Thailand', *Journal of Contemporary Asia*, 38, 1, 2008, 151–3.

28 Pramuan Rujanaseri, การใช้อำนาจเป็นธรรมชาติของมนุษย์ [The Use of Power is Human Nature], Bangkok: Munithi phathana phalang phaendin, 2004.

constitution that had allowed Thaksin as prime minister to avoid parliamentary scrutiny by virtue of his overwhelming parliamentary majority. In 2005, Pramuan was one of nearly 60 MPs from Thaksin's party who signed a petition stating that attempting to remove the Auditor-General was an attack on royal power.[29] In the end, Thaksin retreated. During the stand-off, the issue of royal power took centre stage. To some, the question of how an electorally popular prime minister with an overwhelming parliamentary majority might be held accountable was now answered by reference to royal power. Pramuan emerged as one of the key popularisers of this response.

Pramuan's 2005 book *Royal Power* became a sensational part of a broader ideational debate about the nature of politics after the reform constitution of 1997. The book sold in hundreds of thousands. Crammed public lectures and television panel discussions followed. The book struck a chord and galvanised the sense that Thaksin was turning against both the benefits derived from traditional monarchical moral oversight in modern society and the intentions of the People's Constitution of 1997.

To read *Royal Power* is to peer into a more comprehensive and nuanced account of how one influential citizen mobilised an idealised monarchy to support conservative values and some formally liberal ones. Although the book's apparatus is not scholarly (there are no footnotes), its form of argument is ably structured. The book contrasts Thai culture, beliefs and values, and royal customary traditions with Thaksin's aggressive political transgressions.[30] In the face of these, Pramuan assured readers that, 'His Majesty the King is the harbinger of justice ... Civilians hold onto the King as their last resort, they appeal directly to the king, a tradition and belief that has existed since the Sukhothai era.'[31] The idea of an appeal to the king to rid Thailand of Thaksin was now weaponised.

Pramuan's book might be viewed as an archive of the accumulated sense of the monarchy's place in politics – a compilation of the new conservative common sense of moral guardianship that emerged as the ideology of Democracy with the King as Head of State formed and consolidated in the 1980s and merged with a vision of parliamentary democracy that functioned as the secular institution for the aggregation of the national interest. For conservatives, this moral and spiritual dimension to interpret-

---

29 Connors, 'Article of Faith', 152.

30 Pramuan Rujanaseri พระราชอำนาจ [Royal Powers], Bangkok: Sumet rujanaseri 2005.

31 *Ibid.,* 111.

ing Thailand's democratic development was for some more fundamental than the politics of right or the structures of liberal democracy. Indeed, for Pramuan, the latter had to do the work of cultural accommodation if they were to thrive in the Thai context. As he wrote, 'It is we who must adapt the concepts of power, rights and individualism to be in harmony with the concepts of Dharma, Metta [compassion] and reciprocal relationships.'

ROYALIST REFUGE AND THE
POLITICS OF DEPENDENCY

Saichon Sattayanurak is a leading chronicler and interpreter of Thai conservative thinkers. Since being nominated in the mid-1980s for a national research award for her MA thesis concerning the nineteenth century monarchy, she has emerged as a prodigious scholar working in Chiang Mai University's history department and is an accomplished authority on Thai intellectual history. Her recent award-winning two-volume study of Siamese intellectuals has revitalised the otherwise marginal status of intellectual history in Thailand.[32] Her work is motivated by a desire to understand how past nationalist conceptions continue to shape modern Thailand.

In the article translated for this volume, Saichon brings her astute historical perspective to analyse the anti-Thaksin movement's dependency on royal power and the judiciary. She links the anti-Thaksin movement and its fear of his challenge to monarchy to a collective memory of marginality. Saichon argues that the predominantly urban Sino-Thai middle class's dependence on royal power across different historical periods is contingent on that class's historical political marginality in a system dominated by an ethnic Thai bureaucracy and military that made Sino-Thai capital subject to rentier arrangements. From this perspective, the middle class see the monarchy and its judicial representatives as potential balancers against an extractive ethno-Thai authoritarianism. They provide an especially coveted refuge to the Sino-Thai when their status as ethnic outsiders is mobilised against them by military or political figures from time to time.

Indeed, as recently as 1997, Prime Minister General Chavalit Yongchaiyud, besieged by opposition to his faltering leadership during the Asian economic

---

32 Saichon Sattayanurak 10 ปัญญาชนสยาม เล่ม 1 ปัญญาชนแห่งรัฐสมบูรณาญาสิทธิราชย์ [10 Siamese Intellectuals, Volume I: The Absolute Monarchy Era], Bangkok: Openbook Press, 2014, and 10 ปัญญาชนสยาม เล่ม 2 ปัญญาชนหลังการปฏิวัติ 2475 [10 Siamese Intellectuals, Volume II: After the 1932 Revolution], Bangkok: Openbook Press, 2014.

crisis, admonished the urban middle-class Sino-Thai for their lack of support and warned against a popular uprising from the Northeast in support of his government:

> This country belongs to the Thai people. Those others who came to settle in this land, when they (*mun* in Thai) don't get what they want or suffer some damage, have risen up to make a noise. What they want is to destroy this land. I want the people to stand up for the country. This government will definitely not neglect you because we come from the poor.[33]

In exploring the cultural and historical dimensions of middle-class mobilisation against Thaksin and his successor governments, and their calls for royal intervention, Saichon builds on the political insights offered by Kasian Tejapira that the yellow-shirt politics of the People's Alliance for Democracy were a form of royal patriotism with the Sino-Thai confidently claiming their space in the royal nation.[34] But rather than being a statement of holier than thou royalism, Saichon reads this condition of dependence on royal and judicial authority as an indicator of the structural weakness of the burgeoning middle-class that sought security against a praetorian state or a majoritarian democracy. The security of the monarchy was entwined with their own. She writes:

> The middle class (together with the groups of Sino-Thai capitalists who were deeply concerned about their station in the new 'Thai nation' and about the high costs of business or 'economic rent' that they had to pay to those in power) dedicated themselves to royal powers and supported the construction of royal hegemony, enabling them always to call on *phrabarami*. Given that a military or political party leader's supreme loyalty to the king as head of state is essential to their acceptance of being under the king's supervision, the middle class has been very particular about the 'loyalty' that leaders have for the king.

---

33 Mun is a derogatory pronoun. Cited in Kasian Tejapira, 'The Misbehaving Jeks: The Evolving Regime of Thainess and Sino-Thai Challenges', *Asian Ethnicity*, 10, 3, 2009. Also see the report in *The Nation*, 18 September 1997. Chavalit's party was threatening to bring 1,000,000 protestors from the Northeast of Thailand, in a precursor of the regional/Bangkok divide that would emerge under Thaksin. Chavalit's party, the New Aspiration Party, was already organising around Isan identity, and Thaksin would take this further, benefiting from the merger with Chavalit's party. Of course, Thaksin was a Sino-Thai.

34 Kasian Misbehaving Jeks. See also Sittithep Eaksittipong, 'From Chinese "in" to Chinese "of" Thailand: The Politics of Knowledge Production during the Cold War', *Rian Thai: International Journal of Thai Studies* 10,1, 2017, 99–116.

Saichon provides a contemporaneous reading of a movement that, in conventional democratic terms, was wholly reactionary in its opposition to democratic elections from 2006 to 2014. Her effort to comprehend the historical, ideational and cultural elements of that reaction illustrates that the Bhumibol Consensus was not merely an elite affair but that a mobilised movement could call on the monarchy's service of power regulation and ultimately rely on a supra-constitutional ethos to advance its perceived interests.

CONCLUSION

Pramuan, in this volume, recounts a letter exchanged between King Narai (1656–88) and King Louis XIV (1643–1715) regarding Siamese conversion to Christianity. King Narai wrote:

> I immensely appreciate the King of France for the kind compassion you have for me but to disown the religion that has existed for 2,229 years is not an easy thing to do. If the missionaries could convert all my people to Christianity, I will follow suit. On another issue, I am surprised that the King of France would try to usurp the power of God. Isn't it God's will to have numerous religions in this world? Or else God would have created only one religion.

The response is, of course, salutary; it turns an offence into confidence. More broadly, its reproduction in Pramuan's *Royal Powers* connects to an abiding sense of conservative Thai uniqueness among those who see morality, politics and community as part of a larger cosmic order and who mobilise in that order's protection. The defensive way those influenced by traditionalist thought have reacted to criticisms of human rights abuse, democratic regression and outright dictatorship since the 2006 coup highlights a sensitivity about perceived liberal western imperialism, its purported universality of one secular god – liberal democracy. For such Thais, critics have failed to appreciate, let alone understand, the deeper meaning of Thai politics and the mechanisms required to restore stability – a condition of liberty – to a morally conceived nation-state.

Although the papers gathered here do not use Somchai's notion of a supra-constitution, Somchai named something that was ghosting Thai politics. If one reads the following chapters with supra-constitution in mind, it becomes apparent that the idea need not be restricted to constitutional and extra-constitutional practice in the politics surrounding the monarchy–

military nexus and coups d'état. It is more than an analytical concept, for it broadly points to the logics of extra-constitutional activity that placed moral and political primacy outside the conjunctural constitutional framework. For example, counter-intuitively and presciently, Pasuk's paper, in discussing the broadly liberal-communitarian people's politics behind liberalisation of the Thai state in the 1990s, would view the resulting changes as potentially narrowing the space for political negotiation as politician and bureaucrat became entwined. And as has been clear, many of those progressive forces were in turn seemingly compelled, in response to the narrowing of political space and Thaksin's attack on the 1997 constitution to seek refuge in the monarchy and the judiciary – a form of supra-constitutional politics that led to support of the 2006 coup. We can also observe in the chapters by Kramol, Pramuan, Saichon and Chalermkiat a cultural propensity among those tied to conservative values to embrace strongly ideological-sentimental orientations that provides support to the norms of the supra-constitution.

The idea of Thailand's supra-constitution offers much explanatory power regarding Thailand's prolonged failure to establish a political settlement grounded in shared national ideology and an enduring constitution. Of course, a range of fertile concepts have emerged in the wake of Thailand's crisis to name this political pathology, but these centre on reactive episodic or conjunctural moments, not enduring norms. Being foundational, the idea of a supra-constitution can help order this jumble of competing concepts into an overarching inquiry that explores the endurance of Thailand's conservative strain, its seepage into other ideological currents, and the frequency of political actors' submission to and exaltation of extra-constitutional power.

We hope that the works translated here might in some way assist in the process of social understanding. They do not offer comprehensive explanations, nor do we necessarily share their views. Rather, they do much to illuminate a conservative social imaginary that has powerfully shaped responses to communism, electoral democracy and political corruption. We believe that reading them will illustrate the significance of ideas and political commitments as motivators in the last decade's political struggles and offer insights into the ideological fabric of the Bhumibol Consensus. If the act of translation is unavoidably a deliberative process of cross-cultural communication, and this book deepens understandings of a not well-understood Thai conservatism, then its purpose will have been served.

CHAPTER 2

The Thai Supra-Constitution[1]

Somchai Preechasilpakul

After the change of regime from 'the king above the law to the king under the law',[2] or as it later became known 'change from the regime of absolute monarchy to democracy', there was great hope that the constitution would be the supreme rule specifying the interrelationship of the people, the state, and different state organs. Nevertheless, from 24 June 1932 to 24 June 2007, seventy-five years since the founding constitution, seventeen constitutions have been proclaimed (including those called administrative charters [interim constitutions]).[3] If one calculates, every constitution was in force on average for four years and five months, before being abrogated either by constitutional procedure or by being ripped up.

The frequent cycle of abrogation and promulgation of constitutions might lead to the belief that, in reality, the constitution is not the highest law in governing the country but an instrument that the elite use in competing for and establishing their own power without regard for agreed basic principles. The essence of the constitution can change according to the whim of those who hold power. Although there have been attempts to prevent the constitution from being ripped up as in the case of an article in the 1974

---

1 Originally published: Somchai Preechasilpakul, อภิรัฐธรรมนูญไทย [The Supra-Constitution] Bangkok: Pridi Banomyong Institute, 2007.

2 Pridi Banomyong cited in Malini Khumsupha อนุสาวรีย์ประชาธิปไตยกับความหมายที่มองไม่ เห็น (The Democracy Monument and Hidden Meanings], Bangkok: Samnakphim Wiphasa 2005, 40.

3 Editors' note: While there is no consistent pattern to how constitutions have been designated, most interim constitutions, issued after a coup d'état or the 1932 revolution were named 'administrative charters' [ธรรมนูญการปกครอง]. So named are the administrative charters of June 1932, 1959, 1972, 1977 and 1991. Other coup issued constitutions including 1947, 2006 and 2014 were designated as 'interim constitutions' [รัฐธรรมนูญแห่งราชอาณาจักรไทย (ฉบับชั่วคราว)]. The 1976 constitution, issued two weeks after the October 1976 coup, had no qualification and its preamble described a twelve-year plan to develop democracy. In this translation of Somchai's work, with the exception of the 1976 constitution, all constitutions issued after a coup d'état (or the 1932 revolution) are referred to as interim constitutions to indicate their status, unless they are referred to by official name.

constitution that stipulated that no amnesty be given to coupsters, in the end that constitution was revoked in a coup d'état and an amnesty law was enacted specifically for the coupsters.[4] Thus, constitutional articles in this vein are meaningless.

It cannot be denied that Thai constitutions have suffered setbacks under a constant cycle of drafting, promulgation and abolition by unconstitutional means. Indeed, it may seem as if the constitutional system has yet to be deeply rooted in the Thai polity. Constitutions, rather than being dependable, are like sticks in the political mud: easy to agitate and pull out.

To begin with, the condition of being the supreme law at the same time as being frequently torn up would seem to be a contradiction that is difficult to comprehend. Is there any framework to explain Thai constitutions, especially if considered from a longer-term perspective from the first proclamation of a constitution in the Thai polity to the present?

THREE VERSIONS OF THE CONSTITUTION

From the period since the change of regime led by the People's Party until the present there have been seventeen constitutions. Studies of those constitutions have been limited to specific constitutions to explain their structure and essence. Even though such studies help understand specific constitutions, they are limited in helping understand constitutions in a broader perspective. A broader perspective would illuminate the status of and changes in the body of the constitution.

Studying the Thai constitution from a long-term perspective, Saneh Chamarik analyses constitutions as the autobiography of relations of power, particularly between bureaucrat-politicians [civil servants and military officials in appointed political positions] and professional politicians [elected].[5] In the first period after the change of regime in 1932, bureaucrat-politicians had an important status and role in the constitution but, after the 14 October 1973 Event, professional politicians expanded their

---

4   Article 4 of the 1974 constitution prohibits amnesty for those who seek to overthrow the monarchy or the constitution.

5   Saneh Chamarik, การเมืองไทยกับพัฒนาการรัฐธรรมนูญ [Thai Politics and Development of the Constitution], Bangkok: Thai Studies Institute, 1986, 24. Editors' note: the Thai text refers to 'politician-state officials'. We refer to these as bureaucrat-politicians, as they cover both civil servants and military personnel serving in political office.

constitutional status and role. Somkiat Wanthana proposed to divide constitutions into two categories, namely those that intended to affirm the power and position of bureaucrat-politicians and those that intended to nurture elected professional politicians. Of the latter type, only three pre-1992 constitutions had been drafted to help develop the efficiency and stability of professional politicians.[6]

These approaches can illuminate more broadly the role of the constitution in the development of Thai politics. But if one considers the power relationship of three important groups, namely professional politicians whose basis is in parliament, bureaucrat-politicians whose basis is in the state bureaucracy, and the institution of monarchy, the role of these groups can be variously arranged in terms of their status inter-relationship so that only three constitutional forms appear. To put it another way, in the last seventy five years Thailand has really only had three constitutions: a parliamentary version, an authoritarian version, and a mixed parliamentary-bureaucratic polity version.

The Parliamentary Constitution

One fundamental principle of a parliamentary regime is the supremacy of parliament. This means that parliament possesses legislative power above all other organs. This concept is an important principle in England, stemming as it does from the long struggle between the monarchy and parliament that ended with parliament's victory.[7] In Thailand, the attempt to establish the supreme power of parliament through the constitution is reflected in the following important points.

Firstly, the constitution prescribes that parliament is an institution that has power above other political institutions by making the parliamentary regime the centre of power in both executive and legislative dimensions. In the executive dimension, a parliamentary constitution will place executive power under the supervision and scrutiny of parliament, such as having the parliament oversee the executive as it administers the country, or for exam-

---

6   Somkiat Wanthana, 'ชนชั้นนำกับประชาธิปไตยไทย' [Elites and Thai Democracy], in Suthachai Yimprasert (ed.), 60 ปี ประชาธิปไตยไทย [Sixty Years of Democracy], Bangkok: Creative Publishing, 1993, 95.

7   For more detail on the power struggle between the monarchy and the parliament, see Adam Tomkins, *Public Law*, Oxford: Oxford University Press, 2003.

ple by passing no confidence motions against the policy of the government, particular ministers or the cabinet.[8] Constitutional provisions of this kind aim to position parliamentary power above the executive. Parliament is thus simultaneously a source of support for and control over the executive.

In terms of power to legislate, the parliament is the principal organ charged with the duty of making law. The executive has no legislative power unless granted powers by parliament through acts of parliament. Even though the executive has the power to issue binding emergency decrees to solve urgent problems, these are subsequently subject to parliamentary approval. This is an affirmation of the principle of parliament's sole power to make law.

Nevertheless, apart from considering the relationship between parliament and the government it is necessary to consider the relationship between parliament and the institution of monarchy. Parliamentary constitutions place the status and role of the monarchy outside and above politics. For example, the 1932 constitution stipulated that 'members of the royal family from the rank of prince or princess upwards either by birth or designation have the status of being above politics.' Articles in this manner necessitate that politics is outside the boundaries and duties of the institution of monarchy, with the monarchy playing no role nor taking sides in conflicts that arise among people. For that reason, in any exercise of power by the king there must be a counter-signatory to the royal command. This means that even though an action may have the monarch's signature, it is held that if there are consequences to follow from that action, the responsibility lies with the counter-signatory. This does not mean that the king has no power – for instance, the king still has royal power to delay a draft bill that is proposed by parliament before it is declared law – but that power is not absolute. A bill nonetheless affirmed by parliament is deemed to be a law, even without an assenting royal signature.[9]

---

8   For details on control of the executive by the legislature see Rangsan Thanaphonpan, จารีต รัฐธรรมนูญไทยกับสันติประชาธรรม การแสดงปาฐกถาพิเศษป๋วย อึ๊งภากรณ์ 9 มีนาคม 2550 [Special Lecture: 'The Traditional Thai Constitution and Santiprachatham'], Bangkok: Openbooks, 2006, 198–9.

9   See for example Article 8 of the Administrative Charter (Temporary) 1932 [June 1932] that stipulated that the House of Representatives has the power to legislate. In cases where the king refused to accept legislation, it was returned to parliament after seven days for reconsideration. If a majority still supported the legislation it would be declared law. A similar provision was present in the [December] 1932 Constitution, Article 39, with differences only in terms of processes and duration.

Secondly, establishing parliamentary supremacy requires that parliament itself comes from the choice of the people, whether it be a unicameral or bicameral house. If it is bicameral, consisting of a house of representatives and a senate, then it follows that elections are the clearest affirmation of the people's choice. However, even if the senate is not directly elected, but comes from another method such as indirect elections or by appointment, it may have a part in establishing the parliamentary system if it has less power than the house of representatives. If the senate has an equal power and role, or even a greater position than the elected house of representatives, then this is not a system of parliamentary supremacy. Similarly, with the house of representatives, in the case where there is only one category of members of parliament, MPs must come from elections by the people. If there are several categories, those who come from elections must be more numerous and have the main role and power in that parliament.

Thirdly, in establishing the supremacy of parliament so that it has the principal role in governing the country and is linked with the people, state officials must act as functionaries as if they were one organ of the political system. Those who have a role in the parliament must not have civil service or military positions, and the constitution that aspires to build a parliamentary system will stipulate this. This is especially so in cases of a bicameral parliament, where the senate has a legislative role. For example, the 1946 constitution (Article 24, part 2) stipulated that 'members of the senate must not be state officials.'

The Authoritarian Constitution

The quest for political power by tearing up the constitution and founding new political power is an important factor in the advent of the authoritarian constitution. The essential characteristic of this type of constitution is based on the principle of Power is Right. To put it another way, force is the source of authoritarian political legitimacy and as such it rejects stipulated processes for constitutional amendment.

In founding an authoritarian constitution, the electoral basis of parliament is not important. Legislative organs established during the enforcement of an authoritarian constitution consist typically of appointed members as occurred in the interim constitutions of 1959, 1972, 1976, 1977, 1991 and 2006. If members come from both appointment and election then the status of those coming from appointment is either equal to or even greater than those who are elected, as occurred in the interim constitution of 1947. Generally, the members of the legislative organ are appointed by the leader of the coup group and there are no transparent regulations on the required qualifications for appointment. Indeed, there are no regulations specifying the characteristics of someone who should be barred from membership of the legislative body. Anyone may be appointed. In practice, it may be observed that most of those appointed to legislative bodies come from the high ranks of the state bureaucracy. State officials, civil and military, are the most important social basis of legislative bodies under authoritarian constitutions.

Besides considering the legislative features of authoritarian constitutions, another important characteristic to consider is the absolute power wielded by the executive, first seen in the interim constitution of 1959, Article 17.[10] This mandated that any command or action of the prime minister was lawful. The result of this kind of stipulation was that any action by the prime minister, even though it conflicted with fundamental principles of legal government or the rule of law (such as punishing individuals without due legal process) in effect became law. This acceptance of the arbitrary power of the executive or of a coup group in the authoritarian constitution was preserved in the interim constitution of 2006.

It is understood that authoritarian constitutions are a product of the seizure of power by a coup group that rips up the old constitution and writes a new one. This is accomplished by force. Nevertheless, a coup group's use of force accepts and establishes the importance of the monarchy, which in turn constructs the legitimacy of their regime. This is done by affirming the protection and continuity of the monarchy while overthrowing other political institutions, such as Sarit Thanarat did when he seized power on 20 October 1958 announcing that: 'We elevate the king to a position of eternal worship. This seizure of power is for the eternal preservation of the

---

10 Article 17 of the Administrative Charter of the Thai Kingdom, 1959 stipulated that 'Pending operation of this Charter, if the Prime Minister finds it desirable to prevent or suppress an act giving rise to the subversion of the national security or Throne or an act contributable to the impairment, disturbance or threat against the internal or external peace of the Kingdom, the Prime Minister, upon resolution of the Council of Ministers, shall be bestowed with the power to issue any order or to perform any act whatsoever. Such order or act shall be deemed lawful. Upon issuance of any order or performance of any act in virtue of the foregoing paragraph, the Prime Minister shall inform the Assembly thereof.' Editors' note: This follows the translation of the Charter available at www.thailaws.com.

institution of the king as head of state.'[11] And to affirm their loyalty, the revolutionary group offered a vow to the king:

> In this revolution even though it is necessary to change national institutions, the one thing that the Revolutionary Council will not allow to change is the regime with the king as head of state. The Revolutionary Council will forever stand firm and protect this regime. The Revolutionary Council has already promised this to the people in several announcements and let us offer this to His Majesty once more: the new constitution will securely preserve this regime.[12]

Following this, the royal bureau issued a statement to the head of the Revolutionary Council which was duly reproduced in its 10th Announcement:

> The king has remarked that the declared intentions of the Revolutionary Council to preserve safety, the wellbeing of the nation and develop the country are good. Once you have stated these intentions you should pursue them in good faith, and uphold the general interest. As for what must follow next, give this thorough consideration. When those promised objectives are achieved, we will be grateful.[13]

This reflected not only a stand on preserving the monarchy but also that the monarchy became a customary party in the proclamation of a new constitution once the old one had been torn up. Henceforth, the declaration of a new constitution had to be proclaimed in the name of the king. This was first practised in the Administrative Charter of the Thai Kingdom, 1959, and was followed thereafter so that it became a custom of Thai constitutions.

The Mixed Parliamentary-Bureaucratic Polity Constitution

While the parliamentary constitution nurtures a political system of parliamentary supremacy based on elections and the authoritarian constitution emphasises a political system that is principally based on the bureaucratic polity, the mixed constitution manifests and combines the principles of both. It stipulates that parliament has its basis in elections, it recognises political parties as an important institution in the political system, and elections as an

---

11 ประกาศของคณะปฏิวัติ ฉบับ ที่ 2 ลงวันที่ 20 ตุลาคม 2501 [Announcement 2 of the Revolutionary Council, 20 October 1958].

12 The vow, issued on October 20 is reproduced in คณะปฏิวัติ ฉบับที่ 9 ลงวันที่ 21 ตุลาคม 2501 [Announcement 9 of the Revolutionary Council, 21 October 1958].

13 ประกาศของคณะปฏิวัติฉบับที่ 10 ลงวันที่ 21 ตุลาคม 2501 [Announcement 10 of the Revolutionary Council, 21 October 1958].

indispensable way of choosing individuals for legislative organs. Elections are a source of legitimacy for establishing and changing governments, with MPs from political parties being the determining factor in this political process.

In addition to accepting the parliamentary system's relation to elections, the mixed constitution accepts the parallel power of the state bureaucracy. State officials are able to have a political role in important organs, whether it be in the executive or the legislature. For example, there is no prohibition on serving state officials being appointed to the senate; nor does the prime minister have to be an elected member of parliament. This mixture was exemplified in the constitutions of 1978 and 1991 (before amendment in 1992). In the 1978 constitution there was no requirement that the prime minister must come from an election.[14] Eligibility for appointment to the senate required 'academic or practical expertise in areas which could bring benefit to the national administration'.[15] Typically, state officials were the greater proportion of appointed senators. The respective roles of professional politicians and bureaucrat-politicians were an important factor in this system, and the relationship between them was fluid and changeable depending on political circumstances. Thus, if there is a democratic mood in society the role of professional politicians will be more pronounced. Conversely, if the mood is dictatorial, state officials will play a greater role. Even so, in this type of political system, both groups are required.

Thus, if one considers the role of politicians and state officials under the mixed constitution, before the late 1980s the role of the state officials was quite pronounced, whereas after the late 1980s the role and status of politicians increased. So, for example, the constitutions of 1949 and 1978 stipulated that the president of the senate was the president of the parliament, and the president of the house of representatives was the vice-president of the parliament. This stipulation was preserved in the 1991 constitution, but after the May 1992 Event the constitution was amended and the roles reversed. The amendments also required that the prime minister be an elected member of the house of representatives. These changes reflected that the structure of politics under the mixed constitution was increasingly linked to a parliamentary system based on elections.

---

14 See Article 84, 1978 Constitution.

15 See Article 146, 1978 Constitution.

Under circumstances of episodic struggle between professional politi-cians and bureaucrat-politicians, the monarchy, which had a limited role after the 1932 change of government, came to have greater security both in the written and the traditional Thai constitution.

Regarding written constitutions, the 1932 constitution attempted to found parliamentary supremacy, but the 1949 constitution incorporated the monarchy by legislating that Thailand is a Democracy with the King as Head of State. This was enacted in subsequent permanent constitutions [constitutions that typically succeed interim constitutions], with the exception of the amended 1932 constitution (1952). The legislating of Democracy with the King as Head of State reflects the creation of a unique character to democracy in Thai society by accepting the expanded powers of the king, as evidenced in several laws.

For example, consider the royal prerogative to delay parliamentary bills. In the initial period of constitutional rule, in the event that the king disagreed with proposed legislation, the parliament could reaffirm the legislation and the prime minister resubmit it to the king. If the king still would not give his signature to the legislation, the prime minister could declare it law. This was the case in the interim constitution of 1932 [June 1932], the constitution of 1932 [December] and the interim constitution of 1947. Subsequently, this simple majority requirement was changed to a two-thirds majority in the event that the king would not sign legislation. This expanded requirement first appeared in the 1949 constitution, en-suring that passing legislation against the king's wish was more difficult. Another change was that regarding the prohibition on accusing or suing the king, which was first enacted in the constitution of 1949 and has since been present in every constitution.

As for the customs of the Thai constitution, it became a convention that the establishment of a new constitution was by royal signature after a coup d'état. And even though there is a counter-signature to the royal command by the leader of a coup group, in one respect the meaning was clear: declar-ing a new constitution must be in the king's name, which is equivalent to affirming that the king has the constituent power.

The Future of the Three Types of Constitutions

Even though Thailand has had 17 constitutions, if one considers their substance it is clear that each falls into one of the three constitutional frameworks: parliamentary, authoritarian, or mixed. However, it should be recognised that while it is possible to fit constitutions into this typology, some constitutions are exemplars of one type, and some will combine the characteristics of several types. For instance, some may reflect both parliamentary and mixed elements. A fundamental question that emerges from analysing the three types of Thai constitutions regards the direction in which the Thai constitution is headed.

Regarding the parliamentary constitution there is little possibility of this prevailing owing to its basis in elections. The rise to power of 'wicked' politicians in the recent period from the Chatichai period (1988–91) and Thaksin period (2001–06) has resulted in a negative evaluation of politicians and parties on the part of society. Politicians have become viewed as outcasts who must be subject to extreme control and scrutiny. And not only are they wicked, corrupt and selfish, the parliamentary system which has its basis in election is now transformed, in this view, into a 'parliamentary dictatorship'. Therefore, in the immediate future there is little hope for this type of constitution. Even so, the electoral system is still a fundamental element that has to be accepted and implemented, but this will not entail parliamentary supremacy over other political institutions.

As for authoritarian constitutions, it is possible these will reemerge, provided that the law guarantees the legitimacy of a coup d'état. But such authoritarian constitutions tend to be more and more short term because of the emergence of democratic forces in Thailand, in addition to the international pressure that supports democracy. This leads to the use of absolute power being subject to more scrutiny and the declaration of an authoritarian constitution largely is an interim measure while a new constitution is written.

This is not meant to suggest that the authoritarian constitution will not influence the permanent constitution [then currently being deliberated by a coup-appointed constitutional drafting committee, which was promulgated in 2007]. The lack of trust surrounding politicians will ensure that state officials will have a role in directing politicians who are now stigmatised as outcasts. In the past the power of state officialdom, and especially that of the military, would be expressed through the parliamentary system by having members in the senate. But presently, that force has been transformed into independent agencies that have the duty to scrutinise, oversee and punish politicians. This form of power first occurred in the 1997 constitution, as the vast majority of people who took positions in the independent agencies were former state officials, while those from outside the state bureaucracy were a tiny minority. This was especially so of those agencies that had the power to punish or judge with legal consequence and those who played a role were increasingly from the justice system, including judges, prosecutors and police. Therefore, the new permanent constitution will inevitably be nothing other than a mixed constitution. Nevertheless, the result will be a constitution that arises from the royal prerogative of the king as an institution above politics with the duty to protect the continued existence of the Thai polity by having an important role in supporting both democratic and bureaucratic forces.

THE RULES OF THE CONSTITUTION

Even though there have been many constitutions with different characteristics, making it difficult to understand the basic characteristics of the general Thai Constitution, in time some of these characteristics came to be accepted as the ways things should be done. At first, these may have been novel but subsequently they had to be observed. They became the unquestionable norm. Of the features, or what might be held to be rules, of the Thai Constitution, there are five.

The Constitution is the Highest Law, Temporarily

In governing according to liberal democratic thought, the constitution has the status of being the highest law in determining the relationship of the state and the people, and between organs of the state. In its standing as the highest law, the constitution should be difficult to amend. This is evident in the constitution of many countries where it is harder to amend than other laws. Being the highest law, it must also be secure.

The constitutions written after the change of government in 1932 were intended to be a permanent basis of government. These constitutions from the outset expressed expectations of their longevity, as in this preamble from the 1932 constitution:

> May the constitution of our kingdom be a lasting and effective system
> of laws, the source of happiness, peace and goodness to the people for a
> long time. May it also lead Siam to prosperity and great honour. May the
> members of the royal family, civil and military officials, and the people

be unanimous in observing the constitution into perpetuity with Siam. These are the royal wishes in every respect.

The hope that the constitution would always coexist with the nation, re-appeared in the constitution of 1946[16] and even though that constitution replaced the 1932 constitution, it did so in accord with constitutional processes – thus there was continuity.

Political turbulence led to a seizure of power in 1947 and subsequently the abrogation of the old constitution and promulgation of a new one. This important turning point, which created the temporary character of the supreme law, was a consequence of political change that did not follow the framework of the constitution then in force. After a successful seizure of power, a new constitution was declared that reflected the need for tempo-rary enforcement under an interim coup administration. Temporary law was manifested in two ways. Firstly, it was designated as an interim consti-tution as in the case of the 1947 constitution. Secondly, it was stipulated that there would be an organisation to draft a new constitution, such as in the administrative charters of 1959, and 1972, 1977 and 1991. Because it was clear from the start that the enforcement of this type of constitution was intended to be temporary, there was never any expectation of it being used in perpetuity.[17] If the Administrative Charter of Siam, 1932 [June], is included it will be found that since 1932, eight of seventeen constitutions were interim. The frequent appearance of interim constitutions has worn down hopes that any constitution would be permanent.

At the beginning of the political fluctuations in the mid- to late 1940s it appeared that there was still hope expressed in constitutional preambles that the constitution would be secure. The constitution of 1932 (amended 1952) stipulated that:

> May the constitution of the Kingdom of Thailand serve to ward off the great perils that may attack the nation, religion and the people. May the Thai people unite unanimously in observing the constitution to bring peace to his Majesty's subjects. May the members of the royal family, civil and military officials, and the people be united to live well into perpetuity under democracy and the Thai state. These are the royal wishes in every respect.

---

16 Although in the 1946 constitution the name of the country was no longer Siam, but Thailand.

17 This does not mean that interim constitutions were only briefly in force. The 1959 interim constitution remained in force until 1968.

From the period after the 1932 constitution (amended 1952), hopes that a constitution would endure dwindled. What had once been unequivocal written stipulations on the permanence of the constitution now became ambiguous. And even though the 1968 constitution was written in a similar fashion as the preamble above, it did not embed its hopes in a specific constitution, so much as a constitutional method: 'to nurture a complete constitutional method with stability, as long as possible.' It cannot be denied that this changed sentiment resulted from the serial experience of constitutions being torn up. This made it difficult to hope that any future constitution would avoid the fate of its predecessors. This realisation of constitutional impermanence appeared in preambles in constitutions from 1974 to 1997 which called for people to protect the constitution but had no statement regarding constitutional perpetuity. The 1997 constitution reflected this understanding thus:

> May the Thai people unite in observing, protecting and upholding the Constitution of the Kingdom of Thailand in order to maintain the democratic regime of government and the sovereign power derived from the Thai people, and to bring about happiness, prosperity, and dignity to His Majesty's subjects throughout the Kingdom according to the will of His Majesty in every respect.[18]

The Sanctity of the Constitution

Thai society should be counted as one that uses constitutions profligately, given its record of frequently tearing them up. It has been said that tearing up a constitution is easier than tearing up the facile regulations of some agencies.[19] If those with power consider that a constitution does not reflect their needs or interests when there is a conflict and they amend or tear it up, then it is clear that this constant cycle reflects that the political rules of the game have not been absorbed by different power groups of Thai society. The constitution has not been successful in establishing commonly agreed political rules. And yet, despite this recognised failure, the necessity of hav-

---

18 We have followed the translation of the preamble provided by the Council of State. See www.asianlii.org/th/legis/const/1997/1.html

19 Nidhi Eoseewong รัฐธรรมนูญฉบับวัฒนธรรมไทย [The Thai Cultural Constitution] in Nidhi Eoseewong, ชาติไทย, เมืองไทย, แบบเรียนและอนุสาวรีย์ [Thai Nation, Thailand, School Texts, and Monuments], Bangkok: Matichon, 1995, 136.

ing a constitution co-existent with the Thai polity has become sacrosanct. From this perspective, the 'sanctity of the constitution' means that after the change of government in 1932, no matter what the political circumstances were, however turbulent, whether rule was by dictatorship or semi-democracy, it was still necessary to have a constitution as the supreme law. And while there were non-constitutional intervals, these were only very short-lived before a new constitution would be promulgated.

If one considers all Thai constitutions (excluding the 1932 interim constitution) they may be divided into two groups. The first group consists of those constitutions that can claim continuity, either coming from constitutional amendment or by the establishment of a drafting process in accord with existing constitutional provisions. In this grouping, there is never a void in the enforcement of the constitution as the old constitution only lapses when the new one is declared. The second type of constitution has no continuity and does not spring from an existing constitution. In this case, the power to frame the constitution comes from the seizure of power by force in the form of various types of coups d'état, such as a Revolutionary Council, National Administrative Reform Council, or National Peace-keeping Council. In promulgating a coup-originated constitution, the first act of revoking the old constitution creates a constitutional void in Thai society. Even so, it is possible to separate this second group into three periods.

In the first period from 1932 to 1957 there were two coup-originated constitutions, namely the constitutions of 1947 and 1932 (amended 1952). An interesting observation is that during the process of abolition of a constitution there was no constitutional void. In the first instance, the coup occurred on 8 November 1947 and the new constitution was proclaimed the following day. In the second instance, the coup of 29 November 1951, the proclamation of an interim constitution occurred on the same day.[20] But it was only on 6 December 1951 that the king royally commanded that the 1932 constitution be used. However, Phibun Songkram countersigned a royal command on 30 November to appoint the House of Representatives, applying article 10 of the 1932 constitution. This was, of course, before the royal command noted above. Thus, there was no vacuum, as the constitution was effective one day after the coup.

---

20 คำแถลงการณ์ฉบับที่ 1 ของคณะบริหารประเทศชั่วคราว ลงวันที่ 29 พฤศจิกายน 2494 [Declaration 1 of the Interim National Executive, 29 November 1951].

In the second period between 1958 and 1972, there were two coup-originated constitutions: namely, the interim constitutions of 1959 and 1972. The 1959 interim constitution was a product of the 20 October 1958 coup. After seizing power, the coupsters announced the abrogation of the 1932 (amended 1952) constitution and ruled without a constitution until 28 January 1959. This was a constitutional void of 98 days and was the first time in Thai politics that a coup group had revoked a constitution and not declared its replacement. This occurred again in the self-coup of 17 November 1971, led by General Thanom Kittikachorn, which revoked the 1968 constitution.[21] The coup group did not declare a new constitution and it was not until 15 December 1972 that a new constitution was promulgated. Thailand was without a constitution for one year and 27 days, the longest period since 1932.

In the third period, 1974 to 2006, there were four coup-originated constitutions. The constitution of 1976 was declared 15 days after the coup; the interim constitution of 1977 was declared 18 days after the coup; the interim constitution of 1991 was declared 5 days after the coup; and the interim constitution of 2006 was declared 11 days after the coup. The third period is characterised by there being no long interval without a constitution, unlike the second period.

Bearing in mind the continuities and discontinuities of Thai constitutions it is evident that, in the first period elites understood the importance of the constitution. And even though there were unconstitutional changes of government, new constitutions immediately succeeded those revoked. In the second period, when military dictatorships held power, the importance of the constitution was diminished as evidenced by the long gap between a coup d'état and the declaration of a new constitution and the willingness to use the revolutionary coup group's power, in the interim, to issue many orders and regulations. As for the third period, which followed 14 October 1973, the importance of constitutions was increased by the expansion of democratic forces in Thailand, the convergence and maturing of the parliamentary system and the development of the free market at the international level. And even though the forces in the bureaucratic polity could still stage coups, they were compelled to promulgate a new constitution quickly and

---

21 ประกาศของคณะปฏิวัติ ฉบับที่ 3 ลงวันที่ 17 พฤศจิกายน พ.ศ.2514 [Announcement 3 of the Revolutionary Council, 17 November 1971].

depend less on the exercise of the coup group's power, unlike the era of military dictatorships.

It must be recognised that there is a difference in the Thai polity between having a constitution and having a constitutional regime. In the latter case, constitutionalism establishes a legal system based on the rule of law. In the former case, having a constitution may simply mean having rules that are called the highest law, but the essence of that constitution may gravely conflict with a rule-of-law state, such as legally legitimating a coup group's use of absolute power while not allowing any other organisation to scrutinise or balance that power. Such things can occur in Thai constitutions.

The Tradition of Revoking and Promulgating Constitutions

In the last seventy five years, from the change of government in 1932 to June 2007, there has never been a constitution that stipulates how it can be unconstitutionally revoked to make way for a successor. However, the power struggles and the turbulence of Thai politics has created customary practices in the abrogation and promulgation of a constitution.

From the very beginning of coups d'état in the Thai polity, tearing up the constitution was not something that the coup group did with its own power. The coup of 8 November 1947, which involved the repeal of the 1946 constitution without following constitutional procedure, was the first time this happened in Thai constitutional history. Notably, this was expressed in the preamble to the 1947 constitution:

> The majority of the Thai people and members of the national armed forces are one in respectfully calling for the repeal of the present constitution and for the promulgation of a new constitution, in the hope that by these means the country shall be in a state of progress, the sufferings of the people will be lessened, and the situation will gradually be brought back to normal.

Thus, the abrogation of the constitution by the coup group was done under a royal command that proclaimed the new constitution. A similar sequence occurred in the coup of 29 November 1951:

> Wherefore the Army, Navy, Airforce, Police, Promoters of the 1932 change of government, members of the 1947 Coup Council, as well as loyal citizens, with a steadfast purpose to ensure the continuity of the nation, the Faith and the Chakri Dynasty as well as the constitutional regime,

act in complete accord and unanimity to revive the constitution dated 10 December 1932 for the safety and prosperity of the nation.[22]

The declaration revoking the old constitution and proclaiming a new one was an exercise of the coup group's power, but several days later a royal command was issued proclaiming that the December 1932 constitution be used, with the coup group countersigning the royal command.

At the early stage of coup-making, the use of power to revoke a constitution was not separate from the power to proclaim an interim constitution, accompanied by a royal command. A coup group's self-founding of power by revoking a constitution only emerged in the coup of 20 October 1958. In Declaration 3 of the Revolutionary Council,

> As the Revolutionary Council deems it necessary to newly amend the Constitution of the Kingdom of Thailand, and so as to proceed appropriately, therefore at this point the Constitution of the Kingdom of Thailand 1932 (amended 1952) is repealed.[23]

This form of abrogation by the coup group led by Sarit became a model for future acts by coupsters using their own power to rip up a constitution. For example, after the coup of 17 November 1971, Revolutionary Council Order Number 3 abolished the constitution of 1968 and after the coup of 6 October 1976 Order 3 of the National Administrative Reform Council abolished the 1974 constitution. The practice of coup groups ripping up of constitutions by force has been passed down like a coup tradition even up to the seizure of power on 19 September 2006 when the 1997 constitution was revoked after the Council of Reform with the King as Head of State issued Order 3.

While the custom of abrogation proceeded based on the coupsters' free-standing power, the proclamation of a new constitution was under royal command. And even though the coup group could tear up the constitution in 1958, they had to confer with the king to gain a royal command to proclaim a new constitution. Thus, proclamation of a new constitution was not something the coup group could do with its own power. This has

---

22 คำแถลงการณ์ฉบับที่ 1 ของคณะบริหารประเทศชั่วคราว ลงวันที่ 29 พฤศจิกายน 2594 [Declaration 1 of the Interim National Executive 29 November 1951].

23 ประกาศของคณะปฏิวัติ ฉบับที่ 3 ลงวันที่ 20 ตุลาคม 2501 [Announcement of the Revolutionary Council 3, 20 October 1958]

been the model followed by every subsequent coup; there has never been a constitutional proclamation without a royal command.[24]

Abrogation by coup and proclamation by royal command was not only a cyclical political phenomenon; judicial institutions also played an important role in guaranteeing the legality of the process. In a case from 1952, the prosecution alleged that a defendant had conspired to harm and overthrow the government led by Phibun Songkram from 1 March to 2 October 1948. The defendant contested the charges by arguing that the Phibun-led government was not legal as it had come to power through force. The Supreme Court ruling (Case 1153–1154/1952) found that:

> On the issue that the defendant sought to overthrow the government on the grounds that it was illegal: It is held that overthrowing a government and establishing a new government by use of force, at the first stage is probably illegal until the people accept and respect it. The criminal court found that the government the defendant tried to overthrow was effectively the rightful government, which means that the people accept and respect it. The Appeals court did not overturn this truth. Therefore, the claim that the government is illegal is inadmissible.

The Supreme Court ruling regarding the legality of a government that came to power through a coup noted that at first it arguably may be illegal, but if the people accept and respect it and the group exercising administrative power is able to maintain peace without facing resistance, then that government is rightful by law.

Furthermore, this determination that the legality of a government came from its ability to exercise administrative power was clearly expressed in Supreme Court Case 45/1953 in which the plaintiff, Mr Thongyen Lilaphian, sued the Minister of Finance. The plaintiff claimed that the defendant in his position as minister had sacked the plaintiff according to Order 472/1947 and had withheld his pension. The plaintiff claimed that the defendant did not have the power to remove him from the civil service because the 1947 constitution, which was then in force and under which the defendant had assumed ministerial responsibilities, could not be considered law as it had come from a coup d'état. Thus, the defendant's position as minister was not legal. The Supreme Court found that:

---

24 Thailand has had eight constitutions that have come from coups d'état: 1947, 1951 1959, 1972, 1976, 1977, 1991 and 2006.

The fact is that in 1947 the coup group successfully seized power, and in administering the country in this way it is accepted that the coup group has the power to change, revise, repeal or enact laws according to the revolutionary system so as to give continuity to the administration of the nation. Otherwise, there would be no basis for peace in the country. Thus, the 1947 interim constitution is law.[25]

The Supreme Court's ruling, apart from accepting the seizure of power by the coup group once its seizure of power had been successful, also legalised the coup group's use of power to amend or revoke any law. The approach taken in this ruling by the court became a norm in the considerations of subsequent Supreme Court cases, such as the rulings in 1442/1962, 1234/1980, 2376/1983, which affirmed that the success of a coup d'état was the critical condition bearing on the legality of a coup group's use of power.

Accepting that coup groups had the power to change, revoke or amend the constitution became a basic principle of the judiciary. And this concept has had an important influence in legalising the declaration of orders of a coup group to have the unquestionable force of law, including amnesty laws that erase the coup group's wrongdoing. Therefore, a coup group's cycle of abolition of a constitution and proclamation by royal command has the status of a custom in the Thai polity that is secure and enduring to this day.

The Thai Constitution: The More They are Written, the Longer They Become

A fundamental debate in the drafting of a constitution is the question of whether a shorter or a longer one may be more effectively enforceable. It is not necessary in this analysis to take sides on this question; the purpose is to point out which form Thai constitutions tend to take, and the factors that account for this.

In this analysis of the length of constitutions, emphasis will be given only to those that were considered permanent. Interim constitutions that aimed at legalising a coup group and prescribing the precise steps for making a new constitution are not considered here. They had few articles. The eight interim charters (including the June 1932 constitution) ranged from

---

25 Editors note: The translation of the court's decision draws from Streckfuss, D. 2011. *Truth on Trial in Thailand: Defamation, Treason, and Lèse-majesté*, New York: Routledge, p. 120.

20 to 39 articles, except the interim charter of 1947, whose 98 articles made it much longer than any preceding constitution.

Of the nine constitutions that were drafted with the intent of being permanent it is useful to divide them into two periods, 1932–72 and 1973–2006.

In the first period the length varied from 68 to 183 articles, in general, this was shorter than those in the second period. The 238-article 1974 constitution was the first to have more than 200 articles. Every subsequent permanent constitution had more than 200 articles: 1978 (206); 1991 (223) 1997 (336).[26]

What character did the additional articles take? They took two forms. In the first form there was the legislating of a new principle that was not present in previous constitutions. The 1932 constitution had seven chapters, namely: general provisions, the monarchy, rights and responsibilities of the Siamese people, the house of representatives, the cabinet, courts, and constitutional amendment. In the 1949 constitution, additional chapters covered policy directives of the state and the constitutional tribunal. As for the 1974 constitution, the rights and responsibilities of the Thai people were now divided into separate chapters. The 1978 constitution added a chapter on local government, while the 1997 constitution added chapters on the scrutiny of state power and on the state auditor. Some of the additional chapters expanded either state organs or the substantive matter dealt with under the chapter. It is noteworthy that every new chapter included in a constitution remained in succeeding constitutions.

The second characteristic of constitutional lengthening took the form of elaboration. In this case, there were articles in past constitutions that were considered ambiguous or which were subject to inconclusive debate regarding applicable boundaries. For example, Article 114 of the 1978 constitution gave parliamentary privilege to MPs and senators in statements of fact or opinion to protect them from legal proceedings. It extended protection to those who printed and recorded proceedings according to parliamentary rules. An issue on this matter later arose regarding whether such parliamentary privilege extended to broadcasts of parliamentary meetings and whether a harmed third party could sue. On this matter the constitution was unclear. The 1991 constitution clarified that privilege did

---

26 As for the draft constitution deliberated under the 2006 interim constitution, the draft used at public hearings has 299 articles.

not extend to television or radio broadcasts of parliamentary sessions that were harmful to third parties.[27]

The requirement of greater clarity had the consequence that some articles used in a previous constitution were elaborated or new articles were added to a successor constitution. For example, Articles 15 and 16 in the constitutions of 1932 and 1946 respectively were the same: 'Individuals have the duty to respect the law and to protect the country, assist the crown by paying taxes etc., etc. under conditions and methods that the law prescribes.' Subsequently, in the 1949 constitution, this single article became five.[28]

One basic question is what led to the lengthening of the constitution by elaboration or addition? There were three factors.

The first is that the life cycle of the constitution was short. Given this condition, it was difficult to establish constitutional conventions, by which is meant accepted unwritten rules and practices relating to the constitution. Such conventions would develop over time from a process of competition, struggle and agreement on the rules that must be followed. Constitutional continuity was necessary for there to be acceptance and respect of behavioural protocols such that they became customary. Consequently, the brief lifespan of each constitution has limited the conditions for such conventions and norms to emerge and therefore required that rules be expressly stated.

The second point is that there has been rejection of constitutional interpretation in several matters regarding constitutional enforcement. Differences of constitutional interpretation have occurred because the text is highly general or ambiguous. When this occurs and the matter goes to the relevant agency for consideration, the resulting directive is often not accepted by relevant parties. Thus, when a new constitution is being drafted there will be proposals for clearer wording to avoid former interpretations. This factor highlights that the perceived level of expertise and respect for instrumentalities responsible for issuing acceptable directives regarding the constitution is low.

Thirdly, there is the relationship between the sanctity of the constitution and the proliferation of new provisions within it. The extent of this expansion is evident if one compares the 1932 and 1997 constitutions. Now, in one respect this reflects the increased importance and status of the constitution as the supreme law. That being so, individuals or groups

---

27 Article 125 of the 1991 constitution
28 Pridi Banomyong [Pridi Banomyong and Thai Society], Bangkok: Thammasat University Press, 1983, 391.

will attempt to place issues of importance to them in the constitution, with the hope that the issue will receive greater legal, policy or budgetary consideration from the state. This condition of supplement will have the consequence that the Thai constitution will expand in the future.

The Interim Constitution is of the Elite; the Permanent Constitution (or so it looks) is of the People

The process of drafting interim and permanent constitutions differs. The drafting of interim constitutions is conducted by elites with no importance given to the people. The role of elites, specifically bureaucrat-politicians who monopolise power in this process, is evident, for when a coup d'état occurs an interim constitution is quickly proclaimed and its source is unknown. Apart from there being no clear drafting process, it is not officially known who has played a role in its drafting.

Permanent constitutions have had varied drafting processes because some of them result from the pressure of democratic forces, leading to the elites not being able to monopolise the process. A constitution may be viewed as having come from people's participation, when the drafting process takes three forms.

The model for the first form is the drafting of the 1974 constitution. First there was the appointment of a National Forum consisting of 2,347 members who came from various occupations. Sanya Thammasak, as prime minister, was the king's counter-signatory in its establishment. It then selected 299 members to the National Legislative Assembly, which deliberated on a draft of the new constitution.

While this expanded the selection of those involved in drafting the constitution, the people were not able to choose for themselves those who would draft the constitution. Even in the drafting of the 1997 constitution, which expanded the pool of potential drafters at a provincial level, it was parliament that in the end would select the drafting assembly. The selection of framers in this manner allowed for an image that the elite did not control the drafting process, which would have conflicted with existing democratic forces but at the same time it did not allow the people to choose representatives directly.

The second manner in which a participatory image was formed came in the use of public hearings. This has occurred since the drafting of the 1949 constitution but was not considered of great importance, evidenced by the fact that while some drafting processes were accompanied by public hearings, others were not. Public hearings were an important instrument in the drafting of the 1997 constitution. These were held across the country. Similarly, the 2006 interim constitution provided for public hearings during the drafting of the 2007 constitution.

But the problem with public hearings lay in whose opinions would be heard. Also, forums were typically held in places that only some people could access such as urban areas or large provinces. Also, of the proposals that people put forward, there was no clear process on which would be selected or how they would be screened. Public hearings, then, may not yet be considered as being a medium for the people's ideas to truly pass into the constitution.

The third form of participation is the use of referendum. Regarding the 1997 draft constitution, should parliament have rejected it, there was a provision for the draft to be put to a referendum. This was not necessary as the draft passed parliament. The 2006 interim constitution also stipulates that a referendum be held once a draft has been finalised by the Constitutional Drafting Assembly, but in this case parliamentary approval is not required. This stipulation gives the appearance that the people have the power to accept or not to accept the constitution. However, there is no stipulation for a minimal voter turnout, such that the draft would be proclaimed if it gets a majority of those who voted in the referendum. This raises the question of what happens if only twenty hands are raised while many stay away? Would it be assumed the draft has the people's consent?

THE CONSTITUTION UNDER THE SUPRA-CONSTITUTION

The rules of the Thai constitution, as have been described, have led it to be in a condition of self-contradiction: the drafting of a constitution occurs in the knowledge that it will, sooner or later, be revoked. This founding of the supreme law only for a temporary period opens the possibility of people's participation but under restrictive limits. It also allows for the constitution to be constantly lengthened despite the realisation that it cannot cover all eventualities. This conflicted condition is now so chronic that it is no wonder that at the drop of a hat a constitution may be changed.

This self-contradiction is based on two currents of thought, constitutionalism and authoritarianism. The first aims to found a political system that has a constitution as the supreme law and political institutions derived from the people. The second current is authoritarianism in which the seizure of power is legitimate and the bureaucratic-military forces are at the heart of the political system.

Authoritarian approaches to the Thai constitution are in the mainstream. The alternative approach of constitutionalism exists when the currents of democratic thought are strong. But whenever authoritarianism faces challenges from democracy, it is ready to dominate the thinking of society. Notably, in both currents of thought the monarchy has had an important role to the point of becoming a political institution of great significance. The objective of the change of government in 1932 was to change the absolutist regime to an administration with the king under the law. But under the political power struggles of various groups since then, it is well accepted that the political system has expanded to become one in which parliament, the power of the bureaucratic-military forces and the institution of the monarchy coexist: 'Democracy with the King as Head of State'.

This system is the supra-constitution that soars above, and which directs the changes of the Thai constitution in contemporary Thai politics. The abrogation and proclamation of a constitution, whether it be by another ten coup councils or by 100 law professors, must be under the supra-constitution.

As long as we are under the hegemony of this supra-constitution, the self-contradictory nature of the Thai constitution will continue. To escape this conflicted condition will require more than simply writing another constitution. Rather, it requires awareness of and pressure for change at the level of the supra-constitution, as occurred seventy five years ago.

CHAPTER 3

Political Discourse on Thai Democracy[1]

Nakharin Mektrairat

INTRODUCTION

This article aims to explain how knowledge and understanding of Thai democracy have been institutionalised through the processes of historical change, systems of thought, and the use of power relations in the Thai polity. Here, such institutionalised knowledge shall be referred to as a 'political discourse'.[2] I believe that there are at least two key political discourses on Thai democracy. The first is influenced by the knowledge and understanding derived from a movement that I would like to refer to as the 'Traditionalist School of Thought'. The second discourse comes from another movement that I shall call the 'Western School of Thought'.

The concept of 'political discourse' that I use as a guideline in this research has been considered a powerful explanatory tool.[3] First, it gives importance to the use of language activities to communicate meanings and

---

1   Translation of Chapter 2 นครินทร์ เมฆไตรรัตน์, ความรู้และอำนาจการเมืองในการปฏิวัติ 2475 [Knowledge and Political Power in the 1932 Revolution] 2nd edition, Bangkok: Same Sky, 2003, 78–121 (First edition 1990).

2   I would like to specifically extend my sincere thanks to Somkiat Wanthana for the translation of 'political discourse' and for his recommendation of this conceptual approach to me.

3   Thanet Wongyannawa explained to me that there are numerous schools of thoughts within the two schools that I will explore. Kasian Tejapira also suggested that these schools could be dated back to the classical era of the Western world and, thus, made it even more various. Nevertheless, I greatly benefited from Thanet Wongyannawa's อ่านงานฟูโก้ [Reading the Work of Foucault], วารสารธรรมศาสตร์ [Thammasat Journal], 14, 3 1985, and Michel Foucault, *The Archaeology of Knowledge*, translated by A.M. Sheridan Smith, New York: Pantheon/Random House, 1972; Michel Foucault, *Power/Knowledge: Selected Interviews and Other Writings, 1972–1977*, edited by Colin Gordon, New York: Pantheon/Random House, 1980; Diane Macdonell, *Theories of Discourse: An Introduction*, Oxford: Basil Blackwell, 1986.

express political ideas as well as the control mechanism of such communicative systems on the expression of political thought.

The language activities to communicate meanings and express political ideas in the forms of speech and writing cannot be detached from the prevailing power of a political community. Here, power is conceived as being not confined to those of the elite or the ruling class; it is present at all levels of the political community. Such power is shown through political discursive practices. Each set or each model of political discourse practised in a political community has its own system of thought and system of rationalisation through which political speeches and writings are expressed. The systems provide a framework and model of reality, inquisitiveness, ideas and social position for a person who can be both the subject or the object of a specific discourse. From this point of view, political discourse may be viewed as a political, discursive practice.

Historical processes are not simply a timeline of various historical events but are closely related to a political discourse. In other words, historical processes have influence over the emergence of a political discourse while facilitating its institutionalisation. The institutionalised nature of a political discourse makes political speeches and writings appear rational and consistent. However, as mentioned before, the relationship between political discourse and power is inseparable. Political power is usually exerted to dominate the organising of a historical narrative and the determining of its meanings.

In this article, I shall explain the political discourses on Thai democracy from the viewpoints of two movements. The emphasis will be on understanding these systems of thought and their formation as political discourses within a specific historical process to the point that they became institutionalised. The use of power and the key characteristics of the power relations in the Thai polity, as seen from the framework of each political discourse, will also be examined.

THE TRADITIONALIST SCHOOL OF THOUGHT

The first political discourse on Thai democracy, which is also the most important, is that developed by the Traditionalist School of Thought, which originated in the mid-nineteenth century in a group of thinkers with connections to the royal court and the first generation of nobility influenced by Western ideas. This school of thought would later evolve and became fully established from the early twentieth century to 1932, after which it suffered serious setbacks following challenges from the political discourse of the Western School of Thought. However, since many of the traditionalist proponents were conscientious and accomplished thinkers and many of the Traditionalist School's key characteristics seemed to be compatible with the rise of bureaucrats and militarists, the traditionalists were gradually able to adjust so that their ideas came to frame behaviour and discursive practices to the present.

The fundamental concepts of the Traditionalist School prior to 1932 explained the legitimate status of the monarchy as the most important and longstanding political institution and the source of Thais' accumulated knowledge regarding the culture of governing, among other things. The monarchy's origins and status were traced back to the former paternalistic Father-rules-Child system (*rabob phor pokkhrong luk*).[4] It was explained that certain periods came under the influence of the Khmer and the governing approach turned to emphasise the idea of the Devaraja (God-King) rather than the Dharmaraja (Dharma-King) model. However, the Rattanakosin period [commencing 1782] marked a new era. The Thai monarchy modified itself according to Buddhism, which had long been the religion of the Thais. Specifically, it adopted the Buddhist concept of *aneknikon samosonsommut*, which emphasises the idea that Thai monarchs are put on the throne through the mutual consent of the political community. They reign supreme over their subjects while the rest of the population is considered co-equal. People are not differentiated into social classes; there is only a division of labour. They may be divided into groups of people: those who are loyal or not loyal to the king.

King Mongkut and his group of followers actively created and advanced this idea early in his reign.[5] This was used to assert that his ascent to the throne

---

4   Editors' note: *Rabob pokkhrong luk* is normally glossed as paternalism, but sometimes a direct translation provides a more effective and affective connotation.

5   Namely, Somdet Phra Maha Samana Chao Krom Phraya Pawaretwariyakon, the Buddhist Supreme Patriarch (Sa), and Chao Phraya Thipakorawong Maha Kosathibodi. For studies on the overall ideological changes of this period, see Naruemon Teerawat พระราชดำริทางการ เมืองของพระบาทสมเด็จพระจอมเกล้าเจ้าอยู่หัว [The Political Ideas of King Mongkut], M.A. thesis in History, Department of History, Graduate School, Chulalongkorn University, 1982. For the period's religious movements, see Srisupon Chuangsakul ความเปลี่ยนแปลงของคณะ สงฆ์: ศึกษากรณีธรรมยุติกนิกาย พ.ศ. 2368 – พ.ศ. 2464 [Changes in the Sangha: A Case Study of Dhammayuttika Nikaya, B.E. 1825–1921], M.A. thesis in History, Graduate School, Chulalongkorn University, 1987. For modification of the 'Anakenikorn Samosornsommut'

was through mutual consent of the political community. King Mongkut specifically advocated the Buddhist tradition and the *dharmaraja* concept, which defined the power of monarchs as closely connected to members of the political community. It is the duty of a king and the populace to properly and mutually perform their roles in society for the prosperity and peaceful existence of this community.

King Chulalongkorn and his group worked to preserve and develop these ideas. Most importantly, the king offered a royal judgment that this system of governing had already been institutionalised so there was no need to follow the customs of Europe or elsewhere. He maintained that, 'In other countries, people ask the king to do things. Kings must do them. In our country, it is the king who thinks that things should be done'.[6] The issue of 'kingship' has been comprehensively discussed in many historical research works. Prince Damrong Rajanubhab explained that Thai kings had been the focal point as well as the most trustworthy and influential force behind major changes in Thai history. The idea that the power of a king is connected to the political community has been constantly reiterated among the elite and the royals who have been instilled in the principle of responsibility to one's royal lineage (*khattiyamana*). They are taught to be diligent in their study, and to understand the changing nature of things so that they strive for the betterment of their country. King Chulalongkorn instructed his sons that, 'If you think that by being born a prince you are entitled to enjoy a good life and do nothing all your life, you are not much different from the animals of the lowest born'.[7] Educated people were trained in ethics, morality and 'civic duties' to understand that the political power

---

idea into a theory of modern Thai politics or the ideology of the modern Thai state, see Eiji Murashima, 'The Origin of Modern Official State Ideology in Thailand', *Journal of Southeast Asian Studies*, 19, 1, 1988.

6   พระราชดำรัสในพระบาทสมเด็จพระจุลจอมเกล้าเจ้าอยู่หัวทรงแถลงพระบรมราชาธิบายแก้ไขการ ปกครองแผ่นดิน [The Royal Speeches of King Chulalongkorn on the Explanation of the Administrative Reform], in Chai-Anan Samudavanija and Khattiya Karnasuta (compliers) เอกสารการเมือง-การปกครองไทย พ.ศ. 2417–2477 [Documents on Thai Politics-Administration, 1874–1934], Bangkok: The Textbook Projects, The Social Sciences Association of Thailand, 1975, 124–5.

7   พระบรมราโชวาทในพระบาทสมเด็จพระจุลจอมเกล้าเจ้าอยู่หัว ทรงพระราชนิพนธ์ เมื่อ พ.ศ. 2428 [The 1885 Royal Guidance of King Chulalongkorn] in พระบรมราโชวาท ในรัชกาลที่ 5 พระราชทานพระเจ้าลูกยาเธอ [King Chulalongkorn's Royal Guidance to His Sons] in the cremation book distributed at the royally-bestowed cremation of Rong Ammart Tho Khun Samaksukhakarn, Bangkok: Rungruengtham Press, 1970.

in the country was bound together by the fact that all people performed their proper 'duties'.[8] Kings were comparable to the 'head' of a nation while the people, or 'citizens' as they were called at the time, had different duties. All parties were to work together in harmony to achieve progress, unity and peace of a political society or 'nation' (the word used after the 1890s).

From late in the reign of King Chulalongkorn up to 1932, many foreign political words as well as newly coined Thai words were introduced. This development could be interpreted as the sign of an influx of political ideas from the West and further adjustment of the Thai political system along the line of the Western models. Nevertheless, both the king and his group of scholars remained steadfast while engaging positively with the foreign ways of thinking. King Vajiravudh tried to caution the new generation of Thais through the use of modern language in the way that reflected his deep understanding of and strong bond with the fundamental Thai traditions consolidated during the reign of King Mongkut. King Vajiravudh posed these questions:

> Isn't it true that people of today are happy to boast that they are better than Thais of the old days? But all Thais of the old days have duties to perform for the benefit of the country. If the new Thais do not volunteer to perform such duties, how can they say they are better? The most brazen shortfall of the new Thais is that they want to discard anything old but have nothing to offer as its replacement. They faintly hear the Westerners' words and seize upon them without actually understanding them, blandly repeating their words. There is nothing wrong about behaving like a Westerner if it is a good behaviour. But it won't do to behave in a way that is convenient or beneficial to oneself and neglect what is inconvenient. Westerners love their country, why don't we copy this point and love our country? Why do you prefer others' country and others' language? What is so repugnant about our country that you cannot love it?[9]

With his deep compassion and trust in Thai customs, traditions and culture, in 1915 King Vajiravudh criticised Phraya Suriyanuwat, the author of the book titled *The Science of Property*, for adopting the Western way of thinking and misconstruing that there were social classes in Thailand.

---

8   For works on this topic, see Sumin Chuthangkon การกล่อมเกลาทางการเมือง โดยใช้แบบ เรียนหลวงเป็นสื่อในสมัยรัชกาลที่ 5 [Political Socialisation through Royal Textbooks in the Reign of King Rama V], M.A. thesis in Political Science, Department of Administration, Chulalongkorn University, 1986.

9   King Vajiravudh, ปลูกใจเสือป่า [Instilling the Wild Tiger Ethos], Phranakhon: Maha Makutratchawittayalai, 1963, 35–6.

The king believed that all Thais were equal and it was only kings who were chosen to be head of the political community.[10] Looked at from this perspective, the 'nation', a new political word, only existed with the king as its head. Without a king the nation would suffer grievously to the point of collapse, as would a body expire after its head is lost.

Toward the last period of the absolute monarchy system, before its abolition in 1932, it may be said that King Prajadhipok was steadfast to the ideas and the obligations of power under the absolute monarchy structure that had been firmly established in Thailand since the late nineteenth century, although he and his group of followers recognised the threat to the existing system and the need to play certain 'games' to appease the demands of middle-class people and newspaper columnists in the capital. His idea was that, although royal power was primarily a centralised and supreme power, it had never been exercised at will by any king. Considering the various changes that had taken place, with some intelligence it could be seen that countries all over the world could not adopt one and the same political and administrative system. Rather, that system had to be conceived and developed in compliance with a country's customs and traditions as well as the habits and spiritual characteristics of its people. Prince Dhani Nivat, a young prince educated in Britain, had shrewdly discussed this topic with great insight from a principled point of view in his address to a privy council meeting in 1927 where he said he did not believe that the Anglo-Saxon traditions of government would be suitable for all people in the world. Rather, Thai kings ruled over the people on the Father-Child model and they ascended the throne with the consent of the Thai political community. This model was unique to the Thai society.[11] Any attempt to deviate from the traditional culture would surely create problems and chaos instead of assisting in the further development of Thai politics.

---

10 Aswapahu [King Vajiravudh] ทรัพยศาสตร์ เล่ม 1 ตามความเห็นเอกชนผู้ได้อ่านหนังสือนั้น [Sappayasart (Vol. 1) According to An Individual Who Has Read It] สมุทรสาร [Samutthasarn] 2, 9 September 1915.

11 On this topic, please see government documents at the National Archives Division, Ror.7 RorLor.6/3 (ร.7 รล.6/3) and Ror. 7. RorLor. 6/4 (ร.7 รล.6/4). For a primary source of King Rama VII's political initiative, see his notes on 'Problems of Siam' and 'Democracy in Siam' in Benjamin A. Batson (ed.), *Siam's Political Future: Documents from the End of the Absolute Monarchy*, New York: Cornell University, Southeast Asia Program Data Paper No. 96, 1974. The author would like readers to take note here that the study on this issue needs more research based on extensive readings of documents by researchers with deep knowledge and understanding of the historical and political contexts of the time and not based on arbitrary selection by researchers of quotations devoid of their historical and political contexts.

We cannot really tell whether these words of Prince Dhani Nivat were a prediction of what would happen to Thai politics in subsequent periods or not. The absolute monarchy was already too weak to pull itself together in the period just before 1932. When a group of people calling themselves the People's Party seized power on 24 June 1932, various groups from the old regime had to look out for themselves and safeguard their status under a new set of requirements and restrictions, under the political leadership of the People's Party from 1932 to 1947 and then secondly under the House of Representatives, which served as a central political organ from 1947 to 1957.

Under the atmosphere of abrupt change in 1932, the Traditionalist School did not diminish its endeavours at all. On the contrary, it admirably adjusted its beliefs to fit in with the change. First, the 24 June 1932 Event was re-interpreted as a *patiwat* (revolution), which meant a turning of political foundations from the principles of succession recently adopted in the reigns of King Vajiravudh and King Prajadhipok back to the concept of *aneknikon samosonsommut* once again. This was the explanation put forward by Prince Wanwaithayakon, one of the key thinkers of the Traditionalist School, which contradicted and was directly in opposition to Pridi Banomyong's idea of *aphiwat* [revolution in the progressive sense].[12]

The principle of *aneknikon samosonsommut* was reinterpreted by Prince Wanwaithyakon and other thinkers of the Traditionalist School as an equivalent to the 'democratic system'. At a later date, M.R. Seni Pramoj vehemently asserted that Thai democracy had been in existence since the time of King Ramkhamhaeng and that all Thai kings had had ideas that mostly tended to be democratic'.[13] Not long ago, Sulak Sivaraksa, a contemporary key thinker, also confirmed that *aneknikon samosonsommut* was a democratic principle. He stated that democratic institutions had traditionally existed in the Thai society in the forms of a village community, monk (Sangha) administration and in the Father-Child model at the time

---

12 Krommun Naradhip Bongsprabandh [Prince Wanwaithayakorn Worawan] วิทยา สารานุกรม [Encyclopaedia], Phranakhon: Phrae Phittaya, 1971, 252–3. On this issue, Sombat Chantornvong gave the author the idea that Prince Wanwaithayakorn Worawan was, more or less, influenced by the meaning of the word 'revolution' in the British historical context. The 1688 Glorious Revolution was considered a turning point in the governing system, returning it to the traditional model existing prior to 1648.

13 Malaengwi [Seni Pramoj] เบื้องหลังประวัติศาสตร์ [History Behind the Scene], Phranakhon: Rongphim Sahauppakorn 1947.

of King Ramkhamhaeng.[14] In summary, it can be said that the Traditionalist School agrees that democracy has long been a part of Thai society and there has been a tendency toward this form of administration and Thai kings had long prepared for the introduction of this system. This represents the fundamental conception of one political discourse on Thai democracy.

The interpretations set forth by Prince Wanwaithayakon and other key thinkers of the Traditionalist School regard the principle of *aneknikon samosonsommut* as equivalent to democracy. The restoration of this concept was a major turning point in Thai politics. It is the exercising of political power by the Thai elite to maintain ideological continuity with the old system. Prince Wanwaithayakon provided a clear explanation of why he was interested in conveying the meaning of words and explaining the various meanings of political language. He stated:

> It is the Thai language that will guarantee the continuing security of the Thai nation. If we prefer transliterating foreign words to express our ideas, we may walk too fast. It could be that we directly imitate their ideas instead of first modifying them to fit our ideas.[15]

Prince Wanwaithayakon considered the starting point for such modification to be the political discourse that had emerged from the reign of Mongkut to Prajadhipok, which was of course the Traditionalist School.

After 1932, the problem of how the king could relate to constitutional law emerged. On this, written communications took place between the People's Party and King Prajadhipok. While the former invited King Prajadhipok to ascend the throne 'under' the constitution, he replied that he was willing to become a king 'by way of' the constitution.[16] The difference in the choice of words was unlikely to be in jest or unintended, instead clearly reflecting the deep-seated differences in both parties' principles. King Prajadhipok had earnestly contemplated the problematic adjustment of political institutions and was familiar with the principle of *aneknikon samosonsommut* and those of the proponents of the constitutional system. King Prajadhipok's reply confirmed the original principle that the royal power was entrusted to him

---

14 Sulak Sivaraksa ความคิดที่ขัดขวางและส่งเสริมประชาธิปไตยของไทย [Ideas that Obstruct and Ideas that Promote Thai Democracy], Bangkok: Aksornsarn, 1986.

15 M.C. Wanwaithayakorn Worawan ปาฐกถาพิเศษเรื่องสยามพากษ์ [Special Lecture on the Thai Language] วิทยาจารย์ [Withiyajan] 33, 1, 1932, 67.

16 see Prasert Pathamasukon, (complier), รัฐสภาไทยในรอบสี่สิบสองปี (2475–2517) [Thai Parliament over Forty-two Years (1932–1974)], Bangkok: Chor. Chumnum Chang, 1974, 13.

by the political community and that a small group of people could not violate this traditional agreement. They had neither the 'right' nor the legitimate power to remove the royal power that was his. For him, the true origin of the constitution was that it came from a 'royal bestowal'. The political discourse that explains the 'royal bestowal' status of the constitution has been perpetuated to this day by a certain group of people and especially by traditionalists. The factual evidence that supports this discourse can be found in the government's explanation given at different state functions and in the Royal Statue of King Prajadhipok in front of the new National Assembly building.

Nevertheless, in the view of the traditionalists, although a constitution had come into existence through a royal bestowal, its birth was an unnatural one as it did not come from a slow and steady start but from an abrupt seizure of power by a group of people who breached their duties. Their action set a bad example that would continue endlessly. The idea of certain groups of people to 'limit' the royal power was also appalling as it defied the natural order of things and the existing traditional agreement. It was contrary to the Thai culture, a faulty imitation of the Western culture, and it happened prematurely. What followed after the 1932 seizure of power was the replacement of the single monarch by a 'multiple-monarch' system.[17] The struggle for power that ensued among the group of people who staged the revolution was the starting point of a vicious cycle of subsequent revolutions and coups d'état that continues to this day.

M.R. Kukrit Pramoj, another outstanding scholar in the Traditionalist School of Thought, described the atmosphere in which the multiple-monarch system emerged and the post-1932 struggles for power as if it were a natural consequence of the breach of traditional practice. He stated that,

> Regarding the revolution of 1932, it must have been evident to all of you that the event led to the birth of democracy. In fact, the revolution means the eradication of royal power and such power being tossed into the hands of the revolutionary leaders. Under these conditions, it was not so difficult for the state bureaucracy to adjust. At first, there was some confusion as to who was actually in power, but after a few months it became apparent that it was these people and no one else who had the power. So came Khun Luang, Khun Phra, Phraya, and Thaan Khun [honorifics for officials] for a piece of that power ... Instead of being ruled by a single monarch as in the past, I do not know how many kings we now have. I have failed to count

---

17 This was the opinion of, and the words used by, M.R. Seni Pramoj, *History Behind the Scene.*

them; the number seems innumerable ... But these revolutionary leaders could not maintain their rule forever; they succumbed to the laws of nature. Some lost their power while the others aged or passed away. Initially, these leaders had so much power but soon they began to challenge and undercut the power of each other. They arrested, executed and jailed one another.[18]

Through such an account, thinkers of the Traditionalist School came to regard the period after the 1932 Revolution as the 'Dark Age' of Thai politics. This followed the explanation put forward by Prince Dhani Nivat (Kromamun Bidayalabh Brdihyakorn), in his *Autobiography*.[19] This has been the underlying idea of the Traditionalist School on the development of Thai democracy. It is contrary to the Western School's idea on the same issue, which I will touch upon later. The Western School regards the period after 1932 as the 'Enlightened Age' or the 'Age of Hope' in Thai politics for all individuals and all parties.

In fact, the Traditionalist School's claim that with royal power 'limited' there would ensue a vicious cycle of political turmoil is not totally baseless, as many historical facts and developments support it. For example, Sombat Chantornvong's recent work on the development of the political explanations and political vocabularies in Thai non-fiction political writings revealed some interesting points. He found that after 1946 this genre of writing deviated from the earlier periods in that it was written mainly as narrative accounts. More important is the fact that political writers of this period focused on explicating politics as a struggle for power, using force or deception, among a few political leaders for their own benefit.[20] Notable writings of this genre are such works as *17 Years of Democracy* by Lui Kiriwat, *King Pokklao and the Thai Nation* by Premjit Watcharangkon, *Chao Fah Prajadhipok: The Banished Monarch* by Silapachai Chanchaleom (Nai Honhuay), and *The Political Drama* by Chamlong Ittirong. Whether intentionally or unintentionally,

---

18 M.R. Kukrit Pramoj, การปรับตัวของระบบราชการไทยหลังการเปลี่ยนแปลงการปกครอง [Adjustment of the Thai Bureaucracy after the Change of Government] in Woradej Chandrason and Wanit Songprathum (eds), ระบบราชการไทย: สภาพปัญหาและข้อเสนอจากฝ่ายการเมือง ข้าราชการ นักวิชาการ และธุรกิจเอกชน [Thai Bureaucracy: Problems and Proposals from the Political, Bureaucratic, Academic and Private Sectors], Bangkok: Faculty of Public Administration, NIDA, 2005, 39–40.

19 Kromamun Bidayalabh Brdihyakorn, อัตชีวประวัติ [Autobiography] Bangkok: Rongphim tiranasan, 1974.

20 Sombat Chantornvong, ภาษาทางการเมือง: พัฒนาการของแนวอธิบายการเมือง และศัพท์การเมือง ในงานเขียนประเภทสารคดีทางการเมืองของไทย พ.ศ. 2475–2525 [Political Language: Development of Political Explanations and Political Vocabulary in Thai Political Documentary Writings 1932–1982], Mimeographed document, 1988, 50 and 80.

the political explanations put forward by this group of writers have in effect validated the Traditionalist School's claims on this issue and broadened the circulation of such ideas to a larger number of people.

The political discourse on Thai democracy under the Traditionalist School's movement expanded the scope of discursive practices from the circle of elite thinkers in the old system to thinkers in the new system. Such practices were disseminated through major works by key traditionalist thinkers like Kromamun Bidayalabh Brdihyakorn (Prince Dhani Nivat), Krommun Naradhip Bongsprabandh (Prince Wanwaithyakon), M.R. Seni Pramoj and M.R. Kukrit Pramoj. Another important form of discursive practice has been the dissemination of such ideas through the royal speeches and activities of Their Majesties King Ananda Mahidol and King Bhumibol Adulyadej. The latter discursive practice can be found in the words of HRH Princess Galyani Vadhana, elder sister of the kings, who wrote that the early parenting of both Ananda and Bhumibol had been most influential in instilling the traditional sense of obligation toward their royal powers. The Princess cited an excerpt from one of the Princess Mother's letters:

> The fact that Nanda became king does not make us pleased with the prestige of the royal ranks; we have become extremely weary. The only thing that helps diminish our weariness is the sense of duty to the country. And I have always hoped that by becoming king Nanda will truly be able to benefit the country.[21]

Both King Ananda Mahidol and King Bhumibol Adulyadej recognised and upheld their 'burdens and duties' as their traditional obligations. King Bhumibol Adulyadej, through his royal activities and addresses, expressed his deep understanding. He has said,

> The first role [of a monarch] is to be the symbol of the nation. If this is successfully accomplished, the king will become a living symbol of his country. A king must change with his country but at the same time must be able to maintain the essence of the nation. A king represents all things within his country; he is the spirit of the nation. This means that although

---

21 Princess Galyani Vadhana Krom Luang Naradhiwas Rajanagarindra, เจ้านายเล็กๆ – ยุว กษัตริย์: พระราชประวัติพระบาทสมเด็จพระเจ้าอยู่หัวอานันทมหิดลและพระบาทสมเด็จพระเจ้าอยู่หัว ภูมิพลอดุลยเดช เมื่อทรงพระเยาว์ 2468–2489 [From Little Princes to Young Kings: The Royal Biography of Their Majesties King Ananda Mahidol and King Bhumibol Adulyadej at Young Ages, 1925–1946, Bangkok: The Royal Thai Army and the Siam Commercial Bank, 1987, 221.

the peoples who make up the country may be diverse, all the country's fundamental characteristics must be embodied in the king, who is its head.[22]

Therefore, it may be said that the political discursive practices of the Traditionalist School have been powerfully preserved in royal instructions and activities of a very talented monarch who recognised the obligations of his royal powers and maintained a profound understanding of the obligation of power, the origin of a political community and the necessity of a ruler in the Thai polity.

On the other hand, the political ideas of the Traditionalist School have had a significant influence over the Thai bureaucracy and military, especially over the leaders of the civil servant and the militarist groups who continued to retain power from the time of the political change that took place in 1947. These leaders have accepted the basic explanations of the traditionalist thinkers, who maintain that

> the Thai feudal state differs from those in other countries, both in Europe and Asia. This is because it exists under the absolute monarchy system that contains certain characteristics of a democratic system. Phra Ruang [a king during the Sukhothai period] came to the throne via the consent of the people and ruled for the happiness and wellbeing of the people. In Thailand's regal tradition, kings assume their kingship in the status of *aneknikon samosonsommut*. They are not appointed from heaven.[23]

Thailand, thus, has always tended to evolve towards democracy, as was the intention of the People's Party in 1932, as well. However, one of the most serious mistakes committed by the People's Party was to favour a Western style of democracy. Once the model was adopted, it became apparent that the system did not conform to the existing conditions of Thailand. After 1947, leaders in the state bureaucracy and military shared the viewpoints of key thinkers in the Traditionalist School who considered the period after 1932 as the 'Dark Age' rather than the 'Enlightened Age' of Thai politics for the following reason:

> Thai democracy has become a dragon's head and a dragon's tail. In some periods the dragon's head goes towards dictatorship while in other periods

---

22 This statement came from a royal interview granted to reporters of the ลีดเดอร์ส [Leaders] journal as cited in แนวพระราชดำริเก้ารัชกาล [The Royal Ideas of Nine Monarchs] Bangkok: Academic Department, Ministry of Education, 1984, 268–86.

23 Song Soon Radio Station Broadcasting, ประชาธิปไตยแบบไทยและข้อคิดเกี่ยวกับรัฐธรรมนูญ [Thai-style Democracy and Opinions on the Constitution], Bangkok: Samnakphim chok-chaitewet 1965, 45–46.

the dragon's tail goes towards anarchy ... when Hyde-Park-style speeches were freely staged to publicly and irrationally attack other groups, menacing protesters marched to seize the Prime Minister's Office in such an unruly manner that there was a risk of bloodshed in the city.[24]

Bureaucratic and military leaders joined forces under the leadership of Field Marshals Sarit Thanarat, Thanom Kittikachorn and Prapas Charusathien and influential thinkers like General Sawaeng Senanarong, Krommun Naradhip Bongsprabandh (Prince Wanwaithyakon) and Luang Wichit Wathakan to push forward 'Thai-style democracy'. Thak Chaloemtiarana analyses this undertaking by calling it 'the politics of despotic paternalism'.[25] It is most interesting to note that leaders of the civil servant and the militarist groups tried to create an image of a 'Phor Khun' (Father) for themselves by claiming that their own group could recognise the will of the people without having to go through the rituals of a Western electoral process. The popular and commonly used response to such arguments is that those in power can baselessly claim whatever they wish. But this dismissal of such claims does nothing to shed light on the Traditionalists. To gain a better understanding of this school of thought, we must reconsider the *aneknikon samosonsommut* concept. This holds that a ruler need not come from the Western method of vote counting, but can emerge when people from different walks of life congregate at a meeting and, through traditional culture, offer signs of acceptance that the ruler must, with wisdom, intuite.

However, the fact that traditionalist thinkers were able to exert their influence and transmit their ideas through the bureaucratic and the military systems makes it necessary for us to examine the process of reception of these ideas by the leaders which involves them in the selection of ideas and the use of power to reinterpret those ideas and create a new political language that could be integrated into their practices.

Public opinion [*matimahachon*] is an important concept that can be used as an example to clarify the abovementioned process. Prince Wanwaithyakon initially coined this word at the time of the 1932 revolution. Leaders of the People's Party tried to use it, but without much success. Another influential thinker of the Traditionalist School, M.R. Seni Pramoj, used the word 'public

---

24 *Ibid.*, 49–50.

25 Thak Chaloemtiarana, การเมืองระบบพ่อขุนอุปถัมภ์แบบเผด็จการ [The Politics of Despotic Paternalism], translated by Phanni Chatrapollarak and M.R. Prakaithong Sirisuk, Bangkok: Thammasat University, 1983.

opinion' extensively in his *History Behind the Scene* (1947). The author stated that this writing aimed to explicate and compare the changes of 1947 and 1932. He asserted that the political change of 1932 was in fact a revolution in the Western theoretical sense while the 8 November 1947 incident was a revolution based on public opinion with the goal of creating a unique style of Thai democracy, which has persisted in traditional Thai customs.

Key thinkers in the group of bureaucratic and military leaders like General Sawaeng Senanarong used the 'public opinion' concept for the benefit of their own group. It was employed as a means to interpret the events that took place after the coups d'état of 1957 and 1958 by maintaining that the government established by the Revolutionary Council in 1958 was set up in compliance with such 'public opinion'. General Sawaeng Senanarong provided the following explanation on this matter:

> The problem with Thailand is, to what extent can Western political methods be applied to the Thai context? Can we consider the messages conveyed through newspapers, radio and television broadcasting as well as the opinions of leaders in various fields to be the people's opinions? … We think the views expressed by high-ranking crown servants are an important means of public expression. This is because most of the Thai people do not have a good understanding of the problem at hand. They need to rely on the opinions of specialists with long experiences in dealing with the problems … We only want to point out that to properly identify public opinion in Thailand, it is essential first to learn about how the Thai public opinion is expressed.[26]

This means that under the power structure of Thailand's political community, we can only identify public opinion through Thai methods, which involves the signs given based on the existing cultural and traditional obligations in the Thai society. When it is difficult to identify a public opinion due to the existence of a large number and a great variety of people, those who congregate to choose a ruler will be, in the old political language, '*Khunnang, Samana, Chee, Phram* (the nobility, monks, nuns and Brahmins)' or 'high-ranking government officials and specialists' in today's language. The mutual agreement of these groups of people represents a 'public opinion' to the political community. Based on this logic, leading state officials, civilian and military, can always use their power to speculate what the public opinion

---

26 *Thai-style Democracy,* 238.

will be, as was the case of the 14 October 1973 Event, when it was concluded that the 'public opinion' was 'in essence likely about having the government resign rather than about constitutional problems.'[27]

This idea of 'Thai-style democracy' is based on the Traditionalist School's explanations. Discursive practices were employed alongside the use of power by leaders of the bureaucratic and the militarist groups. It may be said that the Traditionalist School of Thought, its ideas and arguments, have always been powerful, and this was especially so between 1976 and 1991. This discursive practice has profound meaning for the steering of the Thai political community toward national progress, stability, security and peace. Despite the idea that the constitution, parliament, political parties and political elections were considered necessary for Thailand to achieve international acceptance, remaining doubts were aired in various addresses as to whether or not these Western political principles and approaches really bring benefits, wellbeing and people's involvement to the Thai political community. Indeed, Thai people still remember and yearn for the Thai-style democratic administrative system under the leadership of General Prem Tinsulanonda, which has just recently ended.[28] Many still believe that it is possible for such a system to make a comeback.

The transmission of the ideas and influence of the Traditionalist School among the middle class and the educated is extremely interesting. Here, I would like to cite the academic works of Chai-Anan Samudavanija, Kramol Thongthammachart and Rong Sayamanond as examples of those who reject the traditionalists' assumption that there have been some forms of 'democracy' in Thailand since the time of Sukhothai kingdom, and yet these scholars characteristically assume that Thailand has an inherent tendency to become 'democratic' under the leadership of the Thai kings.[29] Chai-Anan

---

27 Sawaeng Senanarong, รวมคำบรรยายของพลเอกแสวง เสนาณรงค์, [A Collection of General Sawaeng Senanarong's Lectures] in อนุสรณ์งานพระราชทานเพลิงศพพลเอกแสวง เสนาณรงค์ [Cremation Volume of General Sawaeng Senanarong], Bangkok: The Royal Thai Survey Department Press, 1977, 49–50.

28 For studies on this topic and parts of an extensive discussion of this idea, see Chalermkiat Phiu-nuan ประชาธิปไตยแบบไทย ความคิดทางการเมืองของทหารไทย 2519–2529 [Thai-style Democracy: The Political Ideas of the Thai Military] a report submitted to the Thai Studies Institute, Thammasat University, 1988, especially chapters 3 and 4.

29 Chai-Anan Samudavanija is the pioneer on the studies related to the plan to promote the establishment of democracy during the reign of King Rama V, including studies on the preparation of the bestowal of a constitution in the reign of King Rama VII. He wrote quite extensively and has written many outstanding works. On this topic see การเมือง การ

Samudavanija, a leading scholar of this approach, explained that some development plans and foundations for the adoption of the 'democratic' administrative system had been laid down since the reign of King Chulalongkorn but stalled in the reign of King Vajiravudh. However, during King Prajadhipok's reign, an earnest preparation for the bestowal of a constitution and the establishment of a democratic system had been in progress.[30] These facts are clearly consistent with the principal ideas of the Traditionalist School. The extensive discussions on the problems relating to this preparation among traditionalists prior to 1973 was likely one factor leading the urban middle class to refer to 'certain parts' of King Prajadhipok's abdication letter in their struggle against the regime of Thanom-Prapas in October of 1973.

The middle class, especially the renowned scholars already discussed, shared another basic assumption of the Traditionalist School regarding the belief that if the constitution had been genuinely bestowed by King Prajadhipok with no 'breach of the existing political tradition', Thailand would have become a true democratic country under moral leaders. This group concluded that between 1932 and 1973, Thailand had been a dictatorship run by a state bureaucratic nobility and militarists. The vicious cycle of power struggle originated because of the 1932 revolution. Nevertheless, this middle-class group differed from the leaders of the state bureaucracy and the militarist groups that, from 1957 to 1973, propagandised Thai-style democracy. Such discrepancy in ideas is probably the result of the middle class's demand to take a greater part in the country's political system by extending the group of 'Khunnang, Samana, Chee, Phram' or 'high-ranking state officials and specialists' to a larger number of participants.

These political discursive practices were highly influential in framing the thoughts of middle-class academics, who still recognise and give importance to the king's role as the head of state. They still believe that the king was able to solve their problems, create a just society and establish Thailand's democracy. The petition, signed by 99 academics [in 1988]

เปลี่ยนแปลงทางการเมืองไทย 2411–2475 [Politics and Thai Political Change 1868–1932], Bangkok: Bannakit, 1980; Kramol Thongthammachart is the author of วิวัฒนาการของระบอบการเองไทย [The Evolution of the Thai Constitutional System], Bangkok: Bannakit, 1981; and Rong Sayamanond is the author of ประวัติศาสตร์ไทยในระบอบรัฐธรรมนูญ [Thai History in the Constitutional System], Bangkok: Thai Wattana Panich, 1977, for example.

30 For additional details, see Chai-Anan Samudavanija, ร่างรัฐธรรมนูญของพระปกเกล้าฯ [Drafts of King Rama VII's Constitution] Mimeographed document, 1975.

and submitted to the king, was an example of the dynamic power of the traditionalists' political thinking.

THE WESTERN SCHOOL OF THOUGHT

Another political discourse on Thai democracy derives from the Western School of Thought, which also originated in the mid-to-late 19th century, among a group of overseas-educated people who were unable to adjust to King Chulalongkorn's administration. They belong to the group that was interested in the disciplines of law and political economy. This school of thought was subsequently promoted by Luang Praditmanutham (Pridi Banomyong) and was passed on by a group of thinkers and writers that was smaller in number than the Traditionalist School of Thought.

The Western School recognised the universal rationality and progress of the Western world. Although they glimpsed some rationality in the Thai system, it was considered mostly antiquated and needed an overhaul rather than a restoration or an improvement. When the young Prince Rapee Phattanasak Kromluang Ratchaburi Direkrit first introduced the British legal system to Thailand he trusted it to be resilient and rational enough to enable Thailand to progress on the same path as other civilised countries. He refused to restore the old codes of law as suggested by the traditionalists which had Prince Damrong Rajanubhab at the helm. After numerous arguments, starting in the late 1890s, the young Prince left the civil service. Phraya Suriyanuwat was another thinker of the Western School who believed in the principles of capital mobilisation, division of labour, modern production system and mutual assistance between producers of different products. His proposal was candidly criticised by 'Aswapahu' [King Vajiravudh's pseudonym] as representing the Western way of thinking.[31]

The Western School became active again when the Law School set up the French Law Section together with the British Law Section. Luang Praditmanutham (Pridi Banomyong) was one of the instructors in the former section. In his book, *Explanations on Administrative Law*, which was published in 1931, Luang Praditmanutham mentioned the 'universal' principle that all persons are born free, equal and in fraternity, explaining

---

31 For further study on Phraya Suriyanuwat as Thailand's first political economist, see Chatthip Nartsupha "ความคิดทางเศรษฐกิจของพระยาสุริยานุวัตร [The Economic Ideas of Phraya Suriyanuwat] สังคมศาสตร์ ปริทัศน์ [Social Science Review] 12, 9, 1974.

that all these 'arise from the common characteristics of being human.'[32] This is the fundamental idea that is not bound to any custom, tradition or any socio-cultural basis. It laid down a foundation of a new way of 'thinking': that all persons should be able to contemplate with their own intellect, whether or not all persons are born free, equal and in fraternity.

The doctrine of separation of powers, another 'universal' principle, maintains that a civilised country must have a separation of the highest powers to provide a proper mechanism of check and balance. It is apparent that this doctrine does not exist in the Thai administrative tradition.[33] As Thailand progressed, it would be necessary for it to adopt this doctrine and revise the old one.

The opinions and explanations of the Western School of Thought are fundamentally different from those of the Traditionalists and are contrary to the same on the important point that there was nothing that could be called 'democratic' in the political, administrative and cultural systems of Thailand prior to 1932. Luang Praditmanutham (Pridi Banomyong) explained that prior to 1932 the distinctive feature of the absolute monarchy lay in the fact that the king had absolute power in exercising supreme powers over the government, and that there was no separation of powers in the Thai political system.

Kulab Saipradit was another key thinker in the Western School. He discussed problems and offered his arguments on this issue in an article titled 'The Meaning of Democracy' in 1944. He was frustrated with the traditionalists' arguments and completely rejected them by saying that the 'Father-Child' system of government could not be compared to or be valued as a democratic system.

> It will not do to say we are citizens of a democratic state while admiring the phor mueang (paternalistic) system of the Sukhothai period or the 'Father-Child' administrative system of the Rattanakosin period as being harmonious with today's democratic system. Students like me and anybody who has cast our votes to elect a representative to rule on our behalf have never intended to elect them to be our fathers.[34]

---

32 Pridi Banomyong, ประชุมกฎหมายมหาชนและเอกชน [Compilation of Public and Private Law], Bangkok: Thammasat University, 1983[1931], 150.

33 *Ibid.*, p. 175.

34 Kulab Saipradit, ความหมายของประชาธิปไตย [The Meaning of Democracy], นิติสาส์น [Nithiisan] June–September 1944, 21.

The refusal to accept that the pre-1932 Thai political and adminis-trative system contains any of the 'democratic' characteristics persists among proponents of the Western School of Thought. For example, although many thinkers in this academic circle may have agreed that the traditional Thai administrative system was unique in many ways, they held that it could not be referred to as a 'democracy'. Saneh Chamarik called this unique system a 'royal patronage society'[35] while political economists called it a 'feudal society'. When the traditionalists perceive the political development from the reign of King Mongkut to 1932 as a democratic system under the concept of *aneknikon samosonsommut* that was progressing toward a truly democratic system, the Western School perceives otherwise. For example, Saneh Chamarik explained the said development as the establishment of a new form of bureaucracy.[36] Likhit Dhiravegin averred it was a progression toward modernisation and a new form of nation state.[37] Nidhi Eoseewong and Somkiat Wanthana similarly agreed and reiterated the emergence of the first truly and fully absolute monarchy system in Thailand.[38] In summary, the works of these Western School scholars considered pre-1932 political development simply as the specific adjustment of political institutions that did not include any 'democratic' features whatsoever.

The Western School of Thought reached its prime around one decade after the 1932 Revolution, when extensive courses on Thai constitu-tional laws and comparative constitutions were offered at Thammasat University with the likes of Luang Prajert Aksonlak, Duan Bunnag and Phairot Chaiyanam as lecturers. Each instructor produced their own textbooks and stressed to their students that the Thai constitutional laws were neither bestowed upon the people by the king nor legislated by the People's Party. They were, however, the result of a compromise between

---

35 See Saneh Chamarik, การเมืองไทยกับพัฒนาการรัฐธรรมนูญ [Thai Politics and Development of the Constitution] Bangkok: Institute of Thai Studies, Thammasat University and the Foundation for the Promotion of Social Sciences and Humanities Textbooks Projects, 1986.

36 *Ibid.,* 66–86.

37 Likhit Dhiravegin, วิวัฒนาการการเมืองการปกครองไทย [Evolution of the Thai Political and Administrative System] Bangkok: Chulalongkorn University, 1987, 199.

38 I had the opportunity to discuss this issue extensively with Nidhi Eoseewong at Chiang Mai University. For Somkiat Wanthana see รัฐสมบูรณาญาสิทธิราชย์สยาม 2435–2475, [The Siamese Absolute Monarchy 1892–1932], Social Sciences Association of Thailand, 1982.

King Prajadhipok and the People's Party.[39] Nevertheless, this notion did not become the mainstream understanding of the historical and political writings of subsequent periods. It only appeared in the legal history writings of the initial period. It should be noted that recent works on the history of the constitutional laws have turned to accept the Traditionalist School's conclusion that the constitution was bestowed upon the people by the king.

Another reason behind the rise to eminence of the Western School of Thought during this period was the dissemination of its presumption through the genre of political non-fiction. Sombat Chantornvong explained this phenomenon as the result of the availability of a large number of political 'textbooks' between 1932 and 1946. Most authors of these texts were absorbed in the new form of administration and wanted to instil among a wider circle of the public the advantages of the new system.[40] Examples of books in this genre are: *History of the Constitution* by M.R. Songsutjarit Nawarat, *Siam and the Administrative Doctrines* by H. Yontrarak, and *Political Stairs* by Luang Saranupraphan.

How does the Western School explain the post-1932 state of Thai politics? How do such explanations differ from those of the Traditionalist School of thought that regard the period after 1932 as the 'Dark Age' of Thai politics? Upon examination, there are several answers to these questions concerned with the problem of establishing a 'rule of law' system in Thai society. Pridi Banomyong explained that there are many steps to establish democracy in a society. In Thailand, it has to advance from a semi-democratic system under the 1932 constitution to a fully democratic system under the 1946 constitution. The word full democracy in the opinion of Pridi Banomyong does not mean only the existence of a constitution and a parliament but includes the fact that all members of the House of Representatives and the Senate must be elected members. However, Pridi Banomyong's full democracy came to an abrupt end with

---

39 Luang Prajert Aksonlak, กฎหมายรัฐธรรมนูญ [Constitutional Law] Phranakhon: Thammasat and Politics University Press, 1934; and Duan Bunnag and Phairot Chaiyanam คำอธิบาย กฎหมายรัฐธรรมนูญ [Commentary on Constitutional Law], 2 volumes, Phranakhon: Rongphim Nithisan, 1934.

40 Sombat, *Political Language,* 23.

the 1947 military coup d'état with the support of the remaining influential groups from the old system.[41]

In general, it may be said that although the Western School realised some of the problems and distorted views of the new administrative system, they still considered and described Thai politics after 1932 as the New Age (of hope and a bright future) rather than as the Dark Age. This type of explanation could be traced back to the points of view initiated by Pridi Banomyong. Another group, the clique of Luang Phibun Songkhram, an opponent of Pridi, that came to power between 1938 and 1944, explained the brighter prospect of the new administrative system in a different manner. Along with the constitution, parliament and political elections, Luang Phibun Songkhram's clique emphasised the ideas of *ratthaniyom* [state preferences], the nation and national independence.[42] Under superficial examination, the *ratthaniyom* may closely resemble Field Marshal Sarit Thanarat's Thai-style Democracy. But upon a closer look, they were extremely different. The concept of *Ratthaniyom* did not claim any connection to or any root in Thai customs or culture; rather, it was connected to a universal doctrine present in both Western and Buddhist thinking, enabling *ratthaniyom* or *dharmaniyom* to serve as a 'law of the spirit and mind' to induce the Thai people to join forces for the creation of a new nation. This idea also claimed that the spiritual unity toward the national progress on the model of other civilised nations had shown itself during the 1932 revolution. The same spirit continued to exist under the idea of *ratthaniyom*, which was introduced with the goal of eradicating spiritual backwardness and underdevelopment from Thai society in order to achieve full progress.[43]

The Western School's ideas of the nation and national independence, especially those endorsed by members of the People's Party, were quite interesting because it was a widely known fact among students of political history that Thailand had never lost its independence. How much political power had been exerted in conjunction with discursive practices to pro-

---

41 See Pridi Banomyong, บางเรื่องเกี่ยวกับการก่อตั้งคณะราษฎรและระบบประชาธิปไตยไทย [Certain Issues Related to the Founding of the People's Party and Democracy] Bangkok: Rongphim nitiwet 1972.

42 Editors' note: literally 'state preferences' or 'statism' which were issued as a series of state decrees concerning individual conduct and politics which aimed to modernise Thai norms and behaviour from 1939 to 1942.

43 I have studied and explicated this issue in Chapter 9. Editors' note: In Chapter 9 of the original text, Nakharin explains the close relationship between Dharmaniyom and Ratthaniyom.

mote this notion? The Traditionalist School maintained that Thailand had never lost its independence because its political community was always ruled by a Thai king. This was contrary to the Western School, especially Luang Phibun Songkhram's clique, who declared that the nation was more important than the king. For this group, whether a nation is independent or not has nothing much to do with the king but with its judicial power, foreign policy, military power and economy. For this reason, the cliques of Luang Phibun Songkhram and Luang Praditmanutham (Pridi Banomyong) agreed that Thailand had never enjoyed being 'fully independent'. On 24 June 1939, Field Marshal Phibun Songkram's government organised an impressive National Day celebration and announced the implementation of the *ratthaniyom* concept, the construction of the Democracy Monument and an annual celebration of the day that Thailand achieved full independence.[44] For this reason, the People's Party political discourse on democracy was marked by ideas of nation, *ratthaniyom* or *dharmaniyom*, and complete independence. This set of political discourses prevailed during the period prior to the end of WWII.

In fact, Thak Chaloemtiarana had already made a comparison between Field Marshal Phibun Songkhram and Field Marshal Sarit Thanarat in various aspects. He concluded that although Field Marshal Phibun Songkhram ruthlessly and aggressively exercised his political power, he kept the parliamentary system, the constitution and the election system. It seems that political leaders of the earlier periods after 1932 still wanted to retain their bonds with Western democratic doctrine. They differed from leaders of subsequent generations who did not have any perceivable ties with such 'universal' doctrines.[45]

Another group of Western School advocates who have steadfastly established themselves in the decade starting from 1947 are the Marxists. Although these thinkers have detached themselves from the ideas above, they can still be classified as belonging to the Western School for the fact that they are partial to universal doctrines. They also recognise that Thai society has more negative than positive aspects to preserve. The word 'democracy' used by this group is also alienated from Thai cultural

---

44 See ไทยในสมัยรัฐธรรมนูญ: ที่ระลึกในงานฉลองวันชาติและสนธิสัญญา 24 มิถุนายน 2582 [Thailand in the Constitutional Period: In Remembrance for the National Day Celebration and the 24 June 1939 Treaty], Phranakhon: Department of Broadcasting, 1939.

45 Thak Chaloemtiarana, *Despotic Paternalism*.

roots. It refers to an economic democracy and a people's democracy that would be created anew and not from a restoration or modification of older institutions.[46]

Marxist and leftist Thais present a picture of 'conflicts' in Thailand's political society. This fundamental notion is contrary to the Traditionalist School's ideas of a harmonious, smooth and unified political society.[47] This group of thinkers regards pre-1932 political society as a feudal society. Some of them suggest that this type of political society possesses an 'Asiatic mode of production', and certainly not a 'democratic' polity in the Traditionalist School's sense. Within this framework, the 1932 revolution was perceived as the Age of New Hope for the fact that progressive noblemen led the change and set up a bourgeois democratic system. However, despite good intentions, the change was carried out under ill-equipped conditions, and the system became distorted and was turned into a military dictatorship and fascist system. This has become one of the conditions that would push Thai society into having a national democratic revolution and 'democracy' in the future.

The transmission of the Western School's ideas and its influence on current writings has proved to be quite problematic. The first problem is quite prevalent and lies in its rather dry explanations of Thailand's political history. In the past, this line of work was carried out by some of Pridi's closest associates.[48] These explanations, also found in the works of several legal experts, normally began with a bland and evidence-free introduction about the basic principles of this school. The works then proceeded to relate the main doctrines and practices in a rather haphazard and inconsistent fashion. For this reason, the Western School's knowledge-building and institutionalisation process has never been properly implemented. There are a lot of discontinuities in the dissemination of its ideas. This is contrary to the dissemination of the Traditionalist School's ideas, which has always been systematically revised and adjusted.

---

46 Nevertheless, recent trends in the movements of academics and activists were more interested in the issues of village community, local wisdom, and Thai intellectual creativity, etc. These new trends among advocates of the Western School should be monitored, studied and analysed. Editors' note: these trends are at the centre of Pasuk's chapter in this book.

47 For a historical discourse study based on the conflicting ideas and opposition to the Traditionalist School of Thought see Craig J. Reynolds, *Thai Radical Discourse: The Real Face of Thai Feudalism Today* Ithaca: Southeast Asia Program, Cornell University, 1987.

48 Such as Suphot Dantrakul and Sawai Suthiphithak.

However, there have been movements to provide opposing explanations about the political history of Thailand, which represent criticisms of the notions championed by the Traditionalist School, especially in the past decade.[49] Even so, these works still explained the political history in a fragmented fashion instead of providing the whole picture. For example, they explained the pre-1932 political system as an absolute monarchy and a new bureaucratic regime. Thinkers of the Western School lacked the vitality to create a systematic and overall understanding of the 'democratic' political development in Thailand, even though some thinkers, such as Saneh Chamarik, strove to achieve this goal. This issue will be discussed in later sections.

Another problem that advocates of the Western School were confronted with was how to convince the public about the worthiness of their doctrines. In certain situations where an explanation to the public was needed, the traditionalists did not remain idle; they would immediately respond to a claim or an attack on their positions by other groups. For example, during the October Revolution of 1973 Pridi Banomyong, a key thinker of the Western School, proposed many alternative principles for Thai politics such as

> people should have the right to impeach members of the House of Representatives; the government should pay compensation to those who travel to cast their votes in an election; the government should introduce a simple voting system; election candidates should not be forced to belong to a political party and there should be only one house.[50]

An immediate reaction to Pridi's message was given by thinkers such as Chai-Anan Samudavanija who was of the opinion that the People's Party, including Pridi Banomyong, did not have a democratic way of thinking. Chai-Anan explained the 14 October 1973 Event by comparing it to the events of October 1933 when Khana Kubanmuaeng (the National Liberation Group) led by Prince Boworadet rose up against the government [led by the People's Party]. He said this group was more democratic-minded than the People's Party. According to the Traditionalist School, the true inten-

---

49 For example, Nidhi Eoseewong and Chatthip Nartsupha.

50 See Pridi Banomyong, รวบรวมบทความบางเรื่องของนายปรีดี พนมยงค์ เกี่ยวกับระบอบประชาธิปไตยไทยและการร่างรัฐธรรมนูญ [A Collection of Miscellaneous Articles on Democracy and Constitutional Drafting by Pridi Banomyong], Bangkok: Santitham, 1975, 10.

tion of the 14 October 1973 revolution aligns it with the October 1933 Event more than the events of 24 June 1932.[51]

Pridi Banomyong had also tried to make a principled argument that only 'an election' should be used as a criterion for full democracy rather than the unwarranted writings or talks to induce the public into believing that the 1974 constitution was democratic. He repeatedly stated that 'the 1974 constitution diminished the House of Representatives' dignity in the eyes of the world' because it was subjected to mechanisms of the senate and state officials.[52] However, through dynamic arguments the Traditionalist School repeatedly reminded the public that people can have rights and liberties only within the limits of the law. The importance of 'duties' was also emphasised. Leading figures in the military and state bureaucracy claimed to have adopted as their guidance His Majesty the King's speech to the cabinet that was granted a royal audience to take an oath of allegiance before assuming their offices on 16 October 1973. An excerpt from this royal speech reads, 'You must perform your duties to achieve the goal of returning the country to normalcy and restoring the democratic administrative system that suits the conditions of the country'.[53] The Traditionalist School's forceful ideology and discursive practices were effective in its continuity and adaptation to the changing political environment.

Some student leaders who favour abstract principles over traditional ways of thinking, such as Seksan Prasertkul, may be classified as belonging to the Western School. During the transitional period toward the end of the Thanom–Prapas regime [1963–73], Seksan proposed that students should become members of the parliament for the following reasons:

> The parliament normally consists of one or two houses, but we may have three houses, namely, a House of Representatives, a Senate and a House of Youth, specifically for students ... There must be several committees to monitor national problems and the working of government, such as the

---

51 On this issue see Chai-Anan Samudavanija, 14 ตุลา: คณะราษฎรกับกบฏบวรเดช [14 October: The People's Party and the Boworadet Rebellion], Bangkok: History Club, the Academic Aksonsat Group, Chulalongkorn University, 1974.

52 See Pridi Banomyong, *A Collection of Articles*, 138–141.

53 Cited in the lectures of General Sawaeng Senanarong on อิทธิพลต่าง ๆ ที่กระทบกระเทือน นโยบายความมั่นคงของชาติ [Several Influences Impacting the National Security Policy], a lecture given at the Thailand National Defence College on 2 February 1977, in *Cremation Volume of General Sawaeng Senanarong*.

economic, education or foreign affairs committees. University students can be suitably assigned to these committees[54]

In Seksan Prasertkul's opinion, this practice would enable students to learn and work for the country while benefiting the people, tertiary education and students' political activities (so that they would not have to skip classes to march in a protest anymore). However, the idea and justification for the Western concept of a parliamentary system seemed meaningless as Thai politics continued to work along the lines of Traditionalist thought.

Into the present, two of the most famous thinkers and successors of the Western School's ideas are Puey Ungphakorn and Saneh Chamarik. For Puey Ungphakorn, captivated with Thai culture and humanist principles, his way of thinking is taken directly from the *farang* (Westerner) model. He believes in the theory of human rationality. The picture of a utopian society that his writings regularly reflect is one of competency, freedom, fairness and compassion.[55] The 'addition' of compassion to his utopian society may seem similar to the traditionalist concept but his main concerns are the first three Western principles. Compassion was added to make the first three principles more complete. From this perspective, it is apparent that his ideas clearly differed from those of the traditionalists, who modify all things foreign to fit with the unique and fundamental aspects of Thainess.

The Western School thus does not always consist of people who are intent on imitating or replicating everything from the West. Its proponents have wanted to add or improve on some of its doctrines as well, but such improvement must not be overpowered or wiped out by the existing cultural forces within Thai society. The Western School's doctrines must be retained while some rational practices may be added. For example, at this point, I would like to return to Pridi Banomyong, the Western School thinker who firmly believed in the principle of separation of powers. However, the highest powers, in his opinion, as represented in the form of the interim constitution of 27 June 1932, could be separated into four elements, including

---

54 Seksan Prasertkul, เอียงข้างประชาชน [Leaning toward the People] Bangkok: Chumrom nangsue saengchan 1974, 30.

55 See Nidhi Eoseewong, ป๋วย อึ๊งภากรณ์: สิทธิมนุษยชนแบบไทย [Puey Ungphakorn: Thai-style Human Rights] จดหมายข่าวสังคมศาสตร์ [Social Sciences Newsletter] February-April 1991, 65–72.

the sovereign power of the king.[56] For Seksan Prasertkul, parliament is the ultimate requirement for full democracy, but the existence of a parliament does not mean that there must be one or two houses; Thailand may have three houses, including *Yuwasapha* (House of Youth).

Saneh Chamarik's opinions are also consistent with the Western School's perspective. To start with, he sees Buddhism not from an institutional state perspective but from the standpoint of universal humanism, imbued with the principles of freedom and human rights. This is a freedom that stresses an individual's creative and inherent potential to choose or not choose to be free; it also relies on the concept of compassion. Changes that aim to emancipate human beings and to free them from the bond of imbalanced power relations is the ordinary state of human beings.[57] These ideas reject the Traditionalist School's notion that the bonds of human beings are determined by their cultural environment. The next issue that puts Saneh Chamarik in line with the Western School's perspective is that of democracy. He does not agree with the traditionalists' view that 'democracy' already existed in Thai society prior to 1932. On the contrary, he considers Thai democracy to have originated in the Siamese Revolution of 1932, the New Age of Hope for all people. In Saneh Chamarik's opinion, Thailand's political problems after 1932 were at the level of principles, not – as postulated by the traditionalists – as mere pragmatic aspects flowing from the power struggle among leaders of the People's Party. He does not see constitutional laws as problematic, as they are the political ways of life shared by all people and they can always be modified to suit changing times and situations. In this way, the Revolutionary Party's announcements were also constitutional laws. According to Saneh Chamarik, the principal problems in Thai politics are those of decisions that the elite and political powerholders make together, as to whether there will be overt rules on the contest for and transfer of power or not.[58]

---

56 Editors' note: the remaining three were the legislature, the executive and the judiciary. Interestingly, the June constitution was not meant to be an interim document, but the king submitted to it on that condition.

57 Saneh Chamarik, พุทธศาสนากับสิทธิมนุษยชน [Buddhism and Human Rights], in รวมบทความ ก้าวต่อไปของสังคมไทย [Collected Articles: The Next Steps for Thai Society], Bangkok: Political Science Student Committee, Thammasat University, 1980.

58 Saneh, *Thai Politics*. For additional information see Nakharin Mektrairat and Thanet Arpornsuwan, สเน่ห์ จามริก กับสังคมราชูปถัมภ์ [Saneh Chamarik and the Royal Patronage Society], วารสารธรรมศาสตร์ [Thammasat Journal], 15, 4 1987.

Thinking in this universalist style (universal, because all countries striving for democracy must undergo such a decision) is a key factor for why this writer considers Saneh Chamarik as within the Western School. We can conclude at this point that proponents of the Western School realise that Thai politics is confronted with many problems after 1932 but they tend to fuse historical and principled explanations on the problems of Thai politics, rather than focus on the problems stemming from the breach of previous administrative traditions.

The power of the Western School's thinking lies in its principle that all humans are born equal by nature, or the view that there will be conflict one way or another in political society. Such ideas are contrary to those of the Traditionalist School. In many cases, thinkers of the Western School aim to perfect their ideas rather than to discuss the problems from a historical process perspective. This tendency results in the discursive practices of discussing their ideas in abstract rationalist ways. The Western School possesses powerful and rational ideology, but the lack of historical dimension in their works make the School's discursive practices somewhat ungrounded and alienated from the Thai political society. There has never been any direct confrontation or clash of ideas between the two schools. Wisut Phothithaen, a scholar in the Western School, tried to explain the ideal democracy as an ideology based on the democratic criteria of people's participation, a system of majority rule that respects minority rights, freedom and equality.[59] These are abstract ideologies that are not bound to any custom or tradition. It should be noted that, unlike the Traditionalist School, scholars of the Western School have never discussed the principle or concept of 'duty'.

Another interesting point is the fact that the Western School's expressing of ideal opinions about democracy is not totally futile or ineffective. In the past, major thinkers of this school usually presented their belief in universal doctrines in a manner that was widely different from the traditional beliefs that overshadowed them. However, it may be said that, even today, there has been very little elaboration of many important doctrines and concepts. For example, there is no written work on the doctrine of right in Thai society even though it is a vital doctrine embraced and researched by all scholars of the Western School. On the contrary, the Traditionalist School's central

---

59 Wisut Phothithaen, ประชาธิปไตย: แนวความคิดและตัวแบบประเทศประชาธิปไตยในอุดมคติ [Ideal Democracy: Ideas and Models of Democratic Countries], Bangkok: Thammasat University, 1981.

ideas of civic duty have been extensively written about and taught in schools and educational institutes for almost a century.

CONCLUSION

Kasian Tejapira recently wrote a compact article titled 'People's democracy must be free from state and capitalism' in which he made a most relevant and forceful conclusion:

> The power to exercise democracy of various groups in Thai society begins with how they define democracy ... [D]efinition is crucial in that it determines the peoples' ideas, beliefs, legitimacy, and contest for democracy. Democracy must, as the first step, begin with the people successfully winning the contest over the definition of democracy.[60]

The present article is also concerned with the 'defining' of democracy. However, the institutionalised knowledge and understanding of democracy cannot happen without continual explanation about its historical processes or a proper knowledge management system of Thailand's political history. Key issues that need to be addressed by both the Western and the Traditionalist Schools of Thought are: Did democracy or something that may be called democracy exist in Thailand prior to 1932? What was the actual status and origin of the 1932 constitution? Was the post-1932 period of Thai politics a Dark Age or an Enlightened Age? Is chaos another form of order or rule?

In addition, a set of 'defining' practices must be implemented based on systematic thinking and fundamental doctrines to adequately confirm the systems of knowledge that will be developed subsequently. The sets of knowledge that the Traditionalist and Western Schools of Thought have previously explicated include: How are rulers connected to their people? How can rulers learn the intentions of their people? What is the purpose of politics? What are the goals of a political community? How are right and duty related? Which is more important?

Defining democracy is a dynamic and powerful means to determine people's ideas, beliefs, legitimacy and practices. A set of defining practices, which this writer has called a 'political discourse', evolves through historical processes until it becomes institutionalised. A discourse analysis explicates historical

---

60 Kasian Tejapira, ประชาธิปไตยของประชาชนต้องเป็นอิสระจากรัฐและทุน [People's Democracy must be Free from the State and Capital] บานไม่รู้โรย [Ban Mairuroei] 4, 8 September 1991, 71.

perception and lays down the basic thinking process. All these are interwoven with the use of power in a political society until they become inseparable.

This writer considers Kasian Tejapira to be a scholar in the Western School based on his explanation that 'Thai society accepted or borrowed democracy later. It was not originated within our own social, economic and cultural settings.'[61] In addition, Kasian has declared a principled view to establish new systems of knowledge, definition and practices related to a new form of democracy, which will be severed from all previous traditions and practices.

Nevertheless, this writer disagrees with the conclusion reached by Kasian Tejapira: that both the Traditionalist and Western Schools of Thought are faced with similar limitations in their perception of the problems of Thai democracy.[62] The reason behind these limitations is because Thai democracy has evolved and already become institutionalised. The reasoning system and the powerful influence of the political discourses set forth by both schools have set their roots and extensively dominated Thai political society for a very long time. This writer agrees with him on the necessity of starting something new again, but a new set of political discourses must be forceful enough to provide explanations and a reasoning system that is 'superior' to the political discourses already offered by both schools.

The last noteworthy point is concerned with the powerful influence of both sets of political discourses. It was again Kasian Tejapira who firmly stated that, 'Democracy in our country has simply been a political tool seized and modified by various groups in the Thai society for their benefits in their contest for political power.'[63] This writer has a different opinion on this point: since the 'tool' here is resilient in nature and can be transferred from one group to another, it must be a 'tool' with some degree of freedom capable of turning into a leading and constraining force over the 'tool' user in the future.

Both the Traditionalist and Western Schools of Thought are likely into the future to have allies and supporters. The distinctive feature of their political discursive practices is their seriousness; they have won interest and attention because they indicate the character of political discourse and the use of political power over humans in everyday life. They reflect the reality of the political society.

---

61 *Ibid.,* 67.

62 *Ibid.,*

63 *Ibid.,*

CHAPTER 4

National Ideology and Development of the Thai Nation[1]

Kramol Thongthammachart

THE MEANING OF IDEOLOGY

*U*domkan [ideology] is such a new term in [Thai] political science that even political scientists have not been able to give it a precise meaning.[2] Although *udomkan* has been used in the same way as the English word 'ideology', the term still has different meanings for different academics, as evident from some of the definitions given by Western philosophers and academics. For Karl Marx and Friedrich Engels, ideology is 'any form of "consciousness" which expresses the basic attitudes or commitments of a social class'.[3] Talcott Parsons explained that ideology 'is a system of beliefs held in common by the members of a collectivity.'[4] Friedrich and Brzezinski viewed ideology as 'a set of literate ideas – a reasonably coherent body of ideas concerning practical means of how to change and reform a society, based upon a more or less elaborate criticism of what is wrong with the existing or antecedent society.'[5] In this view, a core property of ideology is that it has a practical element.

Thai theorists and academics give the meanings of ideology as follows. Anut Arpapirom defined ideology as 'a theory of people and a society

---

1 Kramol Thongthammachart, อุดมการณ์ของชาติและการพัฒนาชาติไทย [National Ideology and the Development of the Thai Nation], in Office of the Prime Minister อุดมการณ์ของชาติ [National Ideology], Bangkok: Office of the Prime Minister, 1983, 29–42.

2 Editors' note: the translation of ideology as *udomkan* in Thai connotes the dual meaning of systematic ideas and ideals to strive for.

3 See Henry D. Aiken, *The Age of Ideology,* New York: Mentor, 1956, 17–18.

4 Talcott Parsons, *The Social System,* cited in Chai-Anan Samudavanija, อุดมการณ์ทางการเมือง [Political Ideology], Kled Thai Press, Bangkok, 1973, 8.

5 Carl J. Friedrich and Z. K. Brzezinski, *Totalitarian Dictatorship and Autocracy,* cited in Chai-Anan, *Political Ideology.*

with specific goals formulated by an agency that results in the creation of legitimate institutions.'[6] Kamol Somwichien, offering a modified version of the meaning given by Webster's Dictionary, proposed that ideology was 'a systematic set of ideas about life and society held by a particular group of people.'[7] Chai-Anan Samudavanija explained the meaning of ideology, drawing on ideas put forward by John Plamenatz, as 'the beliefs about matters that are significant to a group of people who accept and adopt them as the criteria and guidelines for their conduct and their way of life on a regular basis ... These beliefs help unite people in the group.'[8] In addition, a group of academics addressed this matter and defined ideology as 'a systematic set of ideas that provides an inspiration for people to act or refrain from acting with the goal of achieving the finest condition at a particular time'.[9]

Although different meanings of ideology have been advanced by various philosophers and academics, similar characteristics of ideology have emerged from these meanings. They agree that the key characteristics of an ideology are:

1. A system of ideas or beliefs about life and society;
2. A system of ideas or beliefs that a group of people accepts as righteous and noble;
3. A system of ideas or beliefs that a group of people has adopted as guidelines on how to lead their life on a regular basis and as a reference point for combined action to achieve the finest condition.

THE ORIGIN OF IDEOLOGY

The above-mentioned meanings and characteristics of ideology may arise from a set of ideas or beliefs of one or many individuals. For example, religious ideologies usually arise from a system of ideas or beliefs about a single prophet, while political ideologies usually originate from the ideas or beliefs of several theorists or cult leaders. It is common knowledge that

---

6   Anut Arphaphirom, อุดมการและค่านิยมในสังคมไทยดั้งเดิม [Ideology and Values in Traditional Thai Society] in Chatthip Nartsupha (compiler) อุดมการกับสังคมไทย [Ideology and Thai Society], Social Sciences Association of Thailand, Bangkok, 1972, 7.

7   Kamol Somwichian อุดมการกับสังคมไทย [Ideology and Thai Society] in Chatthip, *Ibid.,* 212.

8   Chai-Anan, *Political Ideology,* 9.

9   Chatthip, *Ideology and Thai Society,* 95.

once a prophet or cult leader thinks or believes that they have found the truth or the facts of life and society, they generally disseminate them to other people who accept and adopt them as guidelines for their livelihood and for the achievement of the noblest living conditions. The reasons for people in a society to accept and adopt a set of ideas or beliefs of a certain prophet, theorist or philosopher as guidelines on how to live their life are likely to be the following:

1. The faith or miracle that a prophet or disciples of such prophet or a cult leader or disciples of a cult leader can manifest to others.
2. The ability of a prophet or disciples of such prophet or a cult leader or disciples of a cult leader to meet the emotional or materialistic needs of a group of people.
3. The scientific characteristics of a specific system of ideas or beliefs, including its ability to produce evidence or rational explanations.

THE IMPORTANCE OF IDEOLOGY

Today's religions and politico-economic doctrines come in various forms with their disciples and believers actively propagating their beliefs to other groups for acceptance as a guideline for living. Diverse groups in various countries all over the world can have different religious and politico-economic ideologies. And when certain religions and politico-economic systems sometimes hold conflicting sets of ideologies, this can result in mutual destruction between different groups of disciples as is evident from fatal clashes between Lebanese of the Christian and Islamic faiths or between Vietnamese, Cambodian and Laotian groups of different politico-economic ideologies.

For this reason, societies with serious clashes of ideology usually attempt to mesh shared principles or concepts of different creeds in order to create a common ideology or a national ideology that can provide common guidelines for living. Examples of such efforts can be seen from the cases of India, Indonesia, Malaysia and Burma, where leaders have tried to establish a national ideology that people of different races, politico-economic backgrounds and religious groups can embrace as a way of living. For example, Indonesia has adopted as its national ideology the principle of *Pancasila*, which consists of the political, economic and religious values that are acceptable to all groups. As its national ideology, Burma has the Burmese way to socialism that combined socialist and nationalistic principles. On the contrary, leaders of China, Vietnam, Laos and Cambodia who adhere to Communist ideologies chose to employ various incentives and forms of coercion to have people in their country believe in or accept that communism is the only truth that can solve all problems and achieve a new and better society. These leaders introduced different methods that the people can use as guidelines for the performance of their duties and livelihood. Chinese leaders have been highly successful in using communist ideologies to rally the Chinese people to work for their society over the past twenty years; they had much more success with the creation of a common national ideology than Burmese and Indonesian leaders.

China's higher rate of success in the propagation of national ideology than the other two countries can be attributed to the fact that the Communist Party of China is the country's largest political party with a huge number of zealous party members who work consistently and enthusiastically to induce the mass population to accept and practise the established national ideology. Unlike China, Indonesia and Burma do not have such an influential political party or dedicated party members.

In summary, it can be said that a national ideology capable of creating mass conviction or loyalty which will result in solemn and consistent implementation must have the following characteristics:

1. Being a system of ideas that rests upon a solid foundation of the society's major institutions, or that can be expanded into a social theory or a social philosophy.

2. Being a system of ideas that can explicate the positive social elements that should be upheld and the negative elements that should be eradicated to maintain social justice and the common good.

3. Being a system of ideas that rests upon verifiable rational and scientific principles.

4. Being a system of ideas that can explicate the means that members of the society should adopt and practise to create eventually the most excellent conditions for a society.

5. Being a system of ideas that has been adopted and put into practice on a continuing basis to produce distinctively positive results for the society, a system that can withstand the challenges from other ideologies or opposing ideas.

6. Being a system of ideas that complies to the sentiments, ideas and needs of most of the people in a nation, making it easy for the people to embrace the ideas and trust that they can solve their problems.

If the national ideologies of any country have all six of these characteristics, they will be highly beneficial to the common good of the country and its members. Such benefits include:

1. Providing a common bond to unite the people, making it easy to agree on the national goals.
2. Helping the people to recognise the importance of their relationships with other members of the society, generating a shared desire to improve their society for better living and fairness.
3. Enabling members of the society to recognise the degeneration of their society and to adopt a better way of living in the future.
4. Assisting a slugglishly developing society to become a society with inherent driving forces toward change. Such ideologies are adaptable to changing times and social realities.
5. Enabling members of a society to use such a national ideology as a rationale or a point of orientation for their daily conduct, which will lead to social justice. It can also determine an individual's social duties and social rights.
6. Helping members of a society or a nation to accept the rules and criteria of the existing politico-economic and social systems at the time, and to adopt peaceful solutions to conflicts.
7. Persuading those with strong conviction or faith in such national ideology to act in unison to achieve a better society or to refrain from acting in a certain way that may generate obstacles to the achieving of a better society.

THAILAND'S NATIONAL IDEOLOGY

As it is commonly found, the ideology that has been earnestly promoted and propagated by the government sector, schools and several groups to secure faith and conviction among the Thai people is based on the idea that national security and peace will be achieved if the Thai people have faith in the institutions of the nation, the religion and the monarchy. We may refer to such ideology as the *udomkan trai phak* [tri-allegiance ideology]. It so happens that this ideology has contributed to the forging of the people's unity to achieve certain goals through such activities as sacrificing assets to support public activities or expressing public opinion against the country's external enemies.

However, the key weakness of *udomkan trai phak* lies in the fact that it has put a strong emphasis on loyalty to the three institutions without providing a clear explanation of the practical mechanism to maintain their stability. For example, there has never been a clear explanation regarding which actions truly represent loyalty to the institutions of nation, religion and monarchy so as to defend against affected or opportunistic loyalty that is meant merely to demonstrate to others that one is loyal to the three institutions.

Another weakness of this ideology is that it fails to identify the means by which the existing political, economic, administrative and social problems can be solved. This shortcoming renders the ideology inadequate to assure all groups in Thai society, especially the poor and the disadvantaged, that adopting such an ideology will provide them and their descendants with a better life. For this reason, it is crucial that this ideology be expanded to cover more approaches and solutions to a wider range of problems in Thai society. There should also be guidelines on how to conduct oneself or lead one's life in a way that can be taken as a demonstration of genuine loyalty to the institutions of the nation, the religion and the monarchy. Many academics and researchers have proposed several supplementary ideologies to *udomkan trai phak*, only two of which are cited below.

1. A group of social scientists once proposed that the ideology capable of directing the Thai society toward progress, development and diminished social conflicts should be 'the ideology that can generate development measures that are capable of both transforming the country's economic structures and eradicating economic exploitation, generating social justice and maintaining personal liberty.' The ideology proposed here comes from the economic and political ideology known as liberal socialism. The problem with this proposal concerns how to disseminate this ideology to the masses and how to secure approval for this ideology from the Thai people. These are extremely serious problems for two reasons:

   a. Liberal socialist ideology is mainly practised in northern European countries like Norway, Sweden and Denmark, and most Thai people may find such ideas and practices to be unfamiliar.

b. As all strands of socialism have been criticised by proponents of conservative and feudalistic ideologies as being the same as the communist ideologies, this would make it difficult to propagate and gain approval from the Thai people.

For these reasons, it is the author's opinion that the ideology that can win mass approval and be put into practice is likely to be one that is compatible with the prevailing sentiments, ideas and needs of the majority Thais. Somchai Rakwichit et al. conducted research on this topic and discovered that most Thais share five aspirations as follows[10]:

a. To revere and uphold the nation, the religion, the monarchy and the identity of Thainess.
b. To promote and create stable democratic political institutions that are responsive to the people.
c. To have the country's socio-economic system improved as a stable, just and efficient system of mixed economy that can bring good living and safety of life and property to the people.
d. To upgrade Thailand's social and cultural systems to be capable of providing a simple way of life in which the Thai people can be economical, diligent, ethical and have a high level of social responsibility.
e. To introduce improvement to Thailand's administrative system so that we can have a democratic government that is wholesome, just, and can truly serve the Thai people.

2. Somchai Rakwichit et al. believed that Thai national ideology is capable of merging the strengths of various groups of Thais who are currently dissatisfied with the 'most appalling state' of today's society and must cater to the above-mentioned five aspirations. Sitthithan Rakprathet, a member of Somchai Rakwichit's research team, explained how to implement all five elements of such an ideology in his book, *'Su Sangkhom Mai'* (Toward a New Society).[11]

In applying the first element of the ideology, one must aim to preserve national autonomy and to encourage the Thai people to have strict adher-

---

10 Somchai Rakwichit and General Saiyut Kerdpol, ยุทธศาสตร์เพื่อความอยู่รอดของชาติ [Strategies for National Survival] Bangkok: Pitakpracha, 1976, 245–6.
11 Sitthithan Rakprathet, สู่สังคมใหม่ [Toward a New Society] Bangkok: Amnuayrak kanphim, 1976, 208–254.

ence to religion and respect for the monarchy while preserving the Thai traditions, Thai customs and Thainess.

In applying the second element of the ideology, governmental security must be ensured through a separation of administrative and legislative power and having a prime minister who is directly elected. Moreover, one must provide good persons with the opportunity to enter government through an election and encourage a system of strong political parties through a requirement that a political party with less than 20% of the total parliamentary members must merge with another political party. There should also be financial assistance to political parties.

In applying the third element of the ideology, there must be security for financial investment by laying down the conditions by which a strike may occur. There must also be clear conditions for the distribution of a company's net profits and the allocation of a company's profits to workers. Furthermore, there must be more expansion in different industries, especially in the agricultural industry. The gaps between the rich and the poor must be reduced through improving the status of the poor without degrading the status of the rich. Such gaps can also be reduced by implementing major land reforms to allocate lands to farmers and by a guaranteed increase of the minimum wage for factory workers. Other measures include enough medical and sanitary welfare provision to the poor, provision of wide-ranging education to most people, progressive taxation and introduction of inheritance taxes to force the rich to make larger contributions to the society.

In applying the fourth element of the ideology, which involves the advancement of culture, there should be efforts to create values that allow Thais to appreciate a simple and economical livelihood, pride in the practice of self-help, diligence, hard work and ethical conduct. In addition, there is a need to create a hatred of corruption, love of justice and social responsibility.

In applying the fifth element of the ideology, which involves the improvement of the national administrative system, administrative decentralization should be introduced to allow participation of local people in the decision-making process and local management. In addition, there must be strict prevention and suppression of corruption in the government sector, rotation of government officials to prevent them from holding a single position for an extended period, and control measures to prevent government officials from extravagant or sinful living.

PROBLEMS IN THE DISSEMINATION OF NATIONAL DEVELOPMENT IDEOLOGIES

It can be said that all five ideological elements, as proposed by Dr Somchai Rakwichit and Sitthithan Rakprathet, are so extensive that they encompass institutions and social, political, economic, management and cultural problems that exist in Thai society. Most of these elements are similar to the ones I have already suggested elsewhere. I believe that if all five elements can be implemented, we should be able to get rid of existing problems and conflicts, and to advance Thailand toward a stable and just society. Nevertheless, the key problem that we are faced with is how to disseminate these ideological elements to different groups and gain acceptance among some of the groups that have irrational ideas, or to be accepted by groups with conflicting interests. Adoption of these ideologies will be ineffective if conservative groups that are strongly against modern ideas, or groups with conflicting interests accept only some of these elements. For example, the capitalists may accept only the first and second ideological elements while rejecting the third, which calls for changes in the economic structure that may affect the capitalists' interests. Government officials may not accept the fifth element while workers may not accept restrictions on their right to hold a strike. In such cases, the above-mentioned ideological elements might not be able to prevent the conflicts of interest among different groups, and the hope of proponents of these ideologies to unite the Thai people may fail.

In addition, another key question concerns which organization or institution may be assigned the task of spreading these ideological elements within Thai society. This is because most Thai people do not have much faith in religious, educational, public service or political party institutions. These institutions are generally perceived as ineffective in performing their duties. The absence of capable organizations or institutions for extensive dissemination of these ideological elements will render them marginal ideas or beliefs that are advocated only by a minority of academics or politicians.

These ideological elements will remain dormant if they lack the power and incentives to gain approval and following among the public, making them unable to steer Thailand into successful national development, progress and security.

APPROACHES TO THE DISSEMINATION OF
NATIONAL DEVELOPMENT IDEOLOGIES

As previously mentioned, the People's Republic of China has been highly successful in disseminating Marxist ideology to its people. The Chinese people have accepted and adopted this ideology as a guideline for living and fulfilling their duties and social obligations toward the country. Indonesia and Burma had only minimum success in disseminating the ideology of Pancasila and the Burmese-way to socialism to the people in their respective countries. China's success in this respect has been attributed to the establishment of the Communist Party of China as the country's largest and most highly disciplined political party, with strong influence over the Chinese people's ideas. This success has also been partially attributed to the strong control that the Communist Party has enforced on all types of mass media, enabling the government to effectively block the dissemination of alternative ideologies and beliefs among the Chinese people. The Communist Party of China continues to eradicate all traditional ideas and beliefs that are not consistent with the Marxist-Leninist ideology.

However, although attempts to disseminate the above-mentioned five elements of Thai ideology have been found to be problematic – as political parties and the state bureaucracy are ineffective and cannot command much respect from the Thai public – there seems to be no other alternative. Both institutions have been used to disseminate the said ideological elements as a way of life. This is because Thai political parties have long been performing the roles of collecting data from the people and accounting for the needs and sentiments of particularistic groups of people as they formulate policies under a shared ideological framework. The state bureaucracy has also long been the country's largest institution with close relationships with the people. It is also the sole owner and regulator of all radio and television stations in the country. It is, therefore, a highly effective control mechanism that the political parties who form government must use for political and ideological propaganda. Moreover, all levels of educational institutions are required to take part in the dissemination of national ideology. To ensure maximum success, the government must seek cooperation from newspapers and private organizations in its dissemination of the national ideology.

Hence, if we agree to accept all five ideological elements as the national ideology, as recommended by Dr Somchai Rakwichit et al., we must select short catch phrases to address these elements. For example, the first element may be referred to as the *udomkan trai phak* while the other four ideological elements, addressing the political, economic, cultural and administrative elements, may be collectively referred to as the *udomkan jatumak* (four-path ideology). The explanations and practices of these ideologies must also be presented in short catch phrases to entice the public into adopting them. These techniques were successfully employed by Field Marshal P. Phibun Songkram to propagate leader worship and nationalistic ideologies during the WWII period.[12] For example, there may be an emphasis on the concept that those who pledge their loyalty to the nation, the religion and the monarchy must adopt the following characteristics or ways of life: frugality, honesty, adherence to religious teachings, abstinence from vices, sin and bad deeds, aim to do good, and be willing to sacrifice one's life to protect the nation, the religion, the monarchy and help suppress the enemy of the country.

For the cultivation of faith in and observance of the *udomkan jatumak*, the following information may be used to stress the importance of the ideology in improving people's livelihood and solving problems of the Thai society:

Political aspects

1. For Thai society, democracy is more suitable than any other political system.
2. Democratic practices are more effective than dictatorship in solving conflicts between different groups in a society.
3. Democracy will certainly improve the livelihood of the Thai people.

Economic aspects

4. A mixed economy is the coexistence of public and private sector agencies to promote national progress.

---

12 For example, the phrases: 'believe in the leader and the nation will be safe' or 'Thai made, Thais use'. See การสร้างชาติของจอมพล ป. พิบูลสงคราม สมัยสงครามโลกครั้งที่สอง [Field Marshal P. Phibun Songkram's Nation-building during the Second World War], in Thaemsuk Numnonda, รวม ปาฐกถา [Lectures 1977–1978], Bangkok, Social Sciences Association of Thailand, 1978, 34–309.

5. A mixed economy can better provide justice and suppress conflicts between different groups than any other economic system.
6. A mixed economy does not support state enterprises that do not benefit society.

Cultural aspects

7. Frugality and prudence are parts of Thai culture.
8. Having substance and responsibility towards society are parts of Thai culture
9. Discipline and punctuality are parts of Thai culture.

Administrative aspects

10. Sub-district councils, municipality councils and provincial councils are the administrative instruments used by the people for the people.
11. Honesty in performing their duties and willingness to serve the people are the attributes of good crown servants.
12. Corruption and wrongdoing in the government sector will make Thailand fall behind and, in the end, could lead to the loss of the nation.

It can be said that if the mass media in both the public and private sectors join forces in disseminating these or other similar ideas to build faith in the *trai phak – jatumak* ideologies and consistently urge people to observe them under the directions and examples of political, administrative, business and academic leaders, these ideologies will gain respect and faith in the society. They will also eventually be able to unite different groups of people, create growth, progress and justice in Thai society. Thai people certainly need direction and exemplary conduct from their leaders in different milieus.

CONCLUSION

Ideology is a set of ideas and beliefs about life and society. The ideology that can rally strong conviction from the people will bring different groups together in unity and will lay down acceptable patterns of behaviour for the people. If people benefit from the practising of such an ideology, it will eventually become the key ideology of that society.

The *udomkan trai phak* has already existed in Thailand but its attributes have not yet been extended to include the Thai political, economic, administrative and social ideologies. Clear and precise practices under this ideology have not been established. Since the ideology lacks forceful dissemination it has not sufficiently commanded the Thai people's faith. Such faith and willingness to adopt the practices demanded by such ideology will only emerge when leaders in other sectors have strong faith in the same ideology and take it upon themselves to provide suitable directions and role models that the general population can follow.

CHAPTER 5

Thai-style Democracy: Concept and Meaning[1]

Chalermkiat Phiu-nuan

In the preceding chapters, we studied key principles of the military's political ideas, focusing empirically on the viewpoints and actions of elite military figures who were government leaders and those who were prominently involved in 'politics'. They were all army officers from the era of 'Mythic Democracy', which can be traced to the ideas of the members of the 1912 Rebellion [a thwarted plot by soldiers to introduce constitutional rule], which gave rise to the 1932 Revolution, in part owing to the pressure of a group that we will call 'Constitutional Soldiers'. This marked the dawning of the democratic era of Thai political history, during which the role of the army became prominent, which in turn is one of the most critical factors that hindered Thailand from drawing open the curtain on the 'democracy stage' until the end of the Phibun Songkhram and Sarit Thanarat regimes. This mythic era lasted a full four decades until the 1973 revolution, which symbolised the beginning of the era of mass politics. This change caused elite army officers who were involved in politics at the time – including heads of government and influential ideological groups such as the Thai Young Turks and the Democratic Soldiers; for the sake of brevity we may refer to them as 'political soldiers' – to propose the idea of adaptation by the army in order for it to creatively shape the nation, thereby paving the way to a new era of democracy. The curtain of democracy hence opened again, with new elements ranging from the perspective of the government and military leaders to the liberal style power of the people, all coexisting and struggling through moments of crises up until the present.

---

1 Originally published as Chapter 4 in Chalermkiat Phiu-nuan, ความคิดทางการเมืองของ ทหารไทย 2519-2535 [Thai-style Democracy: The Political Thought of the Thai military, 1976–1992], Bangkok: Samnakphim phujatkan, 1992, 143–186.

We have also seen, in detail, that political soldiers in different eras variously cited 'democracy'. For instance, the Constitutional Soldiers, Phibun Songkhram's and Sarit Thanarat's regimes all spoke from the perspective of a constitutional regime, while Thanin Kraivichien's government referred to 'democracyness' as having the king as the head of state. Pragmatists such as the Young Turks viewed democracy as a functioning administrative system, whereas the Democratic Soldiers called for the establishment of democracy both as a social aspiration and a strategic move against communism. The latter view was expressed in the policies and orders of the government of Prime Minister General Prem Tinsulanonda. It can be seen here that the concept of democracy varies among governments and leading military figures. However, we can consider that the aim of these different concepts of democracy is to establish its 'appropriateness' with Thai society after the inauguration of the era of mass politics in 1973. Having encountered unstable circumstances posed by communist threats at both the domestic and international level, each government during the period seemed to realise that the only solution to the situation is to be democratic. Hence, the term 'Thai-style Democracy' is core to any study of the contemporary military's political thinking.

In this chapter we will attempt to study the core concepts related to democracy that are held to be appropriate to Thailand and that have appeared in the thinking of various military leaders and governments. We begin with a general picture, after which we meditate on the deeper meanings that allow us to comprehend the common basis behind this thinking.

DEMOCRACY: THE CONCEPT

'Thai-style democracy' does not refer only to democracy as a political system for Thailand. Rather, there are specific implications of the term when considered alongside certain facts, such as (1) the claim by Thanin that Thai democracy has the king as head of state; (2) the promise of the government under the administration of 'the National Administrative Reform Council' (NARC), led by General Kriangsak Chomanan, to have a constitution and elections; (3) the determination of General Prem Tinsulanonda's government in 1980 to build democracy by means of Prime Ministerial Order no. 66/2523; (4) the Young Turks reference to a regime that is workable; (5) the proposal by the Democratic Soldiers of ideological and strategic concepts of democracy, based on the assumption that the system is suitable to the conditions and unique character of Thailand; and (6) the emphasis of General Arthit Kamlang-ek on using democracy in accordance with the situation, and General Chavalit Yongchaiyudh's proposition on the universal character of democracy and its responsiveness to the needs of the Thai people. Thus, the term 'Thai-style democracy', in these views derives its meaning from its objectives (i.e., as an ideology, as a compatible component of specific characteristics of Thailand, as a response to the demand from Thai people, or as an effective tool) and from its form and method (i.e., the constitution, political parties, elections, and parliament etc.). We can think of 'Thai-style democracy' as referring to democracy as a form of democratic government that is held to be suitable for Thai culture and traditions and is in accord with the country's situation. We will look at each aspect of this idea.

When we examine democracy from the broad principle of democracy as a political concept that consists of form and method whose essence is government of the people, by the people and for the people,[2] we see at first glance that it is not difficult to say that the ideas of both the governments and the political soldiers have comparably different levels of 'democracyness'. In its short term of office, the Thanin government's National Administrative Reform Council was without the shape or methods of democratic administration, nor were its objectives clear despite having expressed determination to build a complete democratic system. Thus, it is not surprising that the regime was labelled 'dictatorial'. As for the governments of General Kriangsak and General Prem, the 1978 constitution under which they operated exhibited the form and methods of democracy, including having a constitution, an election law, political parties, parliament and holding that a majority is central in decision making. There was some creative substance in the level of political 'democracyness' too, as may be seen in the 1978 constitution and in Prime Ministerial Order no. 66/2523 (66/1980). Still, this period has been called 'half democracy' or 'semi democracy', and in this study it is referred to as statist democracy. While the Young Turks focused

---

2   On democratic principles see Chai-Anan Samudavanija, ประชาธิปไตยสังคมนิยมคอมมิวนิสต์กับ
การเมืองไทย [Democracy, Socialism, Communism, and Thai Politics], Bangkok: Rongphim
piganet, 2nd ed., 1977; M. J. Harmon, *Political Thought from Plato to the Present*, translated by
Saneh Chamarik, Bangkok, Thammasat University Press 1967; William Ebenstein, *Today's
Isms*, Englewood Cliffs, N.J.: Prentice-Hall, 7th ed., 1973; Ernst B. Schultz, *Democracy*, New
York: Barron's Educational Series, 1966; Leon P. Baradat, *Political Ideologies: Their Origins
and Impact*, Englewood Cliffs, N.J.: Prentice-Hall, 1979.

on the results for the majority of the people, who were underprivileged and suffered economically and gave no importance to the form and method, the Democratic Soldiers hoped to be creative in form and method and their prime objective lay in the dimension of political development. Since the emergence of the new era of democracy under the 1978 constitution, the governments often claimed their legitimacy, to a certain degree, by stating that democracy is the system *for the people*. That is, the government came from elections under constitutional law with parliament responsible for legislation, and it ruled for the benefit of the people (such as how all governments from Thanin's regime until today have claimed that their actions were for democracy, or how Kriangsak's and Prem's governments justified their actions on the grounds that they were fighting against poverty). We may say that the governments' legitimacy claims did not achieve their objectives. The most serious problem, which led to constant criticism of governments, was that the system was not truly run *by the people*. The democratic system of the new era was controlled by the principle of statism and its paramount purpose was not the people but national security in which the military was the key institution, not the people. Therefore, we may consider that the people did not truly govern.

There was also criticism that the emphasis on democratic form and method came from leaders and other politically active people who misunderstood democracy. They believed that establishing the form and method of democracy would succeed in creating a true democracy. In other words, they failed to distinguish between democratic methods and democratic goals. Hence, we can see that when a constitution was promulgated, elections held, or parliament formed, some individuals would assume that Thailand had successfully achieved democracy and that there was no need for interest groups to lead protests or demand any more benefits from the government. They would also view political protests as destroying democracy. This exclusive emphasis on democratic form and method overlooked democratic objectives in supporting citizens to achieve contentment by means of establishing a society without wide income gaps and having opportunities to make a living. For instance, there was an emphasis that rights and political equality were based on an elected government and parliament, not on economic equality. Thus, economic development lacked income distribution, while the implementation of democratic form and method in a country with prolonged problems of wide income and life quality gaps further contributed to legitimised exploitation. This factor also allowed in-fluential economic groups to use the name of democracy to direct political power toward supporting their group interests. We may, therefore, say that Thai politics increasingly had the character of a plutocracy.[3] These problems regarding the objectives of democracy were reflected in the army's political ideas, such as the demand of the Young Turks to prioritise economic justice, the proposal of the Democratic Soldiers to develop the national economy under the 'Policy of Democratic Revolution' and General Chavalit's wish to see Thai society take the shape of 'a beautiful egg' – that is, a society bulging with the middle class. After all, these problems have persisted until today and have become key weaknesses of Thai democracy.

The emphasis on form that should be considered here is the establish-ment of a constitution. As is known, the Thai constitution did not gradually evolve as in the case of western countries, but was implemented during the regime change of 1932. Many people and even elements in the People's Party understood that having a constitution was a form of democracy. With the ap-pearance of the constitution in this sudden manner, it could not be expected that the faith and understanding in it would be sufficiently widespread among the population to give it political force as a key political institution, or that dif-ferent political groups would accept its importance and collectively preserve it as the repository of the country's governing principles. Such pragmatic and realist figures as Field Marshal Plaek Phibun Songkhram, Sarit Thanarat, and the Young Turks saw this truth and established themselves as leaders to ad-minister the country in any way they wanted. It is not odd that they thought the constitution was to be employed for various ends rather than being the principal political institution. Instead, they placed emphasis on leaderism (*lathi phunam*) and militarism (*lathi thahan*), taking these as the actual 'par-amount institutions'. Government by law was of less importance than having the appropriate people in office, backed by force.

Scholars who study problems concerning the use of the Thai constitu-tion have made an interesting remark that there are three major sources of constitutions. First, having staged coup d'états, each coup council usually

---

3   Chai-Anan Samudavanija, ปัญหาอุดมการณ์ทางการเมือง [Problems in Political Ideologies], in ในปัญหาทางการเมืองไทยปัจจุบัน, เอกสารการสอนชุดวิชาสาขาวิชารัฐศาสตร์, เล่มที่ 1 หน่วยที่ 2, [Current Problems in Thai Politics, Teaching Materials in Political Science Volume 1, Unit 2], Bangkok, Samnakphim sukhothai thammatirat 1986, 57–8. Chai-Anan straight-forwardly states that Thailand is democratic only in form, but has the characteristics of authoritarianism in essence.

drafted or revived a constitution and used it to temporarily govern the nation with emphasis on its own interest. For example, the 1932 constitution (revived in November 1951) and the 1959, 1972 and 1976 constitutions benefitted the governments of Field Marshals Phibun, Sarit, and Thanom and the judge Thanin, respectively. Thus, we could call these 'oligarchic constitutions'. Second, there usually came pressure from democratic forces for a new constitution some time after an oligarchic constitution was drafted and the power of a coup d'état's Revolutionary Council started to dwindle. For instance, the 1946, 1949, 1974 constitutions were all drafted based on democratic principles, did not facilitate any military groups, and made it possible for political figures with civilian backgrounds to take part in national politics. Thus, we could call these 'democratic constitutions'. However, as the power on the democratic side was not strong enough to secure these constitutions, they were only in use for a short time before being abolished by a coup. Third were charters that resulted from the harmonization of interests between an oligarchic military grouping and democratic forces. This kind of constitution was usually the result of a coup d'état's Revolutionary Council attempting to find support from political groups outside the bureaucracy. They therefore had to allow other interest groups to take part in governing the country. The constitutions of this kind were usually drafted to replace a temporary oligarchical one, but with the Revolutionary Council still playing principal roles in the government. For example, the 1978 constitution secured power for the army by allowing state officials to simultaneously hold political positions for four consecutive years in accordance with temporary provisions. It also allowed the prime minister to appoint senators, thereby creating a 'government party'. Thus, we could call these either 'semi-democratic' or 'semi-oligarchic' constitutions.[4]

When we consider the history of Thai politics from 1932 onwards, we can see that the lifespans of the first and the third kinds of constitutions were far longer than those of the second kind. That is because military groups and the bureaucratic system or statist forces supported them and, in turn, these long-lived constitutions were utilised by the military groups to legally legitimise their political standing. Statists with this legitimacy governed the country as they wished. The weakness of democratic forces and the private

---

4   Kramol Thongthammachart, ปัญหาการใช้รัฐธรรมนูญ [Problems in Applying the Constitution], in *Ibid.*, Unit 4, 135.

sector, of civilians and professional politicians, enabled military leaders to use the constitution in accord with their ideas. For example, leading figures like Phibun Songkhram and Thanom Kittikachorn, both of whom staged coup d'états to abolish the constitution drafted by their own revolutionary councils, tended towards authoritarianism and lacked the qualities required of constitutionalism. They had no belief in the sanctity of the constitution nor regard for governing in accordance with it. On the contrary, military leaders like General Kriangsak and General Prem showed more positive views toward constitutional government even though General Kriangsak's own political role was somewhat questionable as he was involved in the coup attempt of 9 September 1985. As for General Prem, while he openly stated that army support secured his success in leading political administrations, he often commented publicly on his faith in the constitutional system and on how he governed the nation in accordance with its conventions. And while he never ran for election as a member of the House of Representatives, he not only agreed to cooperate with political parties – an act that enabled him to claim that his government came from elections – but he was also accepted among House members who were from the many different parties that joined the government. We can thus say that this regime did exhibit democratic form and methods.

What should be stated again is the appearance of military ideas that emphasised the essence or objective of 'democracy'. Firstly, the Democratic Soldiers and General Chavalit openly contended that the constitution alone did not symbolise democracy, and that the successful founding of a democratic regime should first be done through policies and power; only then can a constitution be drafted. With this approach, the constitution would be democratic and in accord with reality. The true core of democracyness, which is universal, is the sovereignty and freedom of the people. Considering together the idea of establishing true democracy and the wish to shape Thai society like a beautiful egg, General Chavalit may be regarded as being concerned with lifting the quality of socio-economic life of the majority of the people because the middle class is the basis of a democratic society, as seen in liberal democracies in the Western world. After all, true democracyness would guarantee national security and protect the country from communist threats.

Besides being, in the view of General Chavalit and the Democratic Soldiers, a desirable and suitable system, with connotations of being 'an ideal society', 'democracy' was also a strategy to overcome communism under

Prime Ministerial Order no. 66/2523. It appears that since the open and aggressive confrontation between two opposing political ideologies in the era of open mass politics, namely democracy and socialism/communism, democracy was the only option in the view of military leaders and the governments that rejected communism; they thought that communism was not suitable for the country because this doctrine has no place for the monarchy, an issue to be discussed later. Therefore, democracy was indeed strategically significant for the preservation of 'Thainess'. Nevertheless, both the establishment of a democratic society and the strategic use of democracy against communism were, as previously demonstrated, based on the ideas of statism and military force.

The second characteristic of 'Thai-style democracy' is its appropriate alignment with Thai culture and traditions. This is a somewhat vague characteristic because there are many aspects to culture, and this appropriateness need not always be according to democratic principles. The first obvious characteristic is to have the King as Head of State, as the monarchy is viewed as the highest institution of the nation and must not be violated. As discussed, the status of the monarchy had been unstable, as can be seen from, for example, the 1912 rebellion, and the change of administration in 1932 to the period of the Phibun government. However, the Sarit regime managed to restore the monarchy back to its status as the highest institution. The phrase 'Democracy with the King as Head of State' first appeared officially in the foreword of the 1968 constitution as: 'The evolution of the regime with the king as head of state shows that a regime with the king as head of state is forever venerated by the Thai people ... The Constitution Drafting Assembly stipulated the general principle that Thailand is a Democracy with the King as Head of State.'[5] In the era of open mass politics between 1973 and 1976, monarchy, as a mark of 'Thainess', was symbolically used against communist ideologies and 'the leftists'. Then, the NARC claimed the stability of the monarchy as the justification of their 1976 coup d'état. Thanin's government claimed that Thailand succeeded in preserving democracy because of the monarchy, just as did the United Kingdom. The 1978 constitution, drafted during General Kriangsak's administration, specified having the King as Head of State. In addition, the

---

5   Editors' note: The phrase first officially appeared in the 1949 constitution in a slightly different form.

Young Turks and General Prem always claimed their loyalty and devotion to the institution of the monarchy, while the Democratic Soldiers and General Chavalit reasoned that monarchy was a key institution of the Thais since ancient times and constituted a part of Thai culture.

A key feature of this second characteristic is to hold that the country, or the national state is, with the monarchy, the highest institution. In his speech 'The Character of Siamese Administration since Antiquity', Prince Damrong Rajanubhab proposed that the depth of loyalty to the freedom of the nation was one way to gauge the morality of Thai people.[6] This virtue was not simply ancient, as we can see it embedded in the military's political thought, something that statism and national security always prioritised. To protect the nation was a 'sacred' mission because 'the nation is sacred'.[7] There is an interesting point here: for the military to prioritise the nation was equivalent to being loyal to the monarchy, and so when certain figures thought the two institutions were separable, it caused problems – as occurred in the political thought of the soldiers in the 1912 Rebellion, the constitutional soldiers in the People's Party, and in the Phibun Songkhram regime.

The doctrine of the leader or leaderism is the third characteristic that can be examined alongside militarist doctrine. The belief that the nation's leaders should be from the army and that it was appropriate for army leaders to take care of the nation's administration was reflected in the political thought of the Young Turks, the Democratic Soldiers, Prime Ministerial Order no. 66/2523, and the basic ideas in the 1978 constitution, and lay behind coup d'états. Even though the pronounced role of the national leader was first apparent in the era of 'Mythic Democracy' under the Phibun Songkhram regime, its justification was mainly based on the universality or justness that all creatures need strong leaders. The Sarit Thanarat government claimed Thai culture and customs as a justification for its leadership. 'The paternalistic system of rule', which resembles a system of leaderism, reappeared during the government of 'Pa Prem' (Dad Prem) which, although milder,

---

6   Prince Damrong Rajanubhab, ลักษณะการปกครองประเทศสยาม แต่โบราณ ปาฐกถาที่สามัคยาจารย์สมาคม 8 ตุลาคม 2470 [The Character of Siamese Administration since Antiquity, a Speech Given to Samakyajan Samakhom October 8, 1927] in อ่านประกอบคำบรรยายวิชาพื้นฐานอารยธรรมไทย [Introductory Lectures on Thai Civilization] Bangkok, Thammasat University Press, 1971, 52.

7   ประมวลสุนทรพจน์ ฯพณฯ พลเอกเปรมติณสูลานนท์นายกรัฐมนตรีพุทธศักราช 2528 [Collected Speeches: His Excellency, Prime Minister General. Prem Tinsulanonda,1985], Bangkok: Rongphim aksonthai 1986, 275.

despotic power was embedded in his nickname, 'killer of the Chao Phraya River'. The Prem era was similar to that of the Phibun Songkhram and Sarit eras in that the prime ministership was viewed as an institution that could not be challenged and was probably infallible. The only difference lies in the way each ruler subdued dissenters. Militarist doctrine and enduring cultural features such as respect for seniors and a belief in persons over principles were what Squadron Leader Prasong Soonsiri, the former secretary of the prime minister, considered part of the national identity.[8] Thus, Thai citizens had one prime minister who was 'a father' under Sarit and another who was a 'dad' under Prem.

Behind these leaders lay a patronage system, the fourth characteristic. As is generally acknowledged, the patronage system is a remarkable feature of Thai culture that has existed since ancient times and was most widespread in the bureaucracy and in political administrations. This system was based primarily on the mutual benefit between patrons and beneficiaries or leaders and subordinates. In Thai culture, those who do not know their place or do not act in accordance with their social standing could easily be excluded from the patronage system. Field Marshal Sarit Thanarat succeeded in controlling the army by sharing enough benefits with his subordinates. But when field marshals Thanom and Prapas failed to do the same, General Kris Sivara, the Commander in Chief of Royal Thai Army, withdrew his support. Likewise, when Thanin took power and forgot both his rightful place and that he needed support from the NARC or the military, his government collapsed. It is generally known that both General Kriangsak and General Prem came into power mainly with support from the Young Turks and, while the former eventually had to step down when that support was withdrawn, even the latter had to flee an attempted seizure of power. General Prem worked closely with the army and was always ready to be involved in such military matters as assisting in appointing and transferring military officers, as was frequently seen in the news. Many commanders-in-chief, like General Arthit Kamlang-ek and General Chavalit, enjoyed a close relationship with him and accepted his position as 'Dad'. When there were doubts about General

---

8   Sqn. Ldr. Prasong Soonsiri, การเสริมสร้างเอกลักษณ์ของชาติกับการพัฒนาชาติไทย [Promoting National Identity and the Development of the Thai Nation], in รายงานการสัมมนาเรื่อง เอกลักษณ์ของชาติกับการพัฒนาชาติไทย [Report on Seminar on National Identity and the Development of the Thai Nation], Bangkok: National Ideology Subcommittee of National Identity Committee, the Secretariat of Prime Minister, 1985, 98.

Arthit's behaviour as 'a subordinate', he too had to step down. General Prem relied on those he trusted in dealing with public administration, such as Squadron Leader Prasong Soonsiri, a secretary to the prime minister and the administrator of 'the minor cabinet', and the long-serving foreign minister Air Chief Marshal Siddhi Savetsila, who was also the leader of the party that supported Prem as prime minister.[9] Thus, the patronage system should not be overlooked in 'Thai-style' public administration.

Of course, there are still other aspects concerning this broad issue of culture and customs, but since they have not been empirically explored in studies of political ideology, we will not discuss them. However, we will later explore some of their aspects in the critical analysis of the deeper meaning of this concept.

The final characteristic of 'Thai-style democracy' is appropriateness to circumstance or the 'state of affairs'. Military groupings almost always cited the state of affairs as a rationale when they meddled in political activities, including launching coups d'état and in determining policies such as 'The Policy of Democratic Revolution' of the Democratic Soldiers and Prime Ministerial Order no. 66/2523. Of course, the goal in taking such action was the maintenance of national security.

When it is believed that the state-nation is of utmost importance and that the government is its ruling representative institution, the stability and security of the government are then considered equally critical to assessing the state of affairs. Apart from such government adversaries as the Communist Party of Thailand, opposition parties in the House of Representatives were likely to be viewed negatively by the statists. The fight to secure their position as the government against communist groups and political opposition in the parliament was thus part of each state of affairs. In the struggle with the political opposition, and in order to maintain their power or status as rulers, the latter often claimed the current 'state of affairs' as justification for their actions to the public. Only political leaders had the opportunity to play a direct role in driving or creating situations – states of affairs – that favoured them. Citizens were unable to do the same and even risked being used as political tools of the elite. Those who study the topic

---

9 Editors' note: the 'minor cabinet' refers to the officially named Coordinating Committee for Aligning the Work of the State Bureaucracy with Government Policy. Included in this were permanent secretaries of each ministry and military leaders, the police commissioner and Secretary of the Prime Minister's Office (Prasong).

of 'state of affairs' and the power struggle in Thai democracy have come to a specific conclusion that the 'state of affairs' is a key factor in Thai politics, especially during political change.[10]

All of this means that the transitory nature of political situations plays a part in determining the political patterns, objectives, and administrative measures, and even the supporting rules and mechanisms, as well as the resources deployed by the statists to deal with specific states of affairs. For example, Thanin's government believed that its political objectives and its form and method of government were suitable for the state of affairs it faced, while the government of General Kriangsak contended that elections should be held, and that the 1978 constitution was suitable for the political circumstances of the time. Even the political movement of Young Turks, who were the 'elites' in the military organization, was tied up with each specific state of affairs. Similarly, General Arthit thought that democracy itself should adapt to changes and national security – that is, it can sometimes be 'complete' while at other times it can be 'partial'. In that sense, the notion of 'circumstances' is relative to changes in terms of time and the political climate, which might potentially affect both 'democracyness' and 'cultural appropriateness', as seen for example in the comparison between the political concepts of Sarit's regime and Prem's government.

The idea of 'Thai-style democracy' is broad in form and objectives, for this allows flexibility and suitability for a range of 'states of affairs'; its ultimate purpose is to support a concept and practice of national security that has militarism as its foundation. It is no surprise then if those who study the development of Thai politics conclude that 'the development of the political system needs not always progress towards democracy even if we wished as such. The Thai political system may develop towards authoritarianism or semi-democracy'.[11] Democracy as exercised nowadays under the 'Thai-style democracy' framework is, hence, statist democracy.

---

10 See Kanok Wongtrangan, การเมืองในระบอบประชาธิปไตยไทย [Politics in Thai Democracy], Bangkok, Research Publication Program, Chulalongkorn University, 1984, chapter 2.

11 Chai-Anan Samudavanija, ปัญหาการพัฒนาทางการเมืองไทย, [Problems in Thai Political Development], Bangkok, Chulalongkorn University Press, 1987, 1–2.

MEANINGS

In this part, we will review 'Thai-style democracy' in relation to the political thought of the Thai military through philosophical analysis.

Security: The Basis of a Good State

As discussed, one key principle in the political thinking of Thai military leaders is the peak status of the state (or statism). Notably, the words 'country' 'society' and 'state' are used interchangeably to signify one's country. The Thai state is like a living organism, a representative of the spirit of the Thai nation, an indicator of the existence of 'Thainess.' The state is the whole on which the people as a part are dependent. The Thai state needs members who have the full characteristics of Thainess. Here, the state is not viewed in a mechanistic manner as existing for humans, nor as a tool for humans to achieve purposes outside their physical selves such as endowing rights, freedom, property and providing worldly happiness at an individual level. Rather, the state has become an entity with intrinsic value, endowed with a purpose for which individuals may even sacrifice their life. Indeed, according to this notion, those who are tasked with protecting the state may die as a consequence. Such deaths are honourable. Thus, it is not surprising that the army would deem their profession as having the highest honour and would also think that their duties are sacred. As for the government tasked with guarding the state to maintain peace, its status must, therefore, be higher than any other organization. This idea has led to an understanding that the stability of the government is equivalent to the overall security of the state.

'Thai-style democracy' relies on this very idea of the state; it exists for the security of the state (or equivalently, national security). Therefore, how Thai-style democracy manifests itself is subject to changes depending on the state of affairs and what is required to maintain the security of the state. In turn, we can see that 'democracy' is not an end, but merely a 'desirable' means for the greater cause: the preservation of the Thai State.

In the eyes of the military leaders, the preservation and security of the state is of the greatest value. A good state is a secure one, and the most important duties in the life of an individual is to preserve it by protecting major symbolic institutions, namely the nation, religion and the monarchy. In fact, the institution with the broadest definition is the 'nation', which includes sovereignty, territory and people, as well as cultures and customs and government – which is part of the 'state' itself – which also extends to the institutions of religion and the monarchy. Therefore, 'national security' is equivalent to the security of the collective state. It is the sacred burden of the military to accept responsibility for protecting the nation-state from invasion by external enemies while simultaneously maintaining peace and order within the country.

From the analysis above, we may consider that, in general, national security consists of the activities in four principal dimensions, namely politics, economy, social psychology and military.[12] Political security is viewed as core because it is related to the use of administrative power and the distribution of valuable resources within society to ensure national stability and the peaceful coexistence of the people. Domestically, political stability is related to the administrative system – the stability and efficiency of the government – as well as whether it is respected and accepted by the people. We have seen that every government emphasised this point and both the Thanin and Kriangsak governments fell because of deficiencies in these dimensions. Likewise, this emphasis was present in the political thought of the aforementioned military leaders, in the 66/23 Policy, and in today's government and army. As for external matters, the dimension of international politics is concerned with neighbouring countries, such as the attempt to end the war in Kampuchea by solving political problems. Second, economic security is viewed as related to the economic status of the country coupled with the well-being of the people. If economic problems occur, these would affect politics too, just as problems in social-psychological security would impact politics. Social-psychological security gives emphasis as to whether the people feel that their life and properties are protected and that they are treated justly enough by the government and law. One example that reflects this kind of security is Prime Ministerial Order no. 66/2523. While essentially the Order concerned politics, it also focused on practices that led people to believe that the country belonged to them, and therefore, needed their protection, and that the people played a part in governing the country and earned benefit from their roles. The Order also focused on abolishing social

---

12 See Gen. Saiyut Kerdpol, ปัญหาความมั่นคงแห่งชาติ [Problems in National Security], in ปัญหาการเมืองไทยปัจจุบัน, เอกสารการสอนชุดวิชาสาขาวิชารัฐศาสตร์, เล่มที่ 3 หน่วยที่ 12 [Current Problems in Thai Politics, Teaching Materials in Political Science Volume 3, Unit 12], Bangkok, Samnakphim sukhothai thammatirat 1986. See also the essays on national security written by military officials published in Pranot Nanthiyakul (ed.), จิตวิทยาความมั่นคง [Security Psychology], Bangkok: Institute of Security Psychology, 1983.

injustice at all levels, on sharing benefits between people of different social classes, and on urging sacrifice of class interests for the benefit of the majority. The final dimension is military security which concerns the mission of defending the nation from outside threats and maintaining internal peace. The Thai army always focused on strengthening its armaments by means of purchasing warplanes and tanks as well as nourishing the morale of military officers. Nevertheless, we have also seen that the Young Turks called on the army to have a true national ideology rather than use ideology to support cliques to gain political power. Likewise, the Democratic Soldiers regarded that the army belonged to the people and served democratic principles, it was not supposed to belong to a power group that was dictatorial in nature. Still, the army at that time, despite being tasked with establishing democracy, supported General Prem's government according to the principles of statist democracy. The above consideration of security in the four practical dimensions is empirical and helps us see the broader framework and meaning of full national security, which entails that the four dimensions of practice are in equilibrium.

We can further examine the topic of national security from other perspectives and thereby probe deeper into the character of the national security concept. These are the perspective of defence (in the negative sense) and the perspective of development (in the positive sense).

Defence is fundamental because it deals with the preservation of the existing qualities of the state and emphasises the importance of social order and peace. Military leaders have always emphasised these issues, especially in the context of coup d'états. Defence is perceived as a core policy and duty of all governments, the army and the people. There are three aspects to this matter. The first aspect is the defence of key state symbols and major cultural institutions; clear examples are the nation, religion and the monarchy, which are symbols of and institutions of Thainess, two of which – the nation and the monarchy – we previously discussed. Concerning religion, which was not explored in preceding sections, we can say that certain connotations exist in the military's approach, particularly that Buddhism is like a state religion. The King is considered the Defender of the Faith and performs royal religious duties on important occasions. As for the link of religion to the nation, we can all see that one unique feature of Thainess is the idea that the 'Thai are Buddhist'.[13]

---

13 See *Report on Seminar on National Identity and the Development of the Thai Nation* (cited above) and the analysis of Thais as Buddhists in Suwanna Wongwaisayawan, บุญกับอำนาจ":

Under the course of socio-economic and cultural changes, military and government leaders in this period of statist democracy do not share the same sentiments with past leaders, such as how the statist Phibun regime held up the civilised foreign nations as a reference point, or how Sarit's government rigidly reverted to old traditions. The new-era military leaders better understood and accepted socio-economic, political, and cultural changes and they, hence, adapted modern and contemporary practices to the existing context or structure of Thai society. This is the second aspect of defence, which primarily deals with methods by which customs are preserved. There are many examples of the adaptation of the new into the old. In macro-politics, 'Thai-style democracy' reflects an attempt to merge the new concept from the Western civilization with the existing characteristics of Thai society. At a micro level, the military leaders learned the importance of people's demand for political participation from the events in the era of mass open politics, and they tried to find solutions which resulted, for instance, in the 1978 constitution and the 66/23 Policy. Fundamentally speaking, both the constitution and the policies here aimed at the preservation of the two major social institutions and the structure of power, which facilitated military government as the institution responsible for creating a democracy and fighting the threat of nation-destroying communism. The freedom and political participation of Thai people were, in fact, limited under the existing power structure (such as having senators as members of the 'government party', the 'policy above politics' and cultural propagation which focuses on social order and peace. This scenario reflected the principle of harmonisation of interests, which is considered by some as 'a virtue' in Thai society.[14]

To ensure the security of society, Thai military leaders focused on a centralised form of government, and this is the third aspect of defence. Thai governments centralised both Thai politics and education. An important example is the use of village chiefs to govern at the lowest level. The position of the village chief under the Local Administration Act [orig, 1914. By 1989 it had been revised 8 times] is a way to mobilise the natural leaders of the com-

---

ไตรลักษณ์กับลักษณะไทย [Merit and Power: Trilaksana and the Characteristics of the Thai], in Sombat Chantornvong and Chaiwat Satha-anand (eds) ในอยู่เมืองไทย รวมบทความทางสังคม การเมืองเพื่อเป็นเกียรติแด่ศาสตราจารย์เสน่ห์จามริกในโอกาสอายุครบ 60 ปี [Living in Thailand: A Collection of Socio-political Essays in Commemoration of Professor Saneh Chamarik's 60th Birthday], Bangkok, Thammasat University Press, 1987.

14 See Damrong, 'The Character of Siamese Administration', 52–4.

munities to connect with state power. Even though village leaders are elected by the community members, they are subject to the hierarchy and control of subdistrict headmen and district chiefs who are appointed by the central government. It can be said that the appointment of village chiefs is the tangible starting point of power relations at the lowest level because this position is official, determined by the state to fit the well-established concept of natural community leaders. The state also uses these chiefs as bridges to spread their control into rural communities, and concurrently spread educational systems which work to cultivate national and bureaucratic customs to children in addition to knowledge children gain from school. Of course, in some classes, the social values that the state wants to embed would be included in lessons such as knowledge of not only national symbols (the Thai flag and the constitution) but also reflections of state power in civics subjects, for example, on citizens' duty.[15] The significance of centralised power specifically in relation to government is that national security requires fundamental unity, the concept also used in economic and social development schemes. Scholars note that bureaucrats and politicians think political decentralization would jeopardise unity because 'we cannot trust people in the provinces. There is no way to tell whether they are truly loyal.'[16] The idea of centralizing power through a central government would undoubtedly limit political participation of the people, depending on how much the state permits, and this may create the 'bureaucrat-organised mass'. Indeed, the extent to which political freedom is either expanded or limited depends on the suitability of 'circumstances' and its appropriateness to the power holders. For many military leaders, unrestrained democracy that lacks a trusted source of power is deemed greatly dangerous.

The state utilises many measures to embed the notion of security into people's perception and to build trust that the work of the government is appropriate. In turn, it is the duty of the people to protect 'the nation' by following orders from the government. The people are obliged to abide and follow the government rather than have myriad rights outside stipulated boundaries.

This concept of security implies general acceptance of the existing social hierarchy. Considered in the light of the political structure, there is a hierarchical stratification with the governors (government and bureaucratic

15 See Chai-Anan, *Problems in Thai Political Development*, Chapter 7.

16 Surin Pitsuwan, 'The next step for Thailand must be a step into a new direction', in ก้าวต่อไป ของสังคมไทย: รวมบทความ [The Next Steps of Thai Society: Collected Articles], Bangkok: Student Committee, Faculty of Political Science, Thammasat University, 1980.

mechanisms) on the top and the subjects (ordinary civilians) on the bottom as in the Sarit regime. This still exists, though not so obviously. In today's statist democracy, people can elect representatives to work in the cabinet and parliament. However, as we all know, in reality, these professional politicians do not truly hold political power and tend to rely on the *barami* (prestige) of superiors and so, in the end, become supporters of military leaders, as was the case during the various Prem administrations.

Thai governments also rely on state bureaucracy as a mechanism to function rather than on public participation. They also determine what citizens need rather than allowing them to take the initiative. Prime Ministerial Order no. 66/2523 both accepted the existence of classes and demanded only sacrifice from them and mainly operated under the bureaucratic system. This idea corresponds with social hierarchy in Thai cultural sense as well, which holds that senior bureaucrats, or the high class, are distinct from commoners. This condition of hierarchy has endured and not proven to be a threat to national security; thus, it remains in Thai society.

Positive security is development or change issuing from progress. Beginning with the 1958 revolution and the Sarit regime, statists and military leaders brought a new ideology of development into their regime, enabling state institutions and organizations at different levels to legitimately expand their role and political power. Markedly, the Royal Thai Army could wield influence and participate at many levels of political activities to the point that, today, it has founded organizations for local development, and initiated such mega-projects as Green E-san Scheme. We must always remember that the objective of these projects is national security, particularly from the political aspect. For example, the Sarit's government's community development programs in the North-eastern region to General Chavalit's Green E-san scheme, the core idea was always the acceptance that certain sectors of society were flawed and in need of improvement, but the improvement must not be 'revolutionary' nor should it uproot tradition in the manner sought by the Communist Party. Instead, improvement should be *reformative* so that valuable elements from the past could be preserved while the necessary changes can be made step-by-step. Even when we refer to Field Marshal Sarit's perception as 'revolutionary', the actual meaning is still within the reformative sense. That is, he abolished the system and ideologies from the Western world and turned back to traditional paternalistic government. This is clearly not a complete social transformation or a revolution in the conventional sense.

We can see that this positive security is, in fact, based on the negative security previously discussed. Revolutionary and fundamental social transformation was deemed just as undesirable as the preservation of imperfections… But noble cultural traditions that have stood the test of time are worth preserving. When the worth of these traditions are eternal (such as how Buddhist teachings are 'timeless') they cannot be further developed, nor must they be eradicated. What may be subject to improvement in accordance with changing circumstances are the minor elements (such as forms), which, in turn, help preserve the core traditional values. From this outline it may be seen that the 66/23 Policy is one form of reformative thinking aimed at solving some political conflicts in society, as is the 'revolutionary' thinking of General Chavalit.

Nevertheless, the determination to develop national security cannot be overlooked. Military leaders who stepped into the position of political power followed the development ideology that began in Sarit's regime. Development, therefore, became an important ideational state tool. In the political dimension, it was the 66/23 Policy, and in the socio-economic, it was the National Economic and Social Development Plan. In principle, what obstructs or compromises development should be suspended or eradicated, while that which encourages progress should be supported. However, in practice, since the time that both the plan and policy were proposed, no political parties or governments have attempted to do so. Moreover, performance evaluations on the policy and plan were conducted by officials of the army and the NESDB, who were the ones who had initiated them in the first place. Instead, these policies and plans were considered *above politics*. For instance, the idea of amending the constitution in compliance with the policies or certain political activities of the opposition parties were criticised as prompting political instability, which would contribute negatively to national political and economic development. Consequently, development by the state in turn expanded the influence and power of the state's responsibilities, especially that of the military, which constantly demanded moral and financial support.

Even though the law of nature and the Buddhist concept of life indicate that change, uncertainty, and impermanence were natural and even though soldiers know well from first-hand experience that 'war is the battlefield of uncertainty', the military's quest remains that of stability and order. Isn't this contradictory? To this question, their answer, in essence, is that truth should be allowed to follow its nature because this we cannot avoid, and while we cannot create complete security, we should try our best to do so through control and power.

POWER AND LEADERISM BY THE UPPER CLASS

Army life is most certainly well-acquainted with the use of power in the line of command, and military organization depends on this. Loyalty, obedience and seniority are the virtues of the military: falling out of line is degeneracy. Various army leaders express this when they deliberate on political and social cases, and when they exhort people to obey the prime minister or be disciplined. Expected obedience to rulers is unproblematic to the military because they deem hierarchy as the most appropriate approach to politics. Therefore, if the military must get involved in politics, for whatever reason, it should do its best to seize power and establish itself in a superior position.

The notion of security also reflects another motive: power. To secure power, one must be able to protect it, which means that one must hold authority and exercise it. And when it concerns national-state security, one needs the highest level of power. Political centralisation reflects the characteristics of a high concentration of power and unity. As for those who use this power, the state leaders, their mechanism is the state bureaucracy.

National Thai history always makes references to kings and warriors. After the Siamese Revolution of 1932, Thai military leaders concretely exhibited 'physical power' by using their status to step into the highest political office. Field Marshal Phibun Songkhram became the military leader on the side of the government and quashed rebels and used his position and the civil unrest to rule over the country. Then, when Field Marshal Sarit Thanarat became Commander in Chief of the Royal Thai Army, he recognised that based on his experience in participating in successful coups d'états, he had only to wait for 'the right state of affairs' that would facilitate his rise as the absolute political power. Likewise, Field Marshal Thanom also knew that he would be the successor once Field Marshal Sarit was gone. He held the positions of prime minister and minister of defence concurrently (1964–73), while his close friend Field Marshal Prapas was the commander in chief of the Royal Thai Army and deputy prime minister. After the position of commander in chief was transferred to General Kris Sivara, in October 1973 the problem of power emerged and the military's position weakened between 1973–76, in part due to the lack of a strong leader with strength, dignity and self-confidence. Consequently, the adaptive Young Turks, the majority of whom were field commanders, established their standing and supported General Kriangsak as a political leader. Similarly, General Prem, who was 'the dad' of the Young Turks, ascended from the position of commander in chief of the Royal Thai Army to become the prime minister. General Prem took great care of high-ranking military personnel because, as he admitted, he would use the army as the main pillar for the security of his political position. In considering this history there is no need to ponder whether military leaders have power or not, or whether they have the capacity to use that power to support their political status. Their military and political experience teaches soldiers that there is power to be had.

The Phibun and Sarit regimes were authoritarian, as power was absolute. Phibun found excuses in getting both the king and the constitution out of his way, and established himself as 'Supreme Leader' while Sarit made use of the societal acceptance of the king, as head of state and representative of the Thais, to exercise his own power as 'Father' of the people. In both regimes, there was no real opposition party in the parliament: physical force was used against the political opposition and the middle class was weak. The political power of both leaders thus was arbitrary, supreme and singular.

In the era of open politics, the situation changed especially in terms of socio-economic factors. The most important phenomenon was the strength of the urban middle class and its intent to take part in governing the country. In this, a truth was expressed: every human wishes to participate in decision making on issues that directly concern them. Thanin's government was blind to this truth and quickly collapsed when the Revolutionary Council staged the 1977 coup d'état. General Kriangsak understood this reality and it motivated the drafting of the 1978 constitution. General Prem's government also recognised the diversity of groups in society, the pluralistic socio-economic structure, and the power of economic groups outside of the bureaucracy, all of which were unprecedented characteristics of Thai society. General Prem welcomed more professional politicians while trying not to get involved in their conflicts regarding corruption and political ambition. It can be said that from 1976 to 1986, non-bureaucratic power, especially from financial-economic sectors, was more accepted by the military government and by military figures who assumed political roles, such as the Young Turks and the Democratic Soldiers. And so it was that professional politicians came to share state power.

However, this power sharing did not mean autonomy for each group. Even under today's statist democracy in which statist groups no longer hold absolute power, they still possess a status above civilian politicians and extra-bureaucratic and economic forces. The latter's participation meant that they were accepted into the political sphere and tasked with certain responsibilities. But the leader still needed to be the army's prime minister, as in the case of General Prem. Executive and political power was still with statist forces. For example, in the separation of powers according to the principles of democracy, the government or executive has a greater status over others. Challenges by politicians in parliament and extra-bureaucratic groups and economic forces such as merchants and bankers to statist's ruling power were easily absorbed. Such groups lacked free agency and tacitly supported state power. The status of the statists was still more significant to the country than that of the private sector. It is not surprising that General Prem once said frankly, 'I think the cabinet is less important than state officials ... the state bureaucracy is the heart of the country's governance.'[17]

Given this statism, it was inevitable that development plans and the political participation of extra-bureaucratic political forces were within the framework of a centralised approach to security. Development was aimed at mitigating negative security problems, especially to obstruct influence from the communist movement inside and outside Thailand. Similarly, the freedoms and political participation of the people were also placed in the security framework. Statist forces emphasised centralised power and then extended their reach to control local spheres. Pluralistic democracy, therefore, was hard to establish, and the deeper intent was that it should not emerge at all. That is because this kind of democracy requires openness and accepts diversity, which is hard to control and therefore a threat to unity and security. This is the core idea of Thai-style democracy, which clearly manifests in the form of the statist democracy we see today. Statist forces – the army and state bureaucracy – try to maintain unity and to hold the highest political power to rule the country. Other forces may be accepted if they are on the same side and accept statist dominance. As for those who do not, they are labelled as adversaries and eliminated. In the course of so-

---

17 See *Collected Speeches: His Excellency, Prime Minister General Prem Tinsulanonda*, 215–18.

cio-economic changes, the state and its mechanisms accordingly followed the principle that the new should be assimilated into the more fundamental and prior thought. In line with this, the state developed and adapted its roles and duties while simultaneously expanding its network to control different groups that emerged from socio-economic changes. Some examples of this scenario in politics were the use of 'the minor cabinet' coordinated by Squadron Leader Prasong Soonsiri and the 66/23 policy, which was above politics in parliament. As for Prime Ministerial Order no. 66/2523, which mentioned support for the democratic movement, its actual implication was the realization that civilians' political participation must always be controlled by the state. Typically, the army set the rules to determine the scope of relationships, official or not, of activist groups. Establishing mass groups under their control was perceived as an appropriate thing to do.

We have seen that the statist attitude towards political centralization and unity has existed since the time of Phibun and Sarit, which was the 'authoritarian' period; this attitude persists today as a core political idea of military leaders. These leaders may have a more open attitude and allow limited participation from other forces, but they view these forces as merely supplementary elements. Hence, it is not surprising that political scientists who studied the political development of Thailand found that the control and interference behaviours of the state in the semi-democratic regime has both dictatorial and democratic dimensions. These two aspects together foster the impression that the political system has become less authoritarian. By maintaining some characteristics of democracy, politically active groups also feel that they have opportunities and channels for political expression.[18]

The leader of the state is the one who exercises political power. From the above study, we can now see the characteristics of leaderism as practised by military elites. The commander in chief of the Royal Thai Army and other military elites gradually stepped into positions of political power with the army as their support base, though the methods used to acquire power differed from one occasion to another. For example, during Sarit's regime and the NARC period (1976–78), the army openly played the role as the country's ruler. But during General Kriangsak's government and Prem's administration under the 1978 constitution, the army supported the government in the parliamentary system and repressed outside threats. These

---

18 Chai-Anan, *Problems in Thai Political Development*, 34.

military elites played clearly significant roles in directing the course of the politics and in manipulating situations as they wanted. Rank in military organizations, signified power. For instance, the voice of the commander in chief is always heard, except in those cases when certain figures miscalculated their power and situation and faced the consequences, as when General Arthit was removed from his position by the true ruler, General Prem. In today's statist democratic system, the military holds armaments – the source of physical power – and declares that its mission is to protect the nation from foreign threats, to fight against communism and establish full democracy. The army asked for support from people in this latter mission such as General Chavalit's request for the people's permission to stage a 'revolution'. Thus, it is not possible to understand Thai politics without considering the utmost important role of army leaders.

What will be emphasised here is the doctrine of the leader or 'leaderism' by the elite. The term 'elite' refers to high-ranking bureaucrats, who were the equivalent of nobility in the absolute monarchy, and who, as the king's trusted subjects, held both bureaucratic and government positions. To be a bureaucrat is to be 'a royal subject' and, hence, they must be graceful and disciplined both in terms of personality and morality, a persona which connotes 'a person with honour' in the eyes of ordinary people. Those who climb the ladder and become a high-level bureaucrat have the capability to adapt to this system. This quality, coupled with flawless background and loyalty to the monarchy as royal subjects, indicates their lifestyle and discipline is acceptable on moral grounds. Therefore, they are suitable agents in ruling the country, or, in other words, in being the king's eyes and ears as public officials. Field Marshal Sarit was the first and the most prominent example of such a figure. As a military official who fought his way to the top he was undoubtedly a qualified subject in this system. As a colonel he commanded the 1st Infantry Regiment (1945-1948). As a major general he commanded the 1st Division, King's Guard (1948-1950). As a lieutenant general he was commander of the First Region Army (1950-1952) and as general he was Deputy Army Commander in Chief (1952-1954). Finally, as a Field Marshal he was Army Commander in Chief (1954-1963). Undoubtedly, his political role worked to support his professional advancement, a phenomenon accepted in the bureaucratic system. This, coupled with his display of utmost loyalty to the monarchy, granted him the king's trust and, subsequently, the seat of prime minister. Sarit's case was like that of General Prem, though the latter progressed more slowly. As a colonel, he was appointed to command the cavalry divisions (1967). Then as a major general, he was promoted to commander of the Second Army (1968–73) as a general, to assistant chief of the Royal Thai Army (1977–78), and later to commander in chief (1979–81). This, coupled with his flawless background and his loyalty to the monarchy, ensured that he, too, gained support and became a political leader. As generally known, one of the significant reasons why the Young Turks supported him was his reputation for honesty as a professional military official. The Prem government was able to defeat a rebel group in the April 1981 coup attempt because the king trusted him. Being an elite official with an untarnished background who had long and loyally served the king, General Prem was no doubt a suitable figure for maintaining the peace and security of the state and the people.

The notion of leadership by an elite accepted by the Head of State was apparent from the time of the Sarit's regime, in which traditional Thai governance was revived and glorified. Military leaders clearly learned from experience in one respect: if the traditional source of power, symbolised by the monarchy, was destabilised and not well accepted while the power of the revolutionary side [coupsters] was not yet firmly established, there would be a tendency towards chaos caused by a power struggle among the elites. This would affect national security, and did so for example between 1932–57. To solve this problem, it was wiser to refer to traditional power, which had long been accepted by the people. From Sarit's regime on, the status of the monarchy has strengthened. This, in turn, also means that it became impossible for elite state officials to step into the position of political leadership without a degree of consent from the monarchy. Whenever army elites lacked an organizational power base, the elite bureaucrats from other sectors might be nominated instead, as in the case of Thanin Kraivichien. Nonetheless, elites in the Royal Thai Army were fast to adjust and to seize their honour back. To them, the one most suitable for this grand position of power must be the soldier who was successful in his service life. It seems that being the supreme political leader has become the highest 'rank' in the life of a military official.

This elite leadership is also implicit in Thai society's sense of the right political and governmental order. This sense of propriety is based on traditional power, which guarantees ways of life, attitudes and morality of the prospective leader. This political order certainly aims at sustaining the security of the state. The concept 'Thai-style democracy' does not countenance political leaders from outside the state bureaucracy as there appears to be no reason or necessity for this. In the statists' view, to establish a 'proper' political order is held to be a form of social justice, too.

SOCIAL JUSTICE, FREEDOM AND EQUALITY

Based on ideas regarding national order and security, unified and centralised power and leaderism of the elites, we can now discuss another key issue in most political ideologies: social justice. We can consider that the notion of social justice under the framework of the so-called 'Thai-style democracy' consists of three elements: morality, freedom, and utility [benefit]. These are interlinking core ideals under the value system.

The core of morality or virtue is contained in cultural traditions. The custom of 'Thainess' is perceived as an invaluable national treasure and as a force that can solve social conflicts.[19] This is a core element of nationalism. It determines whether an act is right or wrong. In other words, it generates the bond between moral and political truth for Thais. The value of Thai custom is viewed as universal and objective; that is, it is universal in the perception of the Thais who uphold it, and it is a complete set of values, subject to neither temporal nor spatial changes. Likewise, it is not based on whether an individual would believe and accept it, for its value is intrinsic.

This moral principle guarantees social order; it is the principle and standard for irrefutable fairness (that is, 'justice'). The army leaders often express their commitment to righteous traditional values both through words and actions as they, as the high-ranking state officials or 'elites' of this type of regime, are aware of its significance. The case of Field Marshal Sarit is an appropriate example concerning this aspect. In his opening speech for the Annual Conference of Deputy Governors and District Chiefs in 1959, he expressed an idea related to this moral principle:

> No matter how progressive the content of such university classes as modern political science are, one key principle deeply embedded in Thai traditionalist governance will always be invaluable and, hence, should always be practised. That principle is paternalism. A nation is like an extended family with governors, deputy district chiefs, and district chiefs as heads, each

---

19 See *Collected Speeches: His Excellency*, 143–44.

with a different degree of responsibility. Guardians must view people under their care as parts of the same household. People's welfare, happiness, and suffering are, thus, family matters, and it is therefore necessary for the guardians to pay close attention to this family's ups and downs and govern them with love and kindness, as though they were really your kin.[20]

Here, Field Marshal Sarit discusses the value of the principle of traditional governance as sacred and worth preserving. Regardless of the changes in time and social conditions, this principle will always be precious, especially as a moral gauge of, for example, the goodness of a ruler. The importance of tradition appears in policies of every government, though it is not particularly emphasised, perhaps because it is not a key political issue. Nevertheless, the moral principle of traditionalist governance concerning respect for the monarchy institution is always stated. As for the broader and more inclusive sets of political thinking, such as those of the Democratic Soldiers, proposals of a cultural nature were a key element in the 'democratic revolution'.

Of course, traditionalism as a virtue includes religious values. His Majesty the King often gives speeches on morality based on Buddhist principles to the government, bureaucrats and people in general on significant occasions. In one respect, religious values may be considered as restraints against the abuses of power. Even though government power may be considered supreme, rulers are expected to exercise power on moral grounds. In the cultural notions of Thais from ancient times, there have always been concepts of force [*phradet*] and grace [*phrakun*], both of which are based on a religious moral stance. This type of morality is not only a guideline but also a behavioural framework for all people, leading everyone to a decent life in a good society in accord with tradition.

The principle of freedom is also one key element in the concept 'Thai-style democracy'. Social justice requires individual freedom, and, likewise, it is also a principle of 'Thainess'. Theoretically, 'freedom' does not mean the capability to do as one wishes with no limitation. The limit of one's freedom is the principle of morality itself at the level of one's private and social life,

---

20 Field Marshal Sarit Thanarat, คำกล่าวเปิดการประชุมปลัดจังหวัดและนายอำเภอทั่วราชอาณาจักร 27 เมษายน 2502 [Opening Remarks for the National Conference of Deputy Governors and District Chiefs on April 27, 1959], in ประมวลสุนทรพจน์ของจอมพลสฤษดิ์ ธ นะรัชต์, เล่มที่ 1 พ.ศ. 2502–2504 [Collected Addresses of Field Marshal Sarit Thanarat Volume 1, 1959–1961], published by the Cabinet Council on the occasion of Field Marshal Sarit's funeral ceremony on March 17, 1964, 31.

which means being orderly in the state to maintain security. Social control is not only desirable but also necessary. All Thai citizens have the obligation in this aspect, which is instilled in everyday life and political activities. Under the framework of political centralisation for security of the nation and supreme power, political freedom must be limited. This limitation is not based on reasons related to the act of limiting per se, but on the higher and morally superior ground: the preservation of state and society. Laws, orders, and even the acts committed by state's leaders can all be reasoned within this higher ground. We can see that even the freedom to seek happiness or respond to physical pleasure (hedonism) at an individual level is undesirable in that it is viewed as an abuse of individual freedom, thus, morally improper. One should lead one's personal and social life in the same way; that is, a life based on moral grounds (tradition) and on discipline for peace of mind. Orderly social life undoubtedly requires a peaceful mind and life that are equally disciplined. An external sense of calm is often based on internal peace.

It can be easily seen that, profoundly speaking, this perception suggests freedom has no intrinsic value and should not be a goal in one's personal and social life. Tradition and social codes of conduct are more important than freedom. Human nature and the urge to act freely are viewed suspiciously. To set limits is a good precaution for the benefit of the collective. Civilians have the duty to obey the state for a higher cause than mere individual pleasure. In fact, deriving from this notion is the idea that the masses (lower classes) are ignorant, self-indulgent, and thus prone to moral degradation, for they only seek mundane happiness: pleasure for basic comforts. In other words, they are selfish and irresponsible (Indeed, to be responsible under this mindset depends on whether the acts are appropriate in a traditional sense, not on individual logic). These people, therefore, must be taught to be 'good citizens' and 'good persons' through rules and limitations. Also, since they are incapable of realizing or understanding moral codes by themselves for their own sake or for living peacefully in society, it is appropriate that they obey those who have proven their ability to work under the system and to lead a moral life; that is, those who are high-ranking state officials or indeed leaders of the state.

Sarit's regime is a clear example of how the state limited individual and social freedom. His government controlled various aspects of life ranging from cleanliness, appropriateness in clothing and individual behaviours to social and political expressions, making sure that all behaviour was within established moral boundaries. Today's statist democracy is open to freedom to a certain extent, but limits that freedom in the reliable framework of 'Thainess', allowing statists to speak of government by the people in accordance with the law. This is an attempt to employ democratic approaches in the old sense and to continue to cajole moral behaviour while reducing the level of control. This notion of freedom under 'Thai-style democracy' points to how difficult and problematic it would be for the Democratic Soldiers and General Chavalit to establish 'a democratic society' that upholds and manifests the Western concept of people's freedom in reality rather than just in accordance with the law.

There is also a practical component to social justice, and this is the third principle: the principle of utility which has an outcome and an objective which is the fulfilment of an interest, which in this case is state security. This outcome must be based on social foundations and must not contradict moral codes of conduct. The important point is the ability to evaluate the state of affairs, which has already been discussed. The ability to take advantage of the state of affairs or to create situations deemed beneficial is a significant quality of those who seek utility. This can be considered as the ability to 'know time and place' because, within the Thai social context, what is proper in the political sense should be good according to the prevailing conditions. If any conflict is considered a threat to national security, to solve it with a coup d'état is consequently viewed as proper and a concrete political good. The realist military leaders – the NARC, the Young Turks, General Kriangsak, and General Prem all believed that their political roles were 'virtuous' and 'proper', and even 'contributed' to the country. Their political ideas and actions demonstrated that they were pragmatic realists who viewed political situations at the time as reality, and subsequently looked for a way to deal with them through a practical contribution.

This principle of creating utility corresponds to the aforementioned reformist idea. To create change or improve flaws on the ground of traditional morality is perceived as virtuous and correct (in order to preserve security of the public) and requires pragmatism. The utility concept of military officials emphasises concrete outcomes that are truly 'revolutionary'. To completely eradicate the old for the new is neither proper nor possible. To revolutionise the country to establish 'the world of Buddhist Bodhisattva Maitreya' or a utopian society as idealists wish is merely an unattainable and impossible dream. This should not happen as doing so would threaten the security of the existing foundation, which is deemed as already good. It is therefore not surprising that even Thanin's 12-year project to establish a functioning democracy was viewed as 'unnecessarily time-consuming' and not appropriate.

The aim to yield a concrete benefit can be used as an excuse to exercise power and to carry out political duties. This is another connotation of development. All state leaders claim that they govern for the benefit of the people; that is, they intend to develop the country for the welfare of ordinary people. Therefore, the government has legitimacy to exercise political power, and, in turn, civilians must obey and follow the government's orders.

However, the principle of utility has not been fully practised. If it were, the principle of the greatest benefit or happiness of the people would be fully optimised. Other fundamental principles have limited the principle of utility. Although Sarit's regime focused on economic development and General Prem often stated his intention to eradicate poverty, but the underlying concept of security (negative), strong faith in traditions, political centralisation, leaderism by the elites, and the idea of reform all made it difficult to facilitate the interests of the majority, who were the lower classes. The existing economic and political structures made success even more difficult.[21] Of course, Thailand has class differences. For example, there was a clear acknowledgement in Prime Ministerial Order no. 66/2523 of a wide gap in levels of equality. Inequality is a shaped like pyramid, which invites us to think that General Chavalit's image of Thailand in the shape of 'a beautiful egg' is all but impossible to achieve.

The notion of justice discussed here is related to the notion of *equality* in accordance with the principle of 'Thai-style democracy'. There was only one aspect of equality that often received official recognition: lawful equality. Civilians were always told that they were equal under the law and the 66/23 Policy also emphasised this. 'Equality' here did not cover economic and political aspects. Concerning politics, we have seen that equality is not possible under the significant limitations of political centralisation and leaderism of the elite, both of which highlight that not everyone who is successful in life and moral will rise to the position of leadership, and that military leaders always have an edge, for the army is a key political institu-

---

21 Regarding this aspect, see more criticisms in such works as Krikkiat Phipatseritham, การ เปลี่ยนแปลงทางเศรษฐกิจกับปัญหาสิทธิมนุษยชนในประเทศไทย [Economic Changes and Human Rights Issues in Thailand], Bangkok: Thai Studies Institute, Thammasat University; and Chalermkiat Phiu-nuan, ปรัชญาสิทธิมนุษยชนและพันธกรณีในสังคมไทย [Philosophy of Human Rights and Obligation in Thai Society], Bangkok: Religion For Society Coordinating Group, 1987.

tion. Economic equality is 'unnatural' as it contradicts the truth that people are innately unequal in terms of intellect, physical strength, personality and work skills. Therefore, each individual is likely to succeed in accumulating wealth and establish economic status to a different degree. And throughout the course of history, economic equality was not needed: an orderly and stable society does not need this aspect of equality. Thus, this ideal is unreal and alien to natural morality. More profoundly, this concept tends to suggest that economic inequality is inevitable and just, as each individual is different in nature. When such inequality endures and does not lead to the deterioration of security and stability, we should accept this fact and hold inequality as a customary morality.

There is a claim in the statist democratic regime that the state does not rigidly limit economic equality. Rather, one is responsible for struggling and fending for oneself to the extent of one's own ability, and one must do so in accordance with the law. One must also accept unequal rewards as just. The current government showed their admiration for economically successful individuals by granting them 'top business awards'. This act implied that the current economic conditions are good and appropriate, and that it is up to individuals to employ their skills to lead their way to success. Prime Ministerial Order 66/2523's call for personal sacrifices for the common good is an implicit acceptance of economic inequality.

THE SACRED, HUMAN NATURE
AND PRACTICAL REASON

From the aforementioned political and social concepts, it is time to turn to the fundamental problems regarding life and worldview inhering in the principles of 'Thai-style democracy'. Of course, leading military figures have not directly stated these, but the metaphysical and epistemological issues are additional elements that cannot be overlooked. We will examine these elements though inference, studying logical connections from traces in the various strands of ideas discussed in previous parts.

As seen, from the perspective of Thai military figures, the nation is sacred, and, therefore, their mission to maintain national security is also sacred. This idea has great importance according to the principles of customary morality, it is the basis of belief and part of the system of thought. We have seen [in chapter one of the original book] that that *Traibhumikatha – Sermon on the Three*

Worlds, a literary piece considered the foundation of traditionalist political ideology, depicts the structure of its universe as comprising the three worlds, namely the hells, the heavens and the earthly realm. In Buddhist scripts and commentaries, all living creatures in the universe – be they angels, human beings, animals, spirits, et cetera – are stratified under the same hierarchical system in the 'chain of nature', the web of Dharmic interconnectedness. This is the representation of the universe as under the law ('law of nature') that is tied to the principles of morality. This set of laws covers both natural phenomena and human acts. Though it may be difficult to see clearly this aspect among military officials, their belief in the absolute existence of sacred entities aligns with the religious and folk traditions of the people. The importance of these entities, in fact, lies in their power to affect lives and have supernatural influence over humankind. For example, it is believed that they can offer blessing or fortune – a concrete manifestation of strong faith in them.

From a socio-political perspective, to exist, an individual depends on a land or a kingdom, what is called a 'homeland'. The welfare of the people largely depends on the capability of the rulers or kings, as in the saying that compares the ruler to the universe itself, which interpreted from the moral perspective, means the ruler has *barami*, which is to have acquired perfection in the ten virtues. A kingdom or, in modern thinking, the nation-state is thus of utmost importance as people rely on it; this is a profound meaning of the belief that the country is sacred, as is the king as head of state. This view is tied to tradition and religion. An individual relies on one's place of birth and matures under the *barami* of the king. People, bearing gratitude, in turn have a duty to protect important institutions – that is, the nation, religion and king – with their lives. Customary traditions are like a representation of the law of nature, and give it meaning. We can infer from this that 'politics' is not about endeavours to find a way to respond to the needs of individuals or groups. Rather, it functions to achieve the holiest goal: state security as a whole, a purpose, paradoxically, above the realm of politics. It is, hence, not surprising that some military figures with political positions or who are involved in politics would say they are not 'politicians', or that some others heavily criticise professional politicians for their corruption that benefits individuals or political cronies.

The acceptance of the validity of sacred status of the nation (*chart ban muang*) and other key institutions is exhibited in such traditional form of social and religious 'rituals' as saluting the Thai flag, obeying the state's law and regulations, and following customs and moral codes in accordance with the principles of 'Thai-style democracy'. A good citizen indeed refers to an individual who follows laws and traditions, exhibiting the essential quality of 'Thainess'. This behaviour is considered as highly significant because, without any standard or disciplinary restrictions, individual mental stability and national security may collapse. Various government leaders have always asked the people to be well-disciplined from the perspective which holds that humans are flawed in nature. The aforementioned concepts including the negative sense of security, political centralization, limited freedom, social inequality all reflect the negative view of human nature.

Human nature in the conception of 'Thai-style democracy' has nothing to do with intellect, innate virtues, or agency of individuals to lead a full life independently. The reality of society points to the opposite. Humans are capable of doing stupid, evil, selfish things or lose themselves even to the point of conflict and war. Humans are not born perfect; rather, they are full of ignorance and lust, which could lead to degradation. Therefore, they should be cultivated to behave in accordance with rules, orders, prohibitions and traditions. 'Freedom' is corrupting and inappropriate, for it could lead to degeneracy. This also signifies that human will cannot be used as a foundation in politics and morality. Instead, tradition is viewed as a proper choice, because not only does it have absolute and intrinsic value, but it is also 'sacred'. From this perspective, individual responsibility determined by traditions surely precedes and is more important than any other kind of rights. A 'social contract' would be mistaken in emphasising human rights, freedom, and free will. Many may abuse such power, acting against tradition, customs or the law of nature. Tradition and social order should always be priorities to control the inherently evil nature of humans so that they behave properly both in private and public spheres. Political activities should be limited and controllable, and to use force (*phradet*) is necessary and more effective than to rely on individual free will to comply accordingly. In the end, tyranny is better than anarchy. Still, it is expected that rulers would be virtuous because 'legitimacy' in political power and governance is, too, based on tradition, so, under this perspective, ideally, 'dharma is power'.

From the belief in the existence of sacred entities that are superior to such flawed creatures as humans, we can examine related aspects. First is individual responsibility. As discussed, sacred entities in our universe, though supernatural, are equipped with the ability to 'see' the virtuous and evil sides of individual and can influence human life by blessing 'the good' and punishing 'the evil' and 'the unfortunate'. Human life can be determined by certain external and supernatural forces. Buddhist principles on the law of karma also are interwoven with this concept. That is, on one hand, deeds (karma) of a person are important, and thus one should only commit good deeds. In addition, past karma can affect one's present and future in a cause-and-effect manner. On the other hand, there is a belief that it is possible for one to plead that the holy entities help as well as to expiate bad karma by making merit to 'vengeful spirits'. To analyse humans from this perspective, an individual has a certain level of freedom to commit good deeds or to hold a belief and has moral potential to realise the law of nature and other rules of virtues. It depends on individual consciousness and responsibility to choose how to act. At least, this is a major reason behind the tendency to believe that social problems are caused by individuals. Rather than criticise the system, the law, or the environment for causing bad behaviour, people are led to believe that 'wickedness' and 'irresponsibility' (towards virtue and tradition) follow from a lack of discipline and ambition to cultivate oneself, or from a failure to improve oneself. This could also be a reason for the phenomenon of focusing on individuals rather than theoretical principles, our next point.

Another aspect is the concept of social hierarchy in politics. We have seen that with absolute monarchy as a system of governance, there is a hierarchy between rulers (kings), who are related to 'the sacred' (in the forms of god and dharma), and their subjects, who are imperfect and ordinary. Under today's Thai-style democracy this notion has changed in certain respects, yet it is still on the same foundation. That is, although the king does not govern directly, his status as Head of State still symbolises 'holiness' that is worth the highest level of respect into perpetuity. He is also a medium to contact supernatural and sacred entities, for example, in royal ceremonies performed at Bangkok City Pillar Shrine and other religious rituals. The king exercises sovereign power in the name of the Thai people and oversees the government by delegating it to the elites who are the high-ranking bureaucrats. 'Elites' are the ones who advanced well in the bureaucratic system, thus proving their capability and morality. What needs emphasis here is their superiority to others resulting from the belief that, as they have been refined with morality and tradition, they are not only superior to others but also loyal to the sacred. Having attained a higher level of virtue and morality, they are no longer imperfect commoners or, in theory at least, they are less flawed. Indeed, the principle of stratification here follows traditionalist morality.

The meaning of the sacred depends on the belief and acceptance of its concrete and worldly influence over people, which can be felt by experiences and one's understanding of human nature as flawed. The state of the sacred, hence, is abstract, but can be reached through tangible symbols or signifiers (such as the nation, the land, the homeland, rulers, religion-monks, and monarchy-King), which are known by principally relying on experience.

We have discussed the notion of pragmatism to create benefits, and the significance of propriety and circumstance in the military's thinking. The epistemological aspect in relation to these concepts is the use of experience as a foundation. This is the method of learning that relies neither on speculation nor on abstract theories separated from context. The process of reasoning based on one's experience is viewed as more valuable. In fact, human reasoning is limited by imperfection and is prone to deterioration. The right kind of reasoning, hence, should be based on experience in a traditional sense. Political activities must rely on such reasonings and the deep understanding of the state of affairs with the aim of practical outcomes. This is the meaning of 'practical reason' in the subject heading.

Pragmatism that is useful relies on experience and careful reflection to understand a situation. The attempt to create utility or the use of practical reason, which can be distinguished from thinking within theoretical frameworks or claiming valid arguments, is reflected in the cultural mentality of Thais in general. In politics, we have met with such notions as 'policies beyond rules of reasoning', or the idea that the efficiency of government is more important than whether it respects rules or the way it acquires power. Practical reasoning is also employed in the appointment of state officials in the name of 'looking after the situation' or 'to improve the situation', over and above the rules of the system.

One important principle of practical reasoning that is obvious and worth mentioning here is harmonisation of interest, or the 'middle path.' General Arthit Kamlang-ek once stated that the most suitable regime for Thailand is 'the Thai-style middle path'. Nonetheless, the middle path in this sense is not the religious concept of the middle path (*madhyama pratipada*) in Buddhism. The Buddhist notion of middle path refers to a way of life in which a person avoids the extreme states of sensual indulgence and self-mortification. From this definition, we can see that the term 'middle path' in Buddhism does not convey a state between two extremes, but rather is endowed with a clear sense of direction towards attaining enlightenment. In contrast, the 'Thai middle path', or the style that is called utilitarianism which is widely used, is marked by the co-ordination of different interests.[22] This approach bridges divisions by yielding mutual benefits. This is the principle of negotiation by compromise in which the important thing is pragmatism, for if both sides refuse to compromise their stance, none will benefit. On the other hand, if one side wins, the other would 'lose face' for failing to materialise their ideas. The solution in such a conflict, therefore, is to compromise, upholding the notion of 'middle path' to accomplish, for either party, at least some of their interests, however limited.[23] The middle way is, thus, one of the concepts behind practical reasoning, which is characterised by the contingency of circumstances. That is, once the context changes, there must be further negotiation. With this in mind, it comes as no surprise that the political stance of those whose main objective is to attain utilitarian goals such as General Arthit and the Young Turks seems to waver and be contradictory, compared to the more systematic propositions of the Democratic Soldiers.

---

22 Editors' note: the Thai translation of utilitarianism (ประโยชน์นิยม) in this sentence appears to contain a typographical error. Instead of ประโยชน์นิยม the text offers ประชานิยม, which ordinarily would be translated as populism. It is widely believed that this Thai usage for populism began in the late 1990s, a decade after this chapter first appeared. It seems the intended word is 'utilitarianism', and we have corrected the text to this. Indeed, the hierarchism and virtue politics attributed to Thai-style Democracy have little resemblance to populism and the discussion that precedes the use of ประชานิยม concerns interests and benefits. Notably, the Thai word for benefit ประโยชน์ is the root word for utilitarianism. It is not impossible, though, that the author had in mind a people-ism oriented approach to politics among pragmatic soldiers. After much discussion and following the logic of the author's argument we favour correcting what appears to be a typographical error rather than treat this as an early translation of populism.

23 See more in Chalermkiat Phiu-nuan, ทางสายกลาง [The Middle Path], in บ้านไม่รู้โรยนิตยสาร รายเดือน [Baan Mai Ru Roi Monthly Magazine], December 1986.

CHAPTER 6

Civilising the State: State, Civil Society and Politics in Thailand[1]

Pasuk Phongpaichit

O n 9 November last year (1998), a group set out from Chaiyaphum town in northeast Thailand towards two villages whose defiance stands in the way of a dam project. It was an impressive group by Thai provincial standards. The deputy provincial governor. An MP. District officers and other senior officials. Police. *Kamnan* and *phuyaiban* (village heads). Provincial councillors. Representatives of the subdistrict and provincial chamber of commerce and industry association. Other influential figures in the province. All in all, 300 people.[2]

The villages are deep in the forest, and the procession of some 40 vehicles along the narrow, rutted and steep road at the tail end of the rainy season must have been quite an adventure. The two villages are small – about 50 houses each – and very simple. No electricity. No running water. Makeshift wooden houses that can easily be dismantled and transported elsewhere. Only a few small fields, as the villagers live mostly by collecting forest produce: fungi, shoots, red ants' eggs, tree frogs, and the *bai lan* fibre once used as the 'paper' for all of Siam's chronicles and religious texts. Each village is surrounded by a flimsy rail fence with a ramshackle gate hinged by an old truck tyre.

---

1   Originally published in pamphlet form as Pasuk Phongpaichit, *Civilising the State: state, civil society and politics in Thailand*, Wertheim Memorial Lecture, Amsterdam, 1999. (Amsterdam: Centre for Asian Studies, 1999.).

2   This account is based on a document from the Chaiyaphum provincial governor's office entitled 'Khrongkan ang kep nam prong khun petch amphoe bua rahew changwat chaiyaphum' [Pong Khun Petch Reservoir Project, Rahew district, Chaiyaphum province] which details the history of the project and the protests; Sanitsuda Ekachai, 'Villagers complain of arson and death threats', *Bangkok Post*, 22 November 1999; *Sayam Rat Sapdawichan*, 27 December 1998, 88–9; Wanida Tantiwithayaphitak quoted in *Krungthep Thurakit*, 17 November 1998; Phichet Phetnamrop quoted in *Matichon*, 11 November 1998; and eye-witness accounts from villagers involved. Phichet claimed there were 200 armed police, and the invaders called the villagers 'Cambodians' and 'communists'; interview, 24 March 1999.

Exactly what happened next is not clear. According to the official provincial record, they conducted a 'fact-finding mission'. According to villagers and activists, they broke down the gate with a military vehicle, waved weapons in the air, fired off shots, barged into houses, and threatened villagers with worse if they did not stop opposing the dam.

Two weeks earlier, a similar but slightly smaller expedition had been led by one MP, local officials and fifty police officers. Barred from entry to the village, one of the party exclaimed: 'Are these people Thai or not? Are they Buddhists or not?'[3] Two weeks later, officials stage-managed a demonstration in support of the dam. Two MPs proudly sponsored the event. The governor gave speeches. And the crowd deliberately blocked a provincial highway.[4]

On the evidence of the flimsy fence, ramshackle gate, and a crude notice claiming the village would negotiate only with the premier, the villagers were accused of setting up a *rat issara*, a free state. In other words, they had committed a *khabot*, an act of rebellion. In the official record, Thailand's leading human rights lawyer was accused of inciting the villagers to defy the government and cut down trees. At the time cited, he was actually in Bangkok.[5] The Assembly of the Poor, an alliance of NGOs (non-governmental organisations) and local groups that openly supports the villagers, was accused of 'opposing democratic principles, fomenting disunity among the people, stirring up resistance continually and everywhere in Thailand according to an ideology that has never been changed'.[6] In other words, the Assembly was accused of being a communist plot.

I will return to this incident later. Here I just want to raise three queries that arise out of the incident and set the scene for the main discussion of this paper.

First, only a very few years ago, a couple of small, poor and relatively defenceless villages would never have been able to resist such a project. They would have been swept aside. What has happened?

---

3 'Samatcha hoem tapoet no oo po!' [Assembly Dares to Chase off the District Officer]', *Thai Rath,* 2 November 1998; and the provincial governor's document cited in note 1.

4 *Khao Sot,* 5–6 January 1999; Vasana Chinvakorn, 'Diary of a Protest', *Bangkok Post,* 16 January 1999. Shortly after this, a community building in one village was torched. Villagers believe provincial officials were responsible.

5 Thongbai Thongpao, 'Using Old Tactics to Suppress Protesters', *Bangkok Post,* 10 January, 1999.

6 This quote is from the provincial governor's document mentioned above, 'Pong Khun Petch Reservoir Project'.

Second, why is officialdom using the tactics of the mob and the language of the cold war?

Third, this dam (Pong Khun Petch) is a minor project,[7] certainly not a major environmental cause like Nam Choan, Pak Mun, the Yadana pipeline, or the Salween projects.[8] Why are emotions running so high?

My concern is this: what is happening between civil society and the state?[9] In my view, the answers to these three questions about the dam incident are as follows.

First, these little villages can defy the dam because they have the support of new civil society networks, and because there is growing public distrust of government projects on account of their past record.

Second, officialdom has not adjusted to this new situation and resists introducing new procedures such as proper public hearings. Instead, it is fighting back using the same techniques of agitation and demonstration used by protesters.

Third, with the added factor of the economic crisis, this stalemate leads to frustration and high emotions. Such Mexican standoffs, with uniformed and armed personnel facing off against angry villagers (or, in some cases, urban residents), have become a regular feature of the television news and press front pages over the last couple of years.

---

7   The dam was first mooted in 1971 as part of a larger multi-dam project, but dropped as uneconomic. It was revived as a stand-alone project in 1988. The 610 metre earth-fill dam across a shallow valley would create a reservoir of 14 sq.km. (8,750 *rai*) in area now mostly occupied by dry deciduous forest. The total cost is estimated at 318.6 million baht. See the Irrigation Department's report on the project dated Dec. 1988, and its review of the project dated 15 Feb. 1998.

8   The Nam Choan dam project in the western forests was abandoned in 1989 after a long protest campaign. The Pak Mun dam project, sited close to the confluence of the Mun river with the Maekhong, was completed in 1994 in defiance of strong protests by local communities and environmental groups. Protests against construction of the Yadana pipeline, which carries natural gas from Burma through the western forests to Ratchaburi, climaxed in 1997. The project was completed but remains controversial because of continuing environmental damage. The Salween projects are schemes to pump water from the Salween basin into the Chaophraya basin to fulfil increased demand from Bangkok and the agriculture of the central plain. The Chuan II government recently voted a large budget for feasibility studies.

9   I use the terms here according to the way they are used in the discourse I am reviewing, rather than trying to impose a different framework of definition. 'State' refers to government and those parts of society which work closely with and benefit from government. 'Civil society' refers to forms of socio-political association and activity outside official government auspices.

With this incident as background, I want to discuss the changing relations of state and civil society in Thailand. First, I shall talk about the state. Then I shall review the development of civil society. Finally, I will look at the key debate on strategies to change the relations of state and civil society, which I shorthand as civilising the state.

THE DECLINE OF THE STATE

One of the big themes of international political economy in the 1990s has been the decline of the state. Strikingly, analysts approaching from many different disciplines – economics, political economy, geography, cultural studies – and from many different political perspectives, have all tended towards a similar conclusion.

Let me just highlight three of the main arguments.

First, international political economists have argued that the multinational capital has destroyed the major role of the nation-state as the political expression of national capital. Robert Cox has pointed out that the impact of this major change is very different in different parts of the world. In the seats of multinational capital, such as Europe and the US, it is leading to the formation of mega-states. In areas like Latin America, where multinational capital is strong, the state is atrophying. In East Asia, the old developmental states are being broken down. And in some of the poorest and least secure parts of the world – Africa, Eastern Europe – states are disintegrating into a 'new medievalism' of robber barons.[10]

Second, many economists and political scientists have pointed to what Susan Strange calls 'the retreat of the state' in the face of the growing power of market forces. Many have recalled Polanyi's famous treatment of the ascendancy of democracy over the market in the nineteenth century, and have described the growth of neo-liberalism as Polanyi's process in reverse.[11] Susan Strange argues that because technology, finance and much else now flows freely around the world, states have lost many of the powers they

10 Robert W. Cox, 'Critical Political Economy' in B. Hettne (ed.), *International Political Economy: Understanding Global Disorder*, London: Zed Books, 1995. The phrase 'new medievalism' comes from Hedley Bull, *The Anarchical Society: A Study of Order in World Politics*, New York: Columbia University Press, 1977.

11 K. Polanyi, *The Great Transformation*, Boston: Beacon, 1957; Andrew Gamble, 'The limits of democracy', in Paul Hirst and Dunil Khilnani (eds), *Reinventing Democracy*, Oxford: Blackwell, 1996

previously wielded. Some of these powers have shifted from the smaller, poorer states to the bigger and more powerful ones. Some have shifted into the control of market institutions, including international banks, shipping cartels, 'econocrat' institutions like the WTO, and crime syndicates like the mafia. Finally, some powers have simply 'evaporated'.[12]

Third, from cultural studies Arjun Appadurai offers another perspective on state decline. Now that it is much more difficult to believe in the nation as the political expression of a race or people, so the nation-state has lost much of its moral and political authority. Moreover, besides the money and technology now flowing freely around the world, there are also much greater flows of information and of people themselves. With mass migrations, ethnic groups (and ethnic movements) are now scattered across borders. With the communications revolution, people can consume culture from all over the world. There is no longer any 'fit' between a people, a culture and a national boundary.[13] The state is in crisis because it no longer matches a socio-political reality.

Most of this literature comes from the west and often reflects local concerns in that region. But two important contributions are closer to home in Asia.

First, Kanishka Jayasuriya has been asking what will be the particular impact of globalisation on the state in Asia. He argues that the old interventionist developmental state is disappearing and being replaced by a 'regulatory state' in which the administration of the economy is transferred away from government to independent rule-based institutions such as central banks and law courts. Further, he and others argue this is accompanied by the growth of 'illiberal democracy' (or 'authoritarian liberalism') in which power is concentrated in social and technocrat elites, representative institutions are reduced to a meaningless puppet show, and civil society is 'managed'.[14]

---

12 Susan Strange, *The Retreat of the State: The Diffusion of Power in the World Economy*, Cambridge: Cambridge University Press, 1996.

13 Arjun Appadurai, *Modernity at Large*, Minneapolis: University of Minnesota Press, 1996, especially chapter 8.

14 Daniel A. Bell, David Brown, Kanishka Jayasuriya and David Martin Jones, *Towards Illiberal Democracy in Pacific Asia*, New York: St Martins, 1995; Kanishka Jayasuriya, 'Rule of Law and Capitalism in East Asia', *Pacific Review*, 9, 3, 1996, and 'Authoritarian Liberalism, Governance and the Emergence of the Regulatory State in Post-Crisis East Asia', paper for the conference on 'From Miracle to Meltdown: The End of Asian Capitalism?', Murdoch University, 20–22 Aug. 1998.

Second, Chai-Anan Samudavanija, in a famous article, concludes that 'While [in Thailand] the military and bureaucratic elites remain important and will continue to safeguard their diminishing role in society, they will not be replaced; they will be bypassed.' Like many others, Chai-Anan argues that international flows of money and ideas are steadily diminishing the power and space of the nation-state. Hence the Thai elites who have dominated the state will simply decline along with the institution.[15]

This short review is only a sampler. What is most striking about this literature on the decline of the state is that it is huge. On paper at least, the state is already dead.

NEW ROLES FOR THE STATE?

By now I should have telegraphed that I'm going to dissent from this view. Much of this 'death of the state' literature is looking top-down from the Olympian heights of international studies. Certainly, the idea of the nation is crumbling. But to assume this must mean the collapse of the nation-state is to attribute too much importance to a hyphen. Certainly, the argument that the old role of the state in regulating the economy is changing in nature and shrinking in scope is valid. But this is only one aspect of the role of the state. This literature tends to ignore the function of the state as *an instrument of social control*. Here, on the basis of Thai experience, I want to argue that any shrinkage has severe limits. And the expectation of Chai-Anan that we can stand aside while the old military-bureaucratic core of the Thai state is 'bypassed' seems to me overly optimistic.[16]

Let me go back to the dam incident I began with. As I noted, only a few years ago, the Thai authorities could have completed this project with little difficulty. They certainly would not have been deterred by a couple of villages of forest-gatherers. Now they are opposed by local groups, alliances built through the NGO movement, activists who no longer believe in the good faith of the state, and discourses against dams that now abound in the

---

15 Chai-Anan Samudavanija, 'Old Soldiers Never Die, They Are Just Bypassed: The Military, Bureaucracy and Globalisation', in Kevin Hewison (ed.), *Political Change in Thailand: Democracy and Participation*, London: Routledge, 1997.

16 Given that Chai-Anan was active in the movement to pass the 1997 constitution and has since become a judge on the constitutional court, it appears he too believes this 'bypassing' will take some effort.

international literature on environmentalism. To that extent, the growth of civil society – at both local and international levels – has limited the power of the state and created some new political space for opposition.

But as the incident also shows, the authorities are fighting back. And in other recent cases where they used similar tactics – notably the Yadana pipeline and the Pak Mun dam – the authorities ultimately won hands down.[17]

What then is happening to the Thai state? Of course, over the past twenty-five years, the military domination of the state has been driven back and Thailand has built one of the most ostensibly democratic states in Asia. This is an enormous achievement. But if we look at what is happening within this new democratic framework, we begin to see some limitations.

In a famous article written against the background of the 1991–92 political crisis, Nidhi Eoseewong sought the real fundamental working principles of power and politics in Thailand, stripped of all the legal and institutional formalities. Nidhi approached this question using two Thai words: *itthiphon* and *amnat*.[18]

By the word *amnat*, power or authority, Nidhi means the formal power of appointed legal authorities, especially the bureaucracy. By *itthiphon*, influence, he meant the locally-based extra-legal power of village bosses, gangsters, godfathers and businessmen, and their modern incarnations as local councillors and MPs.

Both types of power, Nidhi argues, were basically out to exploit and suppress the people. However, the Thais were saved from the worst excesses of dictatorship and exploitation because both *itthiphon* and *amnat* were severely fragmented and, more importantly, because they could be played off against one another. 'The Thai people', Nidhi writes, 'hate *amnat* because it oppresses them as a matter of course, but the Thai people know the country needs *amnat* because without it there would be nothing to

---

17 These tactics are not confined to big public set pieces. On another dam project, a 'technical meeting' was called for officials and academics to exchange information. Without warning, the officials packed the meeting (in a university seminar room) with local politicians and other supporters of the dam, who held the floor and delivered polemics. No technical information was exchanged.

18 Nidhi Eoseewong, 'Ratthathammanun chabap watthanatham thai [The Thai Cultural Constitution]', originally in *Silpa Watthanatham*, 13, 1, November 1992, reprinted in Nidhi Eoseewong, *Chat thai muang thai, baep rian lae anusawari* [Thai Nation, Thailand, School Texts and Monuments], Bangkok: Silpa Watthanatham, 1995. Nidhi noted that he took the idea from Yoshifumi Tamada, 'Itthiphon and Amnat: an Informal Aspect of Thai Politics' in *Southeast Asian Studies*, 28, 4, 1991.

oppose *itthiphon*. So the Thai people support the survival of both *amnat* and *itthiphon* so the two can fight one another' (164). He concludes that the Thai people survived by playing *amnat* and *itthiphon* off against one another, and that 'this form of struggle is the pure genius, the true wisdom of Thai society' (168).

Using this same model, I want to suggest that over recent years, the space that separates *itthiphon* from *amnat* has drastically narrowed, and the opportunity to play one off against the other has diminished.

Nidhi recognised that *amnat* and *itthiphon* were always ready to compromise with one another. And he pointed out the Thai people fear the army and police because they bridge both kinds of power. But I want to suggest there has been a serious rapprochement of the two sides; that it has occurred at many levels; and that the basis for this rapprochement has been the new framework of democratic institutions.

Let me just give two examples of the process. A decade ago, the Chatichai government (1988–91) extended the authority of ministers to make appointments and promotions at the top levels of the bureaucracy. Since then, career bureaucrats have had to attach themselves to political patrons in order to hoist themselves up the last few rungs of the bureaucrat ladder. Because ministerships change hands quite frequently, often they attach themselves to political parties rather than individuals. And because party politics is an uncertain and expensive business, often these relationships are more about finance than friendship. The buying of senior official positions – for vast sums – has become a common event. And it has spawned a minor industry of agents and fixers to negotiate these deals.[19]

Further, as a result of this new close relationship, the nature of corruption scandals has totally changed. From the Chatichai era until recently, most corruption scandals had been of one particular form: a politician accused of making money from budget spending either as kickbacks on contracts or as skim from direct expenditure.[20] But over the last two years, we have had a flood of corruption scandals of a different pattern: namely, politicians and

---

19 In a landmark case this year, one such agent, an official in the Office of Accelerated Rural Development, was jailed for eighteen months after confessing to accepting 2.4 million baht, allegedly to be paid to a provincial governor to secure a promotion for the agent's client. *Nation*, 25 Feb. 1999. In some ministries, this political alignment filters down through vertical clientages to involve middle and lower ranking officials as well.

20 See Pasuk Phongpaichit and Sungsidh Piriyarangsan, *Corruption and Democracy in Thailand*, Chiang Mai: Silkworm Books, 1996.

bureaucrats *working together* in schemes that are much more elaborate and much more long-term.

In the Salween timber scandal, logs illegally cut in Thai forests were laundered as Burmese imports. This required the connivance of police, customs, military and forestry officials scattered along routes of many hundreds of kilometres. The businessman who masterminded the scheme boasted of his political connections. Some of the suspect logs ended up in the possession of senior politicians and party branches.

In a health ministry scandal, a ministerial order made it possible for senior officials to organise a ring for overpricing the sale of drugs and equipment to provincial hospitals. Political associates of the minister were involved in supervising the implementation by officials at the local level.

In the 'edible fence' seeds scandal, a minister promoted a scheme of free distribution of vegetable seeds to farmers. His officials arranged to purchase the seeds outside normal procedures at vastly inflated prices. Preliminary investigation showed that large numbers of officials were involved, and rumours suggested that the political involvement went very high indeed.

Three features of these scandals are worthy of note. First, they involved large numbers of people, both officials and politicians, and lots of money. Second, the schemes were outrageous, yet those involved seemed confident they could get away with anything. Third, because of the close cooperation between officials and politicians, by and large they *did* get away with it. The media described these schemes in considerable detail, and a handful of ministers and officials were forced to step down. But politicians and bureaucrats were able to close ranks and bury the accusations in a confusing muddle of investigative committees.

At the local level, there has been a similar rapprochement. Since the mid-1980s, each MP has had a fund to spend in his constituency on roads and other civic improvements. Classically this is used to reward localities for their vote. As a result of this scheme, most village headmen probably now make more money as contractors than as farmers. With the formation of the *oboto* (*tambon* or sub-district councils) over the last three years, this system has been extended. The headmen sit on the council. So too does the *nai amphoe* (district officer). Projects funded by central ministries are increasingly implemented through the *oboto*. According to one account, the leakage from project budgets can run at 40 per cent after both *itthiphon* (the village bosses and an MP patron) and *amnat* (the district officer) have taken a cut.[21]

Let me go back again to my example of the Chaiyaphum dam. The procession that travelled into the forest to pressure the two villages is a graphic example of the cooperation between *itthiphon* and *amnat*. On the side of *amnat*, it was led by the deputy provincial governor, who took along district officers, irrigation and forestry officials, and police. On the side of *itthiphon*, there were two MPs, village officers, members of the provincial council, and representatives of the provincial chamber of commerce and industry association.

In sum, whether joining hands in complex and ambitious corruption scams at the national level, or in petty local extraction, or in an intimidating invasion of two irritating villages, *itthiphon* and *amnat* now work closely together.[22] And the ability of the Thai people to play one off against another – the Thai 'genius' for survival in Nidhi's analysis – has been severely diminished.

THE THAI STATE AS REARGUARD

Now let me see if I can drag myself out of the swamp of Thai corruption scandals, escape from Nidhi's culturally sensitive but esoteric framework of analysis, and get back to the evaluation of the state.

Clearly the Thai state is mounting a stubborn resistance to change. Let me give you a few examples. Take the question of bureaucratic reform. All of the last four governments have committed themselves to bureaucratic reform and set up committees to make proposals. But nothing has resulted. The reformist head of the Public Service Commission stated in frustration that there has been no significant reform of the bureaucracy for a century.

---

21 This 40 per cent figure was given by a group of villagers in Yasothon in mid-1998. The group included a long-serving ex-*kamnan* (head of a group of villages) who admitted participating in this leakage.

22 Murder, as Ben Anderson noted, provides great insight into Thai politics. On 27 Febuary 1999, Ubon Bunyachalothon – *jao mae* (Godmother) of Yasothon, ex-MP, loan shark, suspected mastermind of the killing of Saengchai Sunthornwat, *itthiphon* supreme – was shot dead by a sustained burst of AK-47 fire through the window of her Mercedes. The first person to appear at the hospital was *amnat* personified, the provincial governor. It is not clear whether he came in sympathy or to make sure she was dead. See *Thai Rath*, 28 February and 1 March 1999.

The current government announced the intention to downsize and upgrade the bureaucracy, but then drew up proposals to reduce the numbers by just ten per cent over four years.[23]

Take decentralisation. Again this has been a standard policy commitment for over a decade. Recently an adviser to the Interior Ministry told me that the word 'decentralisation' was unmentionable inside the ministry until a few months ago, and can still be uttered only in hushed tones. The project of *tambon* councils is half-hearted and possibly designed to be such a failure that the project will be reversed.

Take the military. Recently it was announced that one-third of all generals (616 out of 1,859) have no active post. Plans were announced to reduce this number by drastically cutting the number of new promotions each year. Last year, they did indeed reduce the length of the promotions list. But they also issued the list twice rather than once in the year. So the net result was more promotions rather than less.[24]

The military has blocked 5.3 million *rai* (0.85 million hectares) of land. The government has repeatedly asked the military to surrender what it does not need, but so far without result. Since 1992, the military has been under pressure to surrender its grip over radio and TV stations. So far, nothing has happened.

Take the police. Pressure for police reform has risen with reports of scandals over bribery, protection rackets, and involvement in gun-running, drug-trading and the flesh trade. The police have responded by weeding out officers who get caught. They insist the problems arise from 'bad people' not 'bad systems' and they strongly resist any structural change.

Now of course all states have an in-built conservatism. Their first instinct is to resist change. Also, the Thai state is a particularly crusty version. It has a century-long heritage as the instrument of royal absolutism and then military dictatorship. But I think the current rearguard action goes beyond normal instincts for self-preservation. The attack is stronger. And hence so is the response.

The period since the relaxation of military controls in the mid-1980s has seen rapid explosion of social and political demands, which had been bottled

---

23 *Bangkok Post,* 25 April 1998. The total number of state employees in 1995 was 1,464,557.

24 *Nation,* 24 September 1998. 218 generals were due to retire and the proposal was to replace only 75 per cent of them. But in the two rounds, 151+93=244 were promoted. The prime minister said the reduction policy 'turned out to be impossible to implement'.

up in earlier years. The resulting expansion of civil society over the past fifteen years has stimulated a defensive reaction. Moreover, this period has been a time of jolting social change, marked by dramatic boom-bust economic cycles, large-scale migrations of people on a temporary and permanent basis, new patterns of work and consumption, and much broader dissemination of ideas and information. These changes have provoked a fear of a major social reorganisation that would threaten long-established interests.

The function of the state as an instrument of social control has been refined to cope with the outburst of social and political demands. Since the 1970s, the old bureaucratic state has been broadened by incorporating big business, both local and provincial, and some sections of the middle class. But there is strong resistance to any form of democratisation that would give greater weight to the rural majority, or to the rapidly growing urban labour force. The conservatism of the state is one line of defence against major political change.

To return yet again to my dam example, when these villages first opposed the dam in 1996, the opposition leader was shot dead – by a policeman.[25] When village resistance hardened, officials resorted to the language of the cold war. Officials claimed the village's flimsy fence, which dogs, kids and chickens pass through regularly without noticing its existence, was evidence of the villagers' attempt to declare a 'free state' – an act of rebellion. And the organisations that lent support to the village were branded as covert communists, working 'according to an ideology that has never changed'.

THE PASSAGE OF HOPE: FROM
DEMOCRACY TO CIVIL SOCIETY

From the 1970s to the early 1990s, reformists believed that the mechanism to change the Thai state would be democracy, meaning representative institutions. During the 1980s, when changes were slow, this tardiness was attributed to an imperfect form of 'semi-democracy' under which electoral

---

25 The police claimed they were raiding a marijuana plantation and the killing happened accidentally during a scuffle. But the villager had just been to lay a complaint against the local headman who was profiteering from land speculation caused by the dam project. He was shot in the back from medium range, which does not indicate a scuffle. The police could produce only a couple of marijuana plants. Suparat Janchitfah, 'Death of an ordinary man', *Bangkok Post*, 4 August. 1996. The case is still in court. Editors' note: The case was dismissed in 2001 for lack of evidence.

parliaments coexisted with much of the culture and practice of military rule. Once the military finally left, it was assumed, change would accelerate.

Hence, May 1992 was a watershed. After the incident destroyed the political aspirations of the military, many reformists were optimistic. Thirayuth Boonmee, the 1973 student leader-turned-'social critic', wrote a book claiming this as a 'turning point' on a scale which occurs only once a century. With the military now out of the way, he foresaw a period of benign change under the leadership of the middle class working through the institutions of formal democracy. He wrote:

> This will lead to a transfer of power and legitimacy from the state to society ... from the bureaucrat group to businessmen, technocrats and the middle class. Society will change from a closed society to an open society, from conservative thinking to a much broader perspective, from narrow nationalism to greater acceptance of internationalism and regionalism, from centralisation to decentralisation.[26]

In mid-1998, just six years later, Thirayuth presided over a meeting of NGOs and local groups to discuss political reforms against the background of the financial crisis. For two days, speaker after speaker detailed local problems, discussed political strategies for seeking redress, and debated agendas for reform.[27] Not one speaker mentioned the formal democratic institutions – parliament, parties, local councils – as representing a proper or promising route to seek redress. In the view of these participants, the parliamentary system had simply been absorbed into the bureaucratic state. The battle was still between the people and the state, the people and paternalist domination, the people and *rabop upatham*, the patronage system which now encompassed not only bureaucrats but elected representatives. What's more, as one speaker pointed out, in the age of mass TV and global communications, the mentality of the people moves ahead much faster than the mentality of state institutions that are big, clumsy and slow to effect change.

---

26 Thirayuth Boonmee, *Jut plian haeng yuk samai* [The Turning Point of the Era], Bangkok; Winyuchon, 1993, 56. For another hopeful view of middle class-led politics see Anek Laothamatas, *Song nakara prachathipathai: naew thang patirup kan muang sethakit pua prachathipathai* [Two Cities of Democracy: Directions for Reform in Politics and Economy for Democracy], Bangkok: Matichon, 1995.

27 Thammarat workshop held at Chulalongkorn University, 25–26 July 1998.

Thirayuth himself defined *thammarat*, the Thai translation of the phrase 'good governance', without reference to the formal institutions of government at all:

> National good governance lies in the power of the movement of local organisations, peoples, and communities to understand problems, be self-reliant, help themselves, reform themselves and, at the same time, be forceful in monitoring whatever is bad and ugly in society.[28]

Take another example of the declining faith in democracy. The student-led revolt of 1973 has often been cited as a landmark of Thailand's democratisation. But in a recent volume published to commemorate the 25th anniversary of the revolt and to analyse its 'lessons', not one of the articles carried the word 'democracy' in its title. The writers, who were mostly veterans of the event, totally ignored the subsequent development of parliament, elections, and parties. Instead, they wrote about social movements, ideology, community, civil society, and the politics of everyday life. The editor's own article concluded:

> The people's movement for community self-rule ... forms a basis for the strength and security, both economic and political, of the community in the future ... To prevent exploitation and to escape the colonialism of the great world powers ... communities must be strong and secure, so the overall society is strong and secure too.[29]

With this declining faith in 'democracy' as the route to a better political future, and in parliamentary institutions as a mechanism of change, the idea of 'civil society' has been seized upon to play the same role: as the repository of hope.

In sum, the hope that democratic institutions will transform the state has dwindled now that unofficial and official power, *itthiphon* and *amnat*, have made a deal. The Thai state is not standing aside to be 'bypassed', but is mounting a rearguard defence. There is thus a growing belief that the state will have to be 'civilised' by civil society.

---

28 Thirayuth Boonmee, *Thammarat haeng chat: yutthasat ku haiyana prathet thai* [National Good Governance: Strategy to Rescue Thailand from Disaster], Bangkok: Saithan, 1998, 31.

29 Pitaya Wongkun, 'Thit thang khabuankan prachachon miti mai: naew santitham lae sang khwam mankhong haeng chiwit' [The Direction of New People's Movements: Peace and Building Life Security], in *Prachaphiwat: botrian 25 pi 14 tula* [People's Revolution: Lessons from 25 Years of 14 October], Bangkok: Withithat, Globalisation Series 7, 1998.

THE STATE OF CIVIL SOCIETY

So let me now quickly review civil society in Thailand.

Let me start by going back to Chaiyaphum, and looking at the linkages which connect these two villages to civil society. The core population of the villages are Chao Bon or Khon Dong, an Old Mon people who probably lived in the Chaophraya basin before the Thai and who have been steadily pushed deeper into the forest.[30] A generation ago, Chao Bon would run away at the sight of an outsider. Now other Isan people have joined the village and married. In the villagers' historical memory, there used to be four villages in this forest. They often shifted location, particularly after an illness or disaster. One villager in his 40s can remember six moves in his lifetime. My point is that this area is very much the periphery: remote from the state, from rice culture, from being Thai, from fixity of residence, from house registrations. But it is now linked into civil society.

The dam project was first proposed in 1988, and initially escaped public attention. It came into view only when, after the Pak Mun dam affair,[31] NGOs began to investigate other dam projects among the Irrigation Department's

---

30 As with many peoples who like to keep themselves remote, what they are called is no problem for the villagers themselves, but a big confusion for everyone else. These villagers favour the form Khon Dong, which simply means forest people in Thai. William Smalley reported they preferred the term Nyah Kur, meaning hill people in their own language (*Linguistic Diversity and National Unity: Language Ecology in Thailand,* Chicago and London: University of Chicago Press, 1994, 264). Nowadays outsiders usually refer to them as Chao Bon, which means hill people in Thai. Previously they were often called Lawa, a catch-all term for Mon Khmer minorities. In 1918, Eric Seidenfaden wrote of them: 'The children in some villages are already ignorant of the language of their parents, and for the rest most of the members of the tribe prefer now to be called Tai for fear of being termed "savage"' ('Some Notes about the Chaobun, a Disappearing Tribe in the Korat Province', *Journal of the Siam Society,* 12, 1918). Smalley noted that this situation, which Seidenfaden assumed was the preliminary to integration, remained the same in the 1970s. In these Chaiyaphum settlements, it is still true in the 1990s. The periphery resists. See also Preecha Uitrakun and Kanok Tosurat, Chaobon: sangkhom lae watthanatham [Chao Bon: Society and Culture], Bangkok: Social Science Association of Thailand, 1987.

31 The Pak Mun dam project was bitterly opposed on grounds that the benefit was enough electricity to supply a small Bangkok department store, while the cost was damage to the fisheries which were important to the protein supply of the lower northeast region. The Irrigation Department faced down the protests and built the dam, incorporating a fish ladder. Protesters claimed the ladder would not work because 'Thai fish cannot jump'. They were right. The dam devastated the fishery potential on the lower reaches of the region's most important river. The credibility of the Irrigation Department was permanently damaged. See articles by Tyson R. Roberts in *Natural History Bulletin of the Siam Society,* 41, 2, 1993 and 43,1, 1995.

plans.[32] In 1995–97, villagers joined the protests under the umbrella of the Assembly of the Poor. In the Assembly's negotiations with the Chavalit government in April–May 1997, the dam was suspended pending review by an independent committee. This committee included the head of the government's environmental watchdog association, who for the first time raised the issue of environmental impact (the project had been designed to fall below the minimum size requiring an EIA, environmental impact assessment). The committee brought in academics who raised doubts over the irrigation benefits and the cost-benefit calculations.

After the Chavalit government (1996–97) fell, local officials and the Irrigation Department quietly reactivated the dam project and prepared to force the villages out. After the November incident mentioned at the start of the paper, several newspapers ran stories on the incident. Most criticized the official aggression. Some raised doubts about the cost/benefit of the project. A local activist lawyer petitioned the Interior Ministry to investigate the governor for abusing human rights, overriding the cabinet order to suspend the project, breaking the law, acting against the spirit of

---

32 The history of the Pong Khun Petch project portrays in microcosm the recent dialectic between civil society and state. 1) When planned in 1989–90, this relatively small project attracted little attention. The Irrigation Department later downsized the project below the minimum size to trigger a mandatory environmental impact assessment. By 1995–96 when protests surfaced, the project had progressed to an advanced stage. The construction contract had been allocated, land for the project purchased, and several villagers had accepted compensation. 2) Opponents queried the project on several grounds: a) The use of the forest for gathering was not costed at all. Not only did the local villagers depend on the forest for livelihood, but other villagers over a wide area also made occasional use of the forest for traditional gathering; b) The irrigation benefits detailed in the project document were vaguely described and probably overstated. The dam would only add a relatively small volume of water to the Upper Chi river, and the same benefit could probably be achieved more cost-efficiently by managing the existing water flow better; and c) Similar small earth dams in the same area had not been effective. 3) When these objections arose, backers canvassed local support for the dam by exaggerating its benefits: a) Several communities both above and below the dam supported it because they believed it would improve their water supply. Yet the project document showed these communities would not in fact benefit; b) Because of drought in 1998, local officials were caught between villages fighting over scarce water. Some began to support the dam in the hope it would make their job easier, even though the project plan allocated the water elsewhere; and c) Local politicians and influential figures lent support for the project to show solidarity with the provincial governor and to gain the kudos of achieving a major local project. In addition, dams traditionally provide profits from land speculation and construction kickbacks. The MP leading support for the dam is said to be close to the construction contractor.

the constitution, and generally 'acting as if Thailand is a jungle'.[33] A human rights NGO visited the villages and established a branch there. Most of the large water storage jars in the villages were spray-painted with clauses from the constitution on human rights, along with text of the 1997 cabinet resolutions on the right of people to live in harmony with the forest.

This is a very small example, but I think it captures some of the key features of the current state of civil society in microcosm: the vital role of the media, the catalytic role of NGOs, the increasing importance of both people's movements and umbrella organisations like the Assembly of the Poor, and the importance of the concept of *rights*. In this last section, I want very quickly to say something about each of these.

The media provide the platform for challenging the powers and actions of the state. This tradition is now well-understood, well-valued and staunchly defended. In retrospect, too, we can see that 1992 was a landmark. Ultimately it strengthened and emboldened the print media. And eventually the events of 1992 willed us one electronic channel outside state control. It is still too early to assess the impact of the first independent television station, ITV,[34] but it has clearly done two things in its first two years. First, it has widened the space available on TV for serious social and political debate, and has forced other stations to adjust in response.[35] Second, it has introduced some investigative journalism that surpasses the standards of the print media. Most famously, it has shown the police accepting bribes on camera. But more importantly, it has documented corruption in the logging industry with full details of how much was paid to whom; traced the paths of amphetamine dealers right back to the production sites in Burma; and much besides.

---

33 The complaint, including this quote, is detailed in the provincial governor's document mentioned earlier.

34 The Chuan Leekpai government (1992–95) initially promised to license several new TV stations to break the state monopoly. However, this promise was diluted and delayed. ITV finally began broadcasting in late 1996. Ownership is spread among a consortium including the Crown Property Bureau. Expertise has come from The Nation press group. Many of the station's most impressive investigations have been presented in the programme *Thot rahat* [Break the code].

35 At the time of writing (Feb. 1999), Channel 7 (army-licensed) is running a drama series called *Dao khon la duang* [Each to his/her Star], which features a godfather, bent policemen and a government minister running a drug-peddling operation. Although the plot celebrates 'good cops', the setting tells a story that would not have been found on this medium a very few years ago.

On the Thai NGO movement, much has been written in recent years.[36] I want to make just one point. Over the last few years, the role of NGO workers has changed. More and more, they are catalysts and facilitators for local groups and local people's movements. They connect local grievances and local aspirations to media platforms, sources of information and expertise, and alliance networks. The power of the NGO movement now comes not so much from its own resources of cash and manpower, but from the underswell of local movements.[37]

The last few years have also seen the growing importance of umbrella organisations, notably the Assembly of the Poor, but also farmers' groups and regional organisations in the north and south. Again, the formal structure of these umbrella organisations is skeletal. They are gradually assuming a larger role in public politics not because of their resources, but because of the underswell they represent.[38]

The concept of *rights* has become central to the project of civilising the state. This is also relatively new. Ten years ago, the concept did not have anything like the importance it has assumed now. As the faith in democratic representation has dwindled, the importance of *rights* has soared.

Over the last few years, this promotion of rights has had two main strands.

The first strand has found its main expression through the movement to draft, pass and enforce the new 1997 constitution.[39] This movement for constitutional change has three main parts.

First, to catalogue a long list of rights as the basis for shifting the balance of power between individual and state. This is probably the easiest of the three. It may seem rather formal and academic. But when you see these clauses spray-painted on water jars in a forest village in Chaiyaphum, you

---

36 Prudhisan Jumbala and Maneerat Mitprasat, 'Non-Governmental Development Organisations: Empowerment and Environment' in Hewison (ed.), *Political Change in Thailand*; Surichai Wun'Gao, 'Non-Governmental Development Movement in Thailand', in *Transnationalisation, the State and the People: The Case of Thailand*, Tokyo: United Nations University, 1985; Thai NGO Support Project, *Thai NGOs: The Continuing Struggle for Democracy*, Bangkok, 1995.

37 See Prudhisan and Maneerat, 'Non-Governmental Development Organisations'.

38 The Assembly of the Poor was formed in late 1995 as an umbrella for many long-standing local movements, especially those connected with the land rights of the poor and dispossessed. In 1997, the Assembly conducted a historic 99-day demonstration in Bangkok. See Prudhisan Jumbala, 'Constitutional Reform Amidst Economic Crisis', in *Southeast Asian Affairs 1998*, Singapore: ISEAS, 1998; Praphat Pintobtaeng. Kan muang bon thong thanon: 99 wan samatcha khon jon [Politics on the Street: 99 days of the Assembly of the Poor], Bangkok: Krirk University, 1998.

39 See Prudhisan, 'Constitutional Reform'; Pasuk Phongpaichit and Chris Baker, *Thailand's Boom and Bust*, Chiang Mai: Silkworm Books, 1998, 273–7.

begin to understand that they have powers of education and empowerment beyond the formal legal system.

Second, to shake up the judicial system so it may become a device for enforcing some of these rights. This is done by setting up some new courts (administrative, constitutional) and quasi-judicial institutions (for instance, the National Counter-corruption Commission) to circumvent some of the failures of the past, and implicitly to challenge the existing court system to act more independently of central power. This is undoubtedly the most difficult and uncertain part of the project.

Third, to break up the alliance of *itthiphon* and *amnat* by changing the structure of parliament, strengthening the judicial monitoring of politicians and bureaucrats, extending decentralisation, and providing greater opportunities for public challenge. Here the provision to allow petitions of 50,000 signatures to begin proceedings against the powerful is the most innovative, most dramatic and most feared provision in the new charter.[40]

The second strand in the promotion of rights is associated with the local movements mentioned earlier. Here too, the catalogue of rights claimed has expanded. Early movements focused on the rights to local resources, in opposition to state claims to monopolise or destroy those resources at will. More recently, movements have asserted rights to *livelihood* – in particular the rights to proper compensation for loss of livelihood, expressed in many dam protests – and the right of access to land, expressed in the land invasion movements that emerged in response to growing unemployment during the crisis. Finally, of course, there is simply the *right to have rights* even if you are only a forest gatherer, faced by the deputy provincial governor at the head of a cavalcade of *itthiphon* and *amnat*.

CIVILISING THE STATE

So, how *to civilise the state*? Over the 1990s, this increasingly urgent debate has come to divide civil society. There are basically two different and opposed approaches.

---

40 Under clause 304, a petition of 50,000 eligible voters obliges the Senate to begin investigation of politicians or senior officials accused of corruption. The exact procedure for such petitions has not yet been defined by law. However, NGOs led by Rossana Tositrakun collected 50,000 signatures to force a proper investigation of those involved in the public health ministry scandal. On submission, she was asked to 'verify' the signatures. Vasana Chinvarakom, 'Sign of the Times', *Bangkok Post*, 27 February 1999.

The first approach puts its faith in further modernisation. It wants changes in rights and rules, such as through the reform of the constitution noted above. More important, it puts faith in economic and social changes. For democracy to work, according to this view, the economy and society must advance further along the lines of western industrialised societies. In this analysis, the continued power of both *itthiphon* and *amnat* rest ultimately on rural society. *Amnat* derives its power from the traditional deference of peasants long submitted to official paternalism. *Itthiphon* has developed this deference into a modern patronage system (*rabop upatham*) which the local lords exploit to gain super-profits from illegal commerce and political power from 'money politics'. The only solution, according to this school, is to modernise Thailand's peasant society out of existence. This can be done by draining the poor away from the villages to the city, and by upgrading the peasants into capitalist farmers through education and technology. As explained by Anek Laothamatas:

> We must first destroy patronage relations, to release the "little people" of the village from the unequal, unfree association with the "big people" or "patrons", so they become "individuals" like the people of the city and other modern classes ... then they can join together in free associations as "civil society", which from the angle of liberalism is an unavoidable condition of democratisation, because only such a "civil society" can deal with the state and truly control and reform the bureaucracy.[41]

This approach has adopted the term *pracha sangkhom* to translate 'civil society', and has been active in strengthening community organisations, especially in provincial urban centres.[42]

---

41 Anek Laothamatas, *Song nakara prachathipathai*, 91–2. The same passage appears in Anek Laothamatas, Seksan Prasertkun, Anan Kanchanaphan and Direk Pathamasiriwat, *Wiphak sangkhom thai* [Critique of Thai society], Bangkok: Amarin, 1995, 75. See also Kamchai Laisamit, *Wichan nung nak setthasat* [One Vision of an Economist] Bangkok, 1998.

42 Chuchai Suphawong and Yuwadi Katganglai (eds), *Pracha sangkhom: tatsuna nak kit nai sangkhom thai* [Civil society: a Thinker's View in Thai Society], Bangkok: Matichon, 1997. There is also an ethno-historical dimension to this debate; see Kasian Tejapira on p. 125: 'If you ask me historically who originated Thai civil society, in my view it was the *jek*, the Chinese who migrated into Thailand and took up new roles inside traditional Thai society, that is as capitalists and workers. This group first established the market economy, and created associations independent of the state, such as the Chinese associations and schools.' The book also reveals a war of words. Chuchai advocates *pracha sangkhom*. Anek, Chai-Anan and Prawase Wasi seem easier using the English version. Thirayuth proposes an alternative, *sangkhom khem khaeng* [roughly, strong society]. Nidhi tries to avoid the concept altogether.

The second approach has less interest and less optimism about changing the state through politics or new rules. Rather, it concentrates on battles within civil society: to defend and extend local rights, to enlarge the political space available to local groups, to break down the culture of dominance by bureaucrat or boss. These battles are fought by demonstrations, protests, networking, and attacks on the dominant cultural discourse. This strategy requires regular skirmishes with the state, particularly over the contested control of local resources of land, water and forests, which are so crucial for livelihood and well-being. My Chaiyaphum dam example fits comfortably within this approach.[43]

Advocates of this approach contend that modern Thai urban society and the more traditional rural society can and should coexist, so the overall society can benefit from the best parts of both.[44] Like those of the first approach, they oppose the persistence of paternalism and the patronage system within rural society. But they believe the way to overturn this system is from below – by enlarging the political space and increasing the political defiance of the 'little people'. The state will become civilised only with pressure from below.[45]

---

43 The movement of *watthanatham chumchon* (community culture) promotes an alternative discourse on the future development of Thai society. See Chairat Charoensin-olarn, 'Kanmuang baep mai, khabuankan khloenwai thang sangkhom rup baep mai, lae wathakam kan phatthana chut mai' [New Politics, New Social Movements and New Alternative Discourses on Development], *Warasan Thammasat*, 21,1, 1995.

44 Some of the *pracha sangkhom* modernists react very emotionally against this. 'They are not prepared to coexist with rural society, but wish to reduce it and make the industrialised urban society supreme. In other words, the rural society must serve the city rather than being able to develop independently. See for instance Kamchai, *Wichan nung nak setthasat*. This amounts to liberalism as intolerance. Interestingly, this debate unites the liberal-modernists with surviving Leninists who believe pro-rural movements are an impediment to the march of history through capitalism to socialism.

45 Yet this approach constantly runs up against the power of the state – particularly its central control over resources, and its new reactive aggression. Two recent major meetings of local movements both raised the same problem. The first was the thammarat meeting of NGOs and local groups convened by Thirayuth Boonmee, mentioned earlier. While no speakers showed any interest in the parliamentary system, several expressed a wish for some kind of central organisation to provide better coordination of local movements, and to create a stronger bargaining position with official agencies. Local movements are all very well, the argument went, but they are too easily picked off one by one. Over two days, this sentiment became one of the major themes of the meeting. The second meeting was the third anniversary of the Assembly of the Poor in December 1998. Over the previous year, the Democrat Party-led government had deliberately and aggressively reversed out the major achievements of the Assembly over the previous three years. The challenge was: will the

The difference between these two approaches to civilising the state is partly a matter of class. The first *pracha sangkhom* approach is largely urban, with roots in the modernist middle class. The second approach is rural and has roots among the poor. But this class difference is blurred by alliances and networking. More importantly, the two have very different visions of Thailand's future. For the first, the state can only be civilised when Thailand's old rural society is modernised out of existence. For the second, the era of globalisation creates opportunities to break down the patronage system from below, which enables both urban and rural society to coexist and achieve greater freedom.

So let me sum up. In my opinion, the reports on the death of the state are greatly exaggerated, especially in the less advanced world. While many of the intellectual and material foundations of the old nation-state are being undermined by worldwide flows of money, people and ideas, the state is acquiring a new role as a bulwark against the social changes which these flows threaten to create. In other words, the state has a growing role as a defence of old hierarchies, privileges, vested interests, and controls over resources.

There is growing intellectual support for a concept of civil society that challenges old hierarchies and exclusions. The growth of local organisations and networks translates this concept of civil society into day-to-day reality. However, the job of civilising the state in Thailand is going to be a long struggle. And the debate on how to civilise the state has become dramatically polarised. On one side, the modernists argue that Thailand's peasantry must be sacrificed to ensure a future for representative democracy. On the other, opponents have lost faith in the ability of representative democracy to civilise the state. They seek instead to limit and diminish the power of the state by strengthening the rights of individuals and communities, including the right of peasant society to exist and to be different. The crux of the debate is whether the Thai village could or should have a part in Thailand's future.

Assembly remain vulnerable and ultimately powerless unless it develops some way to enter the formal political process.

The answer at both meetings was negative. At the first, Banthorn Ondam (a respected senior NGO leader, formerly an academic) argued that forming a central body would result in splits and discord. The strength of local movements lay in the locality. Loose networking remained the best organisational strategy. At the Assembly meeting, the proposal was not formally addressed. But the Assembly represents just the kind of loose networking that Banthorn described, and hence the answer was implicit. Yet the dilemma has been clearly stated. Can such movements civilise the state from the outside? Conversely, if they move inside, will they inevitably be coopted, destroyed or compromised?

CHAPTER 7

Royal Power[1]

Pramuan Rujanaseri

ROYAL CUSTOMARY LAW

Thailand's long-standing royal customary legal traditions (*nitthira-chaphrapheni*) with respect to politics and government are various and a good illustration of the special relationship between the Thai monarchs and the people. Yet no political scientist or academic in a university has considered which of these traditions might suitably be used in 'a Democracy with the King as Head of State'. The stipulation of Article 7 of the current [1997] constitution that, 'Whenever no provision under this constitution is applicable to any case, it shall be decided in accordance with the convention of the constitution in a Democracy with the King as Head of State' confirms the true existence of preceding administrative traditions whose precise nature needs to be identified and studied.

The history of democracy in Thailand has witnessed a number of violent events, the solution of which have not been stipulated in any constitution. The king's sound adaptation and use of such legal traditions to deal with such circumstances has become one part of Thailand's culture of power.

Cultural thinking regarding power in Europe and the United States of America emphasises the principles of individualism (one for oneself), equality, the rule of law and the separation of the spheres of power. Such concepts differ from the ancient and long-standing Thai culture of power, which adheres to the principle of the exercise of power based on the concepts of *dharma*, compassion (*metta*) and reciprocal relationships.

At present, the Thai culture of power can be examined and understood from various aspects of royal customary law regarding the relationship between Thai kings and the Thai people, as described below.

---

1   Originally published as Pramuan Rujanaseri, พระราชอำนาจ [Royal Power], Bangkok: Sumet Rujanaseri, 2005, pp. 97–137. Pramuan cites from royal speeches in this piece, but does not offer references.

First, all Thais have a shared recognition that almost all Thai kings are like a father, constantly guarding over their livelihood. This sentiment is in the blood of all Thais, resulting in a strong and unbreakable bond between the kings and the Thai people. Having placed their faith and confidence in the monarchy, Thais believe that they cannot live without the presence of this institution. True Thais worship and have confidence in the institution of the monarchy.

In one of his speeches, Prince Dhani Nivat asserted that:

> In traditional Thai culture, it was the king's duty to act as a military leader in times of war and as a ruler and a judge in times of peace. The relationships between a Thai king and the people was extremely close.

These words still apply to the Thais of today.

Second, there are royal customary laws for the limited exercise of royal power over the people. For example, kings during the Ayutthaya period repeatedly asked for forgiveness from the people when any law was introduced and enforced. They had to give detailed explanations and reasons for having to introduce the law, citing the need for the common good and happiness of the people together with quotations from the Thammasat (a Pali code of law) obtained by gurus from a faraway land. Such practices confirm that kings could not enact laws at will. Some kings even decreed palace laws to restrict the exercise of their royal power. This is different from early sovereigns in the Western cultures who could enact any law of their desire ... as in the case of Louis XIV, who declared: 'L'état, c'est moi' (I am the state).

The royal customary law for monarchs, in which kings give priority to the people, has been passed on and become the cultural heritage of Thailand. All Thai kings have observed the principle of ruling without adhering to or monopolising the absolute royal powers to which they are entitled. On the contrary, Thai kings have been prepared to give the Thai people a stake in the exercise of their sovereign power since the reign of King Mongkut, Chulalongkorn, Vajiravudh and Prajadhipok of the Chakri dynasty. We must acknowledge that the royal customary law that gives priority to the people is unique to the Thai monarchy.

Third, there is the royal customary law to use *dharma* (Buddha's teachings) as an instrument for governing the people. This can be seen from the king's generosity in allowing the people the freedom to choose and practise a religion of their choice. Other *dharma* observed by Thai kings include *metta* (a compassion for all living things), forgiveness, victory through the practices of *dharma*, self-control, supporting others, refraining from vices, righteous performance of one's social duties as well as the monitoring of people's wellbeing.

Through such a culture of power, all Thai kings must be highly knowledgeable in *ratcha-sat* or the science of being king, *dhammasat* and other disciplines. They must also be good persons who dedicate themselves to bringing happiness to all groups of people, promoting *dharma*, promoting good people and good action, creating peace and prosperity, and caring for and remaining close to the people.

Fourth, there is a royal customary law for monarchs to look after the country's independence and the Buddhist-practising Thai people. Thai kings executed this custom on two occasions following the falls of Ayutthaya, when King Naresuan the Great and King Taksin the Great reclaimed Thailand's independence. The founder of the Chakri dynasty, King Buddha Yot Fa Chulalok the Great, also fought fiercely in many battles to protect the country, while King Chulalongkorn was forced to give up some Thai territories to protect the country's sovereignty from the threat of Western imperialism.

When pressured by King Louis XIV to convert to Christianity, King Narai the Great (r.1658–88) subtly and ingeniously declined the request by stating that,

> I immensely appreciate the King of France for the kind compassion that you have for me, but to disown the religion that has been in existence for 2,229 years is not an easy thing to do. If the missionaries convert all of my people to Christianity, I will follow suit. On another issue, I am surprised that the King of France would try to usurp the power of God. Isn't it God's will to have numerous religions in this world? Or else God would have created only one religion. At this point in time, God must have wished me to continue to remain a Buddhist. I would wait for the day that it is God's will to have me become a Christian. When that day comes, I will convert to Christianity. I would like to let my fate and the fate of Sri Ayutthaya remain in the hands of God. I hope that my friend, the King of France, will not feel slighted by my words.

Fifth, there emerged a royal customary law for a monarch to nurture the wellbeing of the country and the people more than his own. Members of the royal family must fight in a war and visit the people to learn about their problems and sufferings to rectify them. This is particularly true with the present monarch, who prefers to grant a closer royal audience to his people than to state officials or any other person.

Sixth, since the revolution of 1932 a new royal customary law emerged: kings were to become politically neutral and free of political interference. Any political party which came to power would become the king's government. In this way, even when different political parties take turns governing the country, this does not create any problems for the monarchy.

From all the above mentioned six royal customary laws, it can be seen that none of them contradicts or conflicts with the fundamental ideology of Democracy with the King as Head of State. On the contrary, they all support and promote the Thai-style administrative culture. It is we who must adapt the concepts of power, rights and individualism to be in harmony with the concepts of *dharma, metta* and reciprocal relationships.

Present day Thai-style administrative culture is beginning to be influenced by Western theories of power, which creates problems for Thai government. No matter how well the administrative system is adjusted there will always be problems when it is put into practice. An example of this problem can be seen in the current [1997] constitution. In the beginning it seemed to have many good rules and regulations in place but these have now created a monopoly form of parliamentary dictatorship in which the executive cannot be kept in check. This situation has caused great concern about the possibility of another constitutional crisis that will eventually drive the Thai people to rely on the benevolent power of His Majesty the King for a remedy of the situation, as was the case with previous crises.

Upon close and detailed examination of all six royal customary laws, which have been perfectly observed and executed by Thai kings, it is undeniable that the true focal point of Thailand's ideas, spirit, administration and government lies with the Thai monarchy and not the constitution, the House of Representatives, the Senate, the Cabinet or any other independent constitutional organs. Royal power is built upon the monarchy being at the centre of ideas, spirit and government. Thai monarchs have exercised their royal power under royal customary law for monarchs which is not stipulated in the constitution. Since the royal powers have never been compiled or classified for systematic study, I shall try to initiate such compilation for further studies or research in the future.

THE ROYAL POWER TO SOLVE NATIONAL CRISIS

Some national crises that have taken place are not within the responsibility of and cannot be remedied by the government on its own. This is because they arose from critical disputes between the government and the public, as in the events of 14 October 1973 and May 1992.

In the uprising of 14 October 1973, the public came together in mass protests to force from office General Thanom Kittikachorn [then prime minister], General Prapas Charusathien and Colonel Narong Kittikachorn, resulting in Thais killing Thais. The country fell into a state of lawlessness. His Majesty King Bhumibol Adulyadej combined his virtues, compassion and ingenuity with the deep loyalty of his people to successfully rectify the situation and restore peace.

His Majesty the King told all parties involved as follows: 'let all parties and everyone put an end to the cause of violence by exercising the right presence of mind to quickly return the country to normalcy.' He told the government,

> may the government absolutely refrain from hurting school children, university students and the people no matter how infuriating these groups have acted toward government officials. Even if they are the ones who initiate an attack on policemen or soldiers with knives, pieces of wood or even homemade bombs, please do not hurt them in return.

When the violent clashes escalated, people retreated into Chitralada Royal Villa to seek protection from His Majesty the King, who ordered all his royal pages and guards to remove all bullets from their guns. He also advised the incumbent prime minister to resign. After the crisis was over, the king appointed Mr. Sanya Thammasak as the prime minister, and appointed a National Forum to select individuals to act as members of the National Legislative Assembly based on the following justification:

> due to the uncertainty of the situation prior to the promulgation of the constitution, when the government is not sufficiently secure for His Majesty the King to rest assured (of the political situation). It is also His Majesty the King's wish to have the people participate in the laying of the administrative foundation…

At the time of the May 1992 Event, the brewing crisis was quite like the political development of October 1973. Popular protests organised to purge the regime of General Suchinda Kraprayoon turned into fatal clashes with the authorities. His Majesty the King summoned General Suchinda Kraprayoon and Major General Chamlong Srimueang to a royal audience in which he warned them to solve the problems in the following words:

> Today's problems are not the problems of the drafting or revision of a constitution; they are the problems of the people's safety and morale. At present, people everywhere are frightened and fearful of the prospect of a national tragedy, a collapse that will be difficult to remedy ... if we cannot put an end to the crisis of the past three days. Therefore, both of you, General Suchinda and Major General Chamlong, must help one another find a solution by turning towards each other rather than confronting one another. This is because the country does not belong to one or two individuals only; it belongs to everyone. You must turn to one another and not face off ... [W]hen people get worked up and become violent, they usually lose their self-control. They will eventually forget why they got into a fight and what problem the fight was meant to solve. They only think of how to win over the other party. Who will be the winner? There is no winner, only losers and ensuing perils. Both parties will be the loser. Once you confront one another, you have already lost. The worst losers are the country and the people. Not only the people of Bangkok but the people across the country will be the losers. If Bangkok suffers the whole country also suffers. What is the use of your pride in winning if such victory rests upon a pile of ruins?

> Therefore, I have invited both of you here not for a confrontation but for you to turn to one another. You two are representatives not of two parties but of diverse parties which are confronting one another. You are to help each other solve the immediate problem of violent clashes. When this problem is remedied, then we can discuss how to rebuild Thailand and restore peace. This is the reason I summoned you two here. I believe that you understand that you will be the ones who can save and rebuild our country from ruins. It will bring you great personal returns to commit such good deeds.

In both these historic events, when confrontation between Thais led to bloodshed, peace was restored because the majesty of the king had so accumulated trust that he was the true head of state under the royal customary laws. Whenever such a crisis is looming or becoming imminent, all Thais still expect that the king will be able to protect them and the country from all harm.

170

THE ROYAL POWER TO PROVIDE CONSULTATION AND ADVICE

There are two levels for this type of royal power: the governmental level and the organizational/general population level. This type of royal power has never been stipulated in any version of the Thai constitution, but the king's practice of royal customary law has given rise to these Royal Powers, which he legitimately exercises.

The Governmental Level

Relationships between Thai governments and the Thai king have always been smooth. All governments are aware that they are 'the government of His Majesty the King', who exercise administrative power through the cabinet. Therefore, all Thai governments must have royal audiences with the king to present reports on their operations and regularly seek royal advice on different topics. His Majesty the King may initiate an audience or may send words of advice to the prime minister through his secretary. He may also give advice through various mass media on different occasions. For example, His Majesty the King advised the government to use the principles of 'Understand, Access and Develop' to solve the problems of violence that took place in the three southern border provinces. Royal advice may also be given at informal royal audiences during state functions. Royal visits to provincial areas also provided opportunities for the prime minister and his ministers to present their reports and receive royal advice from His Majesty the King.

For example, on the auspicious occasion of His Majesty the King's 25th anniversary of his ascension to the throne in 1971, the government at the time wished to obtain royal permission to erect a monument in his honour, but His Majesty the King advised the government that it was better to construct roads. The government then had Ratchadapisek Road built as part of the city's inner ring road system. When members of a foreign terrorist group stormed and seized the Israeli embassy on 28 May 1971, His Majesty the King gave advice that the then-prime minister applied, and he was able to successfully negotiate the release of hostages.

Organisations and the People

His Majesty King Bhumibol Adulyadej frequently exercises his royal power by giving advice through royal speeches to individuals and groups of individuals on various topics and various occasions. For example, the king usually addresses major national problems in his annual birthday anniversary celebration speeches and gives valuable advice on various topics such as national unity, losses and profits and sufficiency economy, etc. Such royal speeches are also given to military personnel, policemen and civil servants on different occasions. These organisations and their personnel are grateful for the royal speeches and royal guidance.

It should be noted that there has never been any assessment on how much the organisations, individuals, groups of individuals and government officials who have been the recipients of such speeches have put the royal ideas into practice. However, I believe that people have applied some of them on a voluntary basis and not by force.

THE ROYAL POWER TO CAUTION

As head of the nation His Majesty the King exercises legislative power through the parliament, executive power through the cabinet and judicial power through the courts. These entities and other institutions established by the constitution are considered to be performing their duties on the king's behalf. Therefore, the monarch has the royal power to caution them and has done so on several occasions. For example, he usually cautions members of the parliament on the executing of their duties during his speech at the ceremony to open parliament after each election, and to cabinet members when they are sworn in. When during a royal audience, judges as well as personnel of the Justice Courts, the Constitutional Courts, the Administrative Courts, and the Military Courts pledge loyalty to the king, and pledge to perform their duty under his name with honesty, integrity and impartiality, His Majesty the King takes these opportunities to give them guidance and forewarning on the execution of their duties with honesty and strict observance of their pledge.

THE ROYAL POWER TO INITIATE
DEVELOPMENT AND PROVIDE SUPPORT

Following the royal customary law to treat their people in the same manner as a father does his children and to nourish the country and the people, His Majesty the King has introduced numerous development initiatives to solve the problems of his people. He set up different learning centres on the royal-initiated development projects, advised the government to construct dams and large water reservoirs, and launched various projects based on the principles of the New Theory and Sufficiency Economy. Such projects will be discussed in more detail in the section on the majesty of King Bhumibol.

THE ROYAL POWER TO RELIEVE
PEOPLE FROM SUFFERING

Direct submission of a petition to the king is part of the culture and belief of the Thai people that has persisted from the time of Sukhothai Kingdom, when people with grievances could ring the provided bell to make their plight known to the king. During the Rattanakosin period King Mongkut had a drum placed at a gate to the royal palace and announced the rules of people's petition, which allowed an individual to directly present a petition to the king.

These beliefs and customs are our national heritage and persist to this day.

The royal power to relieve the people from their hardship through a request for royal pardon has already been discussed elsewhere and will not be repeated here. But I will outline the royal powers to relieve the people from general distresses as follows:

1. For miseries caused by non-criminal offence such as being penalised by a breach of discipline or regulation offences, His Majesty the King will have the responsible government agency review the case to ensure proper justice.

2. For miseries caused by a government agency's action, His Majesty the King will have the case directed to the government agency concerned for inspection and remedy.

3. For miseries in which the petitioner pleads for justice, His Majesty the King will have the case directed to an organization with the proper authority for a review. In cases of direct appeal to the king, he will deal with it as he deems appropriate. If it is a problem of public interest, he may use different measures to solve it. For example, in response to an appeal for water source His Majesty the King may allocate water from a development project to the petitioner's location or may initiate a new project to deal with the problem.

Some of the royal assistance to his people has not come directly from the king's personal benevolence but through various government agencies that take it upon themselves to remedy people's miseries because of their recognition and high regard for the royal power in this respect.

Although the royal powers under the well established royal customary laws are not stipulated in the constitution, they have long been accepted and respected through a combination of the people's reverence of the royal majesty and the strong faith and devotion that the people have for the exemplary conduct of the monarchs. Thai kings have always been vigilant and protective of the welfare of the country and their people. Whenever they exercise the royal powers to solve national crises, miraculous outcomes generally ensue.

Through the administrative experiences of the present king, the royal power to give advice to the government, the parliament, the courts, independent organizations and the people, the royal power to develop the country and provide royal support as well as the royal power to relieve people from their miseries have been carried out with virtuous intent and compassion. There exists the best of relationships between the king, the government and the people which have not always been formed based on the Western concepts of power, rights and individualism.

Given this administrative legacy and noble culture, all Thais, the government, the parliament, the courts, independent organizations and government agencies should adopt the royal initiatives and adjust their administrative styles and approaches for the happiness of the country and the people.

THE MAJESTY OF KING BHUMIBOL

In studying the majesty of modern-day monarchs, one must remember that they can no longer be judged by their bravery, military skills, military conquests or the ability to make impressive territorial expansion. The royal standing of modern-day monarchs has shifted from the ideal of warrior kings to that of kings close to their people, who can protect and care for them through various political mechanisms such as the cabinet, the parliament, the courts and independent organizations. The majesty of Thai kings spreads far and wide to people in both urban and remote rural areas.

It can be readily surmised from these studies that the present king of Thailand, His Majesty King Bhumibol Adulyadej or King Rama IX, is a monarch whose truly immense majesty allows for the protection and security of the country and the people, and this is the reason behind Thailand's unparalleled progress and prosperity.

THE FIRST ROYAL ADDRESS

On 9 June 1946 at the age of 18 years, six months and four days, His Majesty King Bhumibol Adulyadej ascended the throne in accordance with the palace law on royal succession, B.E. 2467 (1924) and with the consent of the House of Representatives.

The main protocols of the Royal Purification Ceremony or Coronation (พระราชพิธีบรมราชาภิเษก)were as follows: His Majesty the King changed into white attire, a white shawl with gold edges hanging diagonally across his body. He sat on the Atha Disa Udumbara Raja Asana Throne in preparation for the Royal Purification Ceremony. The Supreme Patriarch sprinkled holy water over the king, who was then ritually bathed. The waters used in this ceremony came from the five major and sacred rivers of ancient India, namely, the Ganges, Yamuna, Aciravati, Saraphu and Mahi, mixed with waters from five major rivers in Thailand, namely, the Chao Phraya, Petchaburi, Ratchaburi, Pasak and Bang Pakong Rivers, as well as the waters from the four important ponds of Sa Ket, Sa Kaew, Sa Khongkha and Sa Yamuna, which have been used in coronation ceremonies since ancient times.

At the completion of the purification ritual, His Majesty the King changed into royal coronation attire and took a seat on the Atha Disa Throne (พระที่นั่ง อัฐทิศ), placed under the seven-tiered great white umbrella in Baisal Daksin Throne Hall. Members of the parliament offered the king holy coronation water on behalf of the royal sages. This part of the ceremony was adapted from the former tradition, in keeping with the modern time, to signify that his ascent to the throne was by the consent of the people and Brahmin priests. The next ceremonial stage was the offering of holy water to deities in all eight directions. The President of the Senate offered a blessing to the king in the Pali language and the Speaker of the House of Representatives offered a blessing in Thai, followed by Phra Ratchakhru Warmathepmuni presenting the nine-tiered Royal Umbrella of State to the king.

His Majesty the King then took the Bhadrapitha Throne inside the old Baisal Daksin Throne Hall. The chief Brahmin, Phra Ratcha Khru Vamadeb Muni, chanted homage to the Kailasa Heaven [in Hinduism the physical embodiment of the sacred residence of Lord Shiva] and presented His Majesty the King with the Royal Golden Plaque with an inscription of the king's royal title of 'Phrabat Somdet Phra Poraminthara Maha Bhumibol Adulyadej Mahitalathibes Ramathibodi Chakri Naruebodin Sayaminthrathirat Boromnartbopit'. Also presented were the royal regalia, the royal utensils and the royal sword. The Brahmin priest then proceeded to offer a blessing to the king in the Magadhi language. His Majesty the King gave his first royal speech in Thai by expressing his intention to safeguard all Thais in the following words: 'We will reign with righteousness for the benefit and happiness of all Siamese people'. Phra Ratcha Khru Vamadeb Muni responded to the royal speech in the Magadhi and Thai languages as follows: 'I, the servant of Buddha, accept your majesty's royal command and royal address with my head and the top of my head and may the power of the dust under the soles of your royal feet protect my head and the top of my head." His Majesty the king then poured holy water onto the ground and pledged his intention to execute the royal duties of governing the Thai kingdom with the ten virtues of a righteous kingship, thus ending the coronation ritual.[2]

In executing his royal duties, His Majesty the King has been focusing on the benefits of the country and the people. Such determination was reflected in his response to a question about his regal roles in a documentary titled 'Soul of the Nation', which was broadcast on BBC Television Station in the United Kingdom around 1983:

> The primary issue is security, which is the people's security. Thai people had fought for their freedom and independence. Therefore, it is essential for me to be a good military leader. After the country is somewhat peaceful, there will be peace and order, laws and government. At the same time, there must be sufficient food supply and other necessities for the people to be able to secure good housing and the like, the essentials of living. It should be followed by social order and emotional peace. This means we must be a good person to avoid any chaos since good persons do not cause much trouble. We must also be religious, with the king being a religious leader.

With these words and the first royal address, it can be surmised that His Majesty the King places great emphasis on the ultimate goals of stability, safety and progress for the nation and the people. In managing to achieve

---

2   In translating the section on the coronation ceremony, we have been guided by the translations in Ministry of Culture, *The Royal Coronation Ceremony*, n.d.

these goals, His Majesty the King has never failed to reiterate the 'spiritual' aspects of the Thai people. He has emphasised to the Thai people that the concerned parties:

1. 'must conduct themselves with the best of strength and without persecuting others, and must try to cooperate with one another. If they come across any inappropriate conduct or incident, they should work together to suppress or correct it with honest intention.'

2. must have 'the strength of mind ... to enable the Thai race to continue living with stability and prosperity. If they can do that everyone will live in happiness and convenience. It doesn't matter if the world we live in is in a state of anarchy or our ideas keep changing or someone tries to destroy our unity, the Thai nation will go on if we can keep our strength and unity.'

3. [remember that] '[I]t is the duty of the people who live on our lands to join forces in protecting and maintaining national security at all times.'

4. [can] 'enable the people to manage to safeguard their homeland with full benefits and complete freedom. In doing so, it is the government who has the most important duties of defending and protecting the country's peaceful existence and safety. It must provide the people with academic, technical and socio-economic support so that the people can look after themselves, improve their career and livelihood as well as learn to live together in unity.'

His Majesty has also placed emphasis on 'peace and happiness of the people being the key factors for national security.'

His first royal address, and the national goals as inferred in the royal speeches given on various occasions, as well as the above-mentioned principles have been overlooked by the Thai people and the government in recent times. They fail to examine closely these principles and put them into practice. On the contrary, they have turned to experiment with a variety of governing ideologies, principles and techniques. And these have often been carried out on a trial and error basis, resulting repeatedly in damage to the country and the people. The Thai people and the Thai governments of today should seriously re-examine the words of His Majesty the King's first royal address, royal initiatives, royal speeches and royal guidance and really put them to good use to reciprocate the great love and concern that the king has for his people.

THE ROYAL INITIATIVES

His Majesty King Rama IX has introduced a myriad of royal-initiated projects, 3,298 of them (as of 2003), which range from agriculture to environment, public health, occupational development, water source development, telecommunications, social welfare projects. They are a clear indication of the king's ingenuity in ideas and operation. For the purposes of clarity and benefits to the Thai people and the Thai government, I will compile and classify the royal initiatives of His Majesty King Bhumibol Adulyadej into the following categories:

1. National security

King Rama IX's national security initiatives are derived from his clear perception of Thailand's national security which is as follows:

> A nation is made up of land and people. The land is the place that one is born into and lives in; places where people can find peace, happiness and security. People are united into a nation through their association with the land ... For these reasons, people who live in the land must have the mutual duty of protecting and safeguarding the land for eternal security. It is the direct responsibility of military personnel to safeguard the nation. Their responsibilities are to perform their duties to the point of sacrificing their lives.

This royal initiative should be taken as the principal strategy that the Thai people and the Thai government must observe in their effort to maintain national security. The king has also emphasised that stability of the nation rests upon its people.

> For a nation to have security depends on providing necessary support to help people live in peace and happiness and to be able to achieve progress. Agricultural activities, agricultural-related knowledge and academic knowledge in various disciplines can help the country to become united and stable because they can enable the people to progress and prosper.

> [T]he primary goal of maintaining national security rests upon letting the people have the capacity to maintain and govern their local communities, with proper welfare and complete freedom. In doing so, it is the officials who have the imperative duties of defending and protecting peace and safety. They must provide the people with academic, technical and socio-economic support so that the people can look after themselves,

improve their occupation and livelihood as well as learn to live together in peace and unity.

2. National administration

The royal initiatives of King Bhumibol regarding national administration are as follows:

1. National administration must give priority to national prosperity, peace and stability:

    'National prosperity, peace and stability are of utmost importance that a person should take into consideration and aim for. National prosperity and stability will materialise when all groups of administrators are determined to perform their duties with great virtues of mind and determination that come from cautious reflection and intellect for the common good rather than for the benefits of a specific sector ... '

2. '[T]he Cabinet has the most important duties to perform. National welfare and progress depend mainly on the conduct of the Cabinet. The word government or 'ratthabarn' in Thai refers to those who safeguard and maintain the state. A state is the nation in general. If speaking of the cabinet, ministers are councillors of the state. A councillor is a person with an important role who has knowledge and determination to perform his or her work. The state is the centre of the nation, while ministers are the nation's seniors who can apply their knowledge into practice for the good of the nation. In summary, besides great determination, councillors or ministers must be determined to execute their duties with great honesty in compliance with the pledge they gave before taking office. Honesty is of utmost importance because if a person has great determination to work but lacks honesty, he or she will not have explicit goals to pursue but will be indecisive in his or her mission, stumbling this way and that. Such a person will never be successful in his or her work. Honesty is the foremost priority for ministers; they must realise that the primary goal for their work is to bring progress and prosperity to the country. Each minister has his or her own duties to perform and must employ his or her knowledge and ability for such purpose. One becomes a minister to successfully execute the work in each ministry. In addition, ministers must have what is known as unity or cooperation in work performance to bring success to the country.'

    '[A]ll groups of administrators are determined to perform their duties with purity of mind and sincerity with cautious reflection on the common good rather than for the benefit of a specific sector ... '

3. '[M]embers of the parliament are assigned by the people to consult and discuss about the ways to govern the country in order to bring as many benefits, happiness, prosperity and stability to the country as possible. For this reason, all parliamentary debates should be carried out to serve such purposes and nothing else.'

4. On judicial functions,
    'Those whose duties are to uphold justice or fairness should be most careful in the execution of their duties. They should have a clear understanding that law is not justice itself but is only a means to uphold and deliver justice. Laws must be exercised with the goals of upholding justice and not the provisions of law. And the upholding of justice in this country is not confined to the scope of laws alone but must be extended to include the moral and ethical issues as well as the actual causes and effects of the case.'

5. 'There are both good and bad people in a country. Nobody can make everybody a good person. To keep a country in a normal, orderly and happy state is not to make everybody a good person but to advocate for a good person, to enable a good person to govern the country and to restrict a bad person from obtaining power so that a bad person cannot cause troubles and chaos.'

And what can we say about today's governance???

3. National development and progress

The key principles observed by King Bhumibol in these aspects are:

All types of progress must be originated from a study of the existing foundations. Once we are clear about the pros and cons of the situation, we can keep the positive foundations and try to improve them through proper academic principles and cautious reflection. This must be carried out with rational thinking and honesty to cultivate gradual and stable progress as deemed suitable for each situation. It should also be carried out in accordance with the available energy, capability and economic means. In this way, all works in the country will continue to progress with no interruption. Any other approach to development will bring only obstacles and delay, which will result in a waste of energy, brain power and financial resources that can never be redeemed.

What is the approach of the development projects of today???

4. Education

His Majesty the King's vision on the provision of education is as follows:

What are the objectives of education? In brief, its objectives are to provide an individual with a means or instrument for complete and sufficient living in terms of academic knowledge, critical thinking, emotional and moral conducts as well as diligence, perseverance and proper competence. These components will enable such individuals to really work on his or her own. Education will enable them to have a happy, secure and prosperous livelihood so that they can benefit society and the country in accordance with their status.

His Majesty the King aims to have educated people contribute to the greater good of the society.

THE ROYAL SPEECHES AND ROYAL GUIDANCE

Throughout his reign of almost 60 years, King Bhumibol delivered so many royal speeches that represent his serious concern over many of the ongoing problems of this country. He warned the Thai people and the Thai government on how to lead their life and with honesty and integrity. Examples of such royal speeches are shown below:

National development needs to be launched in proper steps, starting from creating a solid foundation of relatively decent livelihood where most people can get by through economical means and equipment. Once a stable and practical foundation has been established the next step is to promote a higher level of prosperity and economic growth. If we focus on achieving rapid prosperity and economic growth without having any action plans that are in keeping with the current state of the country and the people, it will eventually result in unbalanced development, difficulties and failures.

Let us consider the following royal speech that His Majesty the King gave to provincial governors, styled as CEOs:

You must govern. The word govern here means you must manage to have your subordinates and the people lead an orderly life and to be able to live well. To achieve these goals, you must be knowledgeable in various disciplines ... from the art of administration from the political science and legal points of view to the sciences of how to make a living and economics. The three disciplines of political science, law and economics cannot be overlooked. Any of you who are knowledgeable in these fields can make a living. But it will be hard to work on your own. You need to engage people with knowledge in other fields in your work too, especially in the major fields of agriculture ... and economics ...

[G]overnor means one who does the work of the crown, and work of the crown is the work of the king ...

'You will become a CEO provincial governor when the word CEO is taken to mean anyone who issues an effective order. But here the word CEO is used in a commercial sense where CEO is expected to make money for a company. But the role of a CEO provincial governor is not to make money for a company; your role is to generate growth in your responsible areas and localities, and especially for your people, bringing them progress, food and the ability to make a living. You may realise that my speech contains strong words about your duties to bring growth and make local people richer ...

'[A]nother point about CEO duties is to build collaboration, which is to bring people to work together and not to work against one another. The latter is quite a common experience. There is also the problem of corruption. How can we suppress corruption? You cannot just say that corruption is the responsibility of the police, the courts, the monks. It is the issue of the CEO provincial governor. Do not allow corruption by state officials of any level or any rank because corruption either by state officials or ordinary people will bring destruction to the country. Thailand has previously collapsed because of corruption ... When we say our economy is on the rise now, we should realise that corruption is also escalating ... When we say Thailand will be more progressive in the next 10 years, we should know that corruption will be more advanced too. Therefore, you must stop corruption from happening and you will be a very efficient CEO provincial governor ... CEO provincial governors must be honest. They cannot be dishonest. I put the damnedest of curse on anyone who shows even a tiny trace of dishonesty. This may sound rude, but may misfortune fall upon dishonest people. For honest and fair-minded people, may they be blessed with a long life of up to 100 years. They shall be blessed with longevity and good health. Honesty will free Thailand from serious harms ...

From His Majesty the King's speech given during the celebration of his birthday in 1992:

Although Thais normally favour a life of convenience and self-indulgence, deep down almost all of them are rational, disciplined and sincere people with a strong sense of patriotism. These are the characteristics that keep us united and keep our country free and independent to this day. They have also been the vital forces behind the creation of numerous outstanding national heritages. At present, the country has continued to be confronted with persistent problems and obstacles in almost all sectors. These are disturbing indicators that it is time for all parties to seriously put aside their pride and self-indulgence and to turn toward rationality, righteousness and social responsibility to eliminate prejudice while promoting mutual compassion and unity. This is the way to work together and expedite work success, unity and reciprocity for the maximum benefits of maintaining national freedom, sovereignty and Thainess for a long time to come ... (Saturday 5 December 1992).

Vinee Chiengthien's thesis that analyzes the royal speeches of King Bhumibol Adulyadej given on his birthday anniversary celebrations between 1950–99 revealed some interesting points of the royal speeches. The royal speeches between 1950–56 focused on the issues of morality, unity and honesty which were consistent with the ongoing power struggles at the time. The royal speeches between the beginning of Field Marshal Sarit Thanarat's regime in 1957 until the 14 October 1973 Event, which was the period of rising communist infiltration in Thailand, focused on the issues of morality, royal guest receptions, events that took place in each year and the danger of Communism. For example, in the royal speech given on New Year's Day, 1966, the king stated:

'[W]hile our country is moving forward, a terrible event has occurred. Those from the opposite side have made it clear that Thailand is the target of their invasion. They have already started such a mission through propaganda, provocation, infiltration and violent acts wherever they can. Political tensions have developed all over the world and among our neighbouring countries. The situation is of great concern especially if we cannot prevent and suppress such assaults ...

The royal speeches between 1973–76, during the period of rising democracy after a long period of dictatorship, still focused on the issues of morality and national affairs, as evident from one of the king's speeches in 1974:

'[M]ay everyone wish for a Thailand that has enough to live and eat. The country does not have to be extremely prosperous but there should be adequate livelihood and peace in comparison to other countries. If we can preserve such a livelihood, our country will be able to rise to the apex of progress. Other countries worldwide are failing and facing difficulties following their striving toward being a superpower in military might, economics, industry and doctrine. Therefore, may all of you join forces in maintaining our adequate livelihood. I would like to reiterate that it should be reasonably good, adequate and peaceful living. Don't let others take away these characteristics from us. This shall be a valuable and ever-lasting birthday gift to me ...

The royal speeches between 1976–88 still focused on the issues of morality, unity, good deeds and national development, especially on flood solutions, rice banks and cattle banks, aid for farmers and the people, and rural development. The royal speeches between the 1988–99 also focused on the issues of morality, unity, corruption, persistence, perseverance and national development with special emphasis on flood problems and the royal-initiated projects.

ROYAL DUTIES

The royal duties and the royal tasks carried out by King Bhumibol through-out almost sixty years of his reign, which are widely known to the Thai people, are so numerous that they cannot be fully mentioned and described here. His Majesty the King has carried out his royal duties and royal con-ducts in a way that 'exceeds the obligations of a monarch'. He has carried out both the royal duties that are and are not stipulated in the constitution. The latter includes his sharing in the people's happiness and sorrow and his effort to alleviate their miseries and problems. The king has dedicated himself to making personal visits to people in remote and arid areas.

The work principles of His Majesty King Bhumibol Adulyadej as related by Her Royal Highness Princess Maha Chakri Sirindhorn can be summa-rised as follows:

1. The primary mission that His Majesty the King is currently working on is to implement as many national development projects as possible.
2. His Majesty the King must have prior knowledge about the geograph-ical features of the area and other aspects of an area before launching a developmental project.
3. His Majesty the King prefers to drive a vehicle to a target destination, or to walk if such destination can be reached by foot, to really get to know the area. When traveling by helicopter, the king takes the opportunity to check and correct area maps.

4. Besides maps, aerial photography is another important tool that His Majesty the King uses to improve water sources and agricultural activities.

5. While traveling by helicopter, he takes several photography series and creates his own composite aerial photographs by putting them together with scotch tape and glue, for use in his development efforts.

6. He uses meteorological satellite photographs while developing water sources and agricultural activities.

7. For each flood prevention plan, His Majesty the King relies on lessons learned from previous floods. He searches for and uses the oldest area maps that he can obtain to study changes in water flows in and out of Bangkok. He leads government officials from diverse work units on inspection tours of the actual flooded areas for close observation of each location.

8. He takes relevant factors for flooding into consideration and puts everyone he knows to work, even if they are ordinary people and not engineers. Some of these people may work in fields that are not at all related to engineering work, such as policemen. He tells them to go out to measure the water levels and report back to him. He sometimes specifically orders his friends in the flooded areas to take daily water level measurements near their homes and report directly to the king. If he has no personal acquaintances in a flooded area, he appoints someone he knows to be a contact person, and that person asks his or her friends to measure the area's water levels every morning and evening. In this way, His Majesty the King has become familiar with different areas and canals of Bangkok. He developed better understandings of the tide patterns, characteristics, problems and dangers of each canal. He has learned that some waterways cannot be used as conduits because they are clogged with banana trees.

9. His idea was to establish a database system from all collected data, using multi-dimensional rather than unidimensional approaches to problems. For example, he did not look at flood problems from the point of view of a water resource engineering alone because there are many contributing factors involved in any flood flooding such as meteorological elements, inundation from the northern region and rising tide of the sea water. His Majesty the King acquired hydrological, meteorological and irrigational data as well as data from the electrical

authority units and put them together to obtain the overall picture of the problems.

10. On 18 November 1986, the king's principal private secretary, M.L. Taweeson Ladawan, stated that His Majesty the King generally initiates new approaches to problem solving. He spends his own money to fund various studies and experiments until he is certain that his initiatives are workable and useful; only then do other agencies put them into practice. He initiates the ideas and projects for the government agencies. Many experimental projects such as these were initially set up on the grounds of Chitralada Villa. There have been experimental water management and experimental agricultural projects on Yang Na plantation, including rice growing and tilapia fish farming. The latest project at Chitralada Villa is an experimental project on plant tissue culture techniques which are the latest technology in plant cultivation for the plants that cannot be cultivated with the traditional grafting methods.

THE ROYAL DESIGNATION OF 'THE GREAT'

In 1996, Thais from all over the land filed a petition to offer the royal designation, 'the Great', to the king on the auspicious occasion of the 50th Anniversary of His Majesty King Bhumibol's Accession to the Throne, in recognition of his royal benevolence and majesty that has steered Thailand out of many national crises. This is the ultimate gesture of gratitude that the Thai people can express for his continuing efforts to rid people in remote areas of their hardship and suffering, his numerous royal speeches and valuable guidance on national development, his royal visits to aid and be close to his people. Testimonies of the signatures on this petition are currently kept at the National Library, at Wasukree Pier, Bangkok.

CHAPTER 8

Historical Legacy and the Emergence of Judicialisation in the Thai State[1]

Saichon Sattayanurak

INTRODUCTION

This article gives importance to considering the culture of Thai political thinking by emphasising the ideas and meaning concerning 'Thai-style government' that were constructed and reproduced amidst protracted political struggles. These are embedded in middle-class consciousness and became the foundation for the rise of 'judicialisation'. The middle class perceives the judiciary's political role as legitimate even though judicial power is, unlike in other countries, unconnected to popular sovereignty, and the values and principles of liberal democracy including people's rights and liberties.

Explanations for the emergence of 'judicialisation' (*dulakanaphiwat*) often note how the royal speech delivered to the presidents of the Supreme Administration Court and the Supreme Court on 25 April 2006 by His Majesty King Bhumibol Adulyadej led to a movement among judges, lawyers and academics to respond to the king's wishes.[2] This is not contested. But this article also agrees with explanations that see the 'judiciary's

---

1 Originally published as สายชลสัตยานุรักษ์ มรดกทางประวัติศาสตร์และการบังเกิด"ตุลาการภิวัฒน์" ในรัฐไทย, [Historical Legacy and the Emergence of Judicialisation in the Thai State] วารสารนิติ สังคมศาสตร์มหาวิทยาลัยเชียงใหม่, [Journal of Law and Social Sciences Chiang Mai University, 9, 1, 2016 pp. 8–58.

2 See Kasian Tejapira, รัฐประหาร 19 กันยายน พ.ศ. 2549 กับการเมืองไทย [The 19 September 2006 Coup d'état and Thai Politics] รัฐศาสตร์สาร [Ratthasatsan], 29, 3 2008. Editors' note: the king responded to calls to intervene after an election boycott in April 2006 by calling on the judiciary to determine whether the election was democratic.

identity' of being 'good, intelligent and noble people' as a source of judicial political power. This Thai judicial identity has been constructed and
reproduced over several decades.[3] This article adds to these explanations by
noting that cultural heritage, which is to say the culture of political thinking
of the middle class, provides a fertile foundation for the construction and
modification of the various political meanings that led to the rapid rise and
legitimacy of 'Thai-style judicialisation'.

THE CULTURE OF POLITICAL THINKING
OF THE THAI MIDDLE CLASS

The source of the culture of political thinking of the Thai middle class can be
found in the knowledge and meanings of Thai politics and Thai government
that have been constructed by mainstream Thai intellectuals.[4] The essence
of such ideas is based on deference to leaders who are 'good persons'. Being
'a good person' means one must be a moral person or be steadfast in the
ten virtues of righteous kingship, especially those virtues regarding intellect
and having compassion towards the people. Such thinking simultaneously
holds that the majority of Thai people are uneducated and incapable of
reasoning in an election or in political participation. Therefore, the Thai
people should accept the existing social stratification and perform their
duties without claiming any rights. The legitimacy of such leaders is partly
based on the concept of *anekchonnikon samosonsommut* or *mahachonnikon
samosonsommut*, which provide for an elected ruler.[5] This concept has
persisted even after the revolution of 1932, because certain groups of the
Thai elite[6] who had active roles during the transitional period hoped that a
recognition of some links between the old and the new systems of government would facilitate compromise and acceptance of the new system by all
parties.[7] It was also hoped that people would prefer gradual changes over

---

3   See Kritpatchara Somanawat, อำนาจแห่ง อัตลักษณ์' ตุลาการ [Power of the Judiciary's Identity]
    นิติสังคมศาสตร์ [Nithisangkhomsat], 7, 1, 2014.

4   See Saichon Sattayanurak, 10 ปัญญาชนสยาม เล่ม 1 และ 2 [Siamese Intellectuals, volumes 1
    and 2] Bangkok: Open Books Press, 2015.

5   These words are the suffixes of the official titles of King inscribed on the Royal Golden
    Plaques of King Rama IV and Rama V, respectively.

6   For example, Phraya Manopakon Nitithada and Phraya Sriwisarnwaja. See Somchai, *Debates
    on the Monarchy*, 15–18.

7   Beside referring to the principle of 'Elected Kingship' intellectuals such as Prince Naradhip
    Bongsprabandh (Prince Wan) also included the concept of 'Dhammaraja' in the royal
    designation of King Vajiravudh, adding the word 'Nittidhammikarajathiraj' in hopes that the

root and branch changes that would end in bloodshed, as in the cases of the French and Russian revolutions.[8]

Although after the revolution of 1932 the government of the new system emphasised 'public opinion', such 'public opinion' was not to come from existing people who had freedom of thought. The government adopted the *manutsapathiwat* (human revolution) policy with the goal of altering the citizen's mind and body through the practice of governmentality, so that the national leaders themselves become 'the public opinion whose words and conducts will be emulated by the people'.[9] This definition of 'public opinion' envisaged a system of government in which people could participate, or in which there was a system of checks and balances over the exercise of power by rulers.

The Thai middle class expanded significantly in the 1950s and 1960s, and the idea of 'electing a good person to rule' or 'electing a leader who is a good person' gained ground. The middle class placed their hopes on being able to rely on the virtues of a ruler to regulate political leaders as they themselves had neither the 'power' nor the 'influence' to do so. Their 'elected representatives' were also ineffectual in keeping the government in check, while freedom of the press had long evaporated. The middle class would endeavour to fight against dictatorship with the idea that if rulers 'are not a good person' there should be an election to replace them. The alternative was to *phueng phrabarami* (rely on the king's virtuous prestige) to obtain 'a royally appointed prime minister' from the king.[10] The middle class has been highly successful in this respect, as evident from the protest to restore

---

King would consent to rule as a constitutional monarch. [*Nitti* adds the connotation of law to the concept of a righteous king].

8 On the preference for gradual change in the Traditionalist School of Thought see Nakharin, 'Political Discourse on Thai Democracy'.

9 See Saichon Sattayanurak, มติมหาชน: ฐานทางความคิดของระบอบประชาธิปไตยในยุคเชื่อผู้นำ ชาติพันภัยสายชล สัตยานุรักษ์, [Public Opinion: The ideational Basis of the Thai Democracy in the Age of 'Believe the Leader, Keep the Nation Safe', in Sirilack Sampatchalit, Siripon Yotkamolsat (eds), คือความภูมิใจ: รวมบทความวิชาการในวาระครบรอบ 60 ปี ศาสตราจารย์ ดร. ฉัตร ทิพย์ นาถสุภา เกษียณอายุราชการ [With Pride: Collected Articles to Commemorate Professor Chatthip Nartsupa's Retirement], Bangkok: Sarngsan, 2002.

10 Editors' note: *Barami* has been variously translated as charisma, prestige, perfection, all of which are held to rise from an individual's past and present attainment of moral virtues and the associated aura, or prestige, that attaches to that person. Jory's *Thailand's Theory of Monarchy* (pp.34–38) offers an extended discussion of a surprisingly underexplored concept even in the Thai non-religious literature. A possible translation of *phueng phrabarami* would be 'rely on the royal moral perfections.' We have opted for 'rely on the king's virtuous prestige', an imperfect but serviceable translation that binds karmic merit with public affect.

a constitution that led to the 14 October 1973 Event, the fight against the extended hold of power by a non-elected prime minister in 1988 and the march against the government of General Suchinda Kraprayoon in 1992.

Some decades later, the middle class was protesting against the holding of elections. The Thai Rak Thai party of Thaksin Shinawatra absorbed three medium-sized political parties and went on to a landslide victory in the 2005 election. A political crisis unfolded. In the election the opposition garnered only 175 seats in a house of 500, which disallowed it from proposing no-confidence motions against the prime minister.[11] Opposition to proposed early elections in 2006 led to the restoration of the idea that Western or electoral democracy is not suitable for Thai society because villagers are uneducated and susceptible to being 'bought' or 'deceived' by politicians. It was believed that to hold an election under these circumstances enabled powerful political business interest groups to monopolise political power and unscrupulously reap benefits at an unprecedented scale.[12]

Regarding the checks and balances between the executive, legislative and judicial branches, the middle class does not expect the parliamentary system to be able to efficiently check the executive branch system because 'politicians are bad and incompetent' and 'political parties are weak'. They understand and realise that in order to retain their impartiality and justice 'the judiciary' should be aloof and should not intervene with the executive or the legislative branches. The political role of the judiciary, according to the middle class's expectation, are to be legal experts, participate in the drafting of the constitution and to judge, under the king's name, cases in which the accused are powerful people.

It can be said that after the 1932 revolution the Thai middle class, who have neither 'power' nor 'influence', have had to rely on the monarchy's 'influence' or *phrabarami* to keep the 'power' of the rulers in check, in accordance with the theory of 'power' and 'influence' that was proposed by Yoshifumi Tamada and Nidhi Eoseewong.[13] At the same time, the middle

---

11 Phaet Phichit (pseudonym), รัฐบาลทักษิณเข้าข่ายระบอบอำนาจนิยมหรือไม่ [Has Thaksin's Government Entered the Camp of Authoritarianism], *Matichon Weekend* 18–24 March 2006, 55. The 1997 Constitution stipulated that a confidence motion against the Prime Minister was allowed only when two-fifths of the 500-member House of Representatives sign the motion request.

12 See the construction of the meanings of these issues proposed by the academics who support judicialisation in later sections.

13 Yoshifumi Tamada, อิทธิพล และ อำนาจ การเมืองไทยเต้นที่ไม่เป็นทางการ ['Influence' and 'Power': The Informal Dimension of Thai Politics] in Amara Phongsapich and Preecha Kuwinpant (eds) ระบบอุปถัมภ์ [The Patronage System], Bangkok: Chulalongkorn University

class also hoped to be able to rely on the judiciary's trial judgments which are conducted under the king's name. They have faith that the monarch will be steadfast in the ten virtues of righteous kingship in all royal conduct, including 'royally-initiated projects'. The royal speeches given on significant occasions, especially during past political crises, not only instilled among the middle class a strong sense of gratitude to the royal benevolence and profound loyalty to the monarchy, but also made the people more confident that the king would effectively oversee and regulate political leaders' exercise of power. The middle class (together with the groups of Sino-Thai capitalists who were deeply concerned about their station in the new 'Thai nation' and about the high costs of business or 'economic rent' that they had to pay to those in power) dedicated themselves to royal powers and supported the construction of royal hegemony, enabling them always to call on *phrabarami*. Given that a military or political party leader's supreme loyalty to the king as head of state is essential to their acceptance of being under the king's supervision, the middle class has been very particular about the 'loyalty' that leaders have for the king.

Furthermore, this idea has historic roots in the pre–1932 period. Nidhi noted that as 'the middle class believed it had a certain level of control over absolutist power through the legal means of commercial and criminal laws',[14] they gave importance to the judiciary's qualifications of being 'a good person' and possessing the virtue of loyalty to the king. The Thai middle class and the Thai judiciary share similar social and political outlooks and values, which have been cultivated under the same culture of thinking. For this reason, together with the judiciary's unique identity, which resonates with Thailand's powerful national culture, the middle class has more confidence in the judiciary than in any other state organ.[15] The

---

Press, 2000. Nidhi Eoseewong applied Yoshifumi Tamada's concepts of 'influence' and 'power' to his analysis of the Thai cultural constitution. Although Nidhi did not touch on the monarchy's 'influence', he argued that 'Thais may not give much thought to the controlling of 'power' from the legal mechanism and civil right perspectives, they tend to focus more on the use of 'influence' to control 'power' and how to use superior 'influence' to counter the hostile 'influence' against them'. See Nidhi, 'The Thai Cultural Constitution', 159, 163.

14 Nidhi Eoseewong วัฒนธรรมทางการเมืองไทย, [Thai Political Culture], วารสารสถาบันวัฒนธรรม และศิลปะ [Culture and Art Institute Journal, Srinakharinwirot University], 12, 2, 2011, 59.

15 King Prajadhipok's Institute surveyed public attitudes towards the Thai judiciary. In 2001, 73.4% of the respondents had confidence in the Courts of Justice. The confidence level increased to 86.7% in 2004 (75% in 2002 and 83.2% in 2003). See Pattama Supkampang, สถาบันตุลาการไทย [The Thai Judiciary]. Assessed 2 March 2016, wiki.kpi.ac.th//index..php ?title=สถาบันตุลาการไทย.

emerging political role of the judiciary is thus readily welcomed by the middle class, especially when it is widely known that such a role and related power were instigated by the royal addresses. This also helped to deepen the middle class's trust in the judiciary.

It should be mentioned that reliance on the *phrabarami* of the institution of monarchy in political struggle appeared in the late 1940s, when 'the royalist group' opposed General Phibun Songkhram's government. The royalist group had drafted a constitution in 1949 in which 'Article 59' stated that 'the military forces belong to the country and are under the supreme command of the king. They are not subservient to any private individual, group of persons or political party.'[16] In 1953, as Field Marshal Sarit Thanarat started to detach himself from Phibun's government (before becoming the Royal Thai Army's commander in chief), he organised the first 'pledge of allegiance ceremony and military parade of the royal guard units'.[17]

To maintain their power and the notion that their duties are performed in the name of the king, the judiciary also relies on the king's *phrabarami*. Nidhi Eoseewong noted that, 'after 24 June 1932 … power was transferred to either elected politicians or leaders who came to power through military might. Since then, the judiciary has tried to win freedom (and succeeded) from the executive branch of power and is the only branch of power that has been able to preserve the 'sacredness' of their positions. Nevertheless, the sacredness of the judiciary continued to be tied to the monarchy, as in the time of the absolute monarchy.'[18]

Reliance on *phrabarami* has also been exploited by students and scholars to oppose military dictatorships on several occasions. Apart from the 14 October 1973 Event, in 1988, 99 academics sent a letter 'requesting an opportunity to inform His Majesty the King' on matters of 'current political

---

16 See the 1949 constitution.

17 Field Marshal Sarit Thanarat used to be the commander of the important First Infantry Division that guarded the king. In 1950, he was appointed Chief Commander of the 1st Region Army. On 1 November 1953, the first 'pledge of allegiance to the king ceremony and military parade of the royal guard units' were held to celebrate the anniversary of the establishment of the First Infantry Division King's Guards. This is responsible for the safeguarding and honouring of His Majesty the King and members of the royal family. The pledge of allegiance ceremony and the royal guard's military parade were suspended between 1954–60. It was restored to celebrate the King's birthday anniversary in 1961 and has been held annually to the present day.

18 Nidhi Eoseewong, พิพากษ์ศาลศาลเจ้า [Judging the Judiciary], Bangkok: Matichon, 2012, 19–21.

chaos', stating 'the country needs to have a transition to parliamentary-style Democracy with the King as Head of State.' This was an act of relying on *phrabarami*, with the goal of requesting that an elected prime minister replace General Prem Tinsulanonda.[19] When the 1992 'May Massacre' took place, the media and the public intellectuals also depended on *phrabarami* to appeal to the king to dissolve the parliament and appoint a 'neutral', 'royally appointed' prime minister. They petitioned the king to appoint a 'mirror assembly', which relied on royal power to establish a national assembly to assist parliament. The media and public intellectuals called for the dedication of royal power to the cause of 'political reform.' They proposed that monarchy take part in selecting leaders to prevent parliament from determining the course of events. The ideas that the printed media and the public intellectuals proposed to the public during this period had three distinctive messages: 'the monarchy can better represent the people's will than can elected politicians … the monarchy is better than politicians in leading and determining important social agendas and … a proposal that there should be increased royal power in the constitution.' They also suggested that the power of politicians should be limited.[20]

During the political crisis of 1992, a group of 42 academics (such as Prawet Wasi, Thirayut Bunmi, Charnvit Kasetsiri, Somkid Lertpaitoon, Surapol Nitikraipoj, etc.) 'petitioned' the king in the form of a 'Petition of Opinion on the National Situation' sent to the Secretary General, Bureau of the Royal Household. The letter was based on the culture of thinking of the middle class and thus reiterated the importance of the monitoring of corrupt practices and the notion that 'a good person' must have no desire for 'power.'[21] For example, the petition accused military leaders of breaking their promises to address the problem of corruption and not to assume the prime-ministership. It also stated that the Thai people were misled into participating in an election to legitimise the military government.[22] This

19 Cited in Thanaphol Ewsakul, เสาหลักทางจริยธรรมชื่อเปรม [The Pillar of Ethics Called Prem], ฟ้าเดียวกัน [Same Sky] 4, 1 2006, 110.

20 Kittisak Sujittarom, ทัศนะของสื่อหนังสือพิมพ์และปัญญาชนสาธารณะที่มีต่อสถานะและบทบาทของสถาบันกษัตริย์ ระหว่าง พ.ศ. 2535–2540 [The Views of Newspapers and Public Intellectuals on the Status and Role of the Monarchy between 1992 and 1997] M.A. thesis in History, Faculty of Liberal Arts, Thammasat University, 2014.

21 See Saichon Sattayanurak, คึกฤทธิ์กับประดิษฐกรรม 'ความเป็นไทย' เล่ม 2 [Kukrit and the Invention of 'Thainess', vol. 2], Bangkok: Matichon, 2007, 47.

22 Kittisak, 'The Views of Newspapers and Public Intellectuals on the Status and Role of the Monarchy', 69.

'petition to the king' indicated that 'the monarchy is the only institution that can unify all people in the nation and the only institution capable of settling the present crisis ... The monarchy has the royal power, under the traditional constitution of Democracy with the King as Head of State to advise and admonish the government. One possible solution is for the king to give royal advice to the prime minister to dissolve the parliament and hold a new election.'[23]

Several liberal academics have also remarked on the importance of the practice of relying on *phrabarami*. For example, Nidhi Eoseewong wrote in one of his articles that, 'Without the *phrabarami* of His Majesty the King it is uncertain how this brutal massacre would have ended'.[24] Charnvit Kasetsiri stated, 'We think the monarchy is the only institution capable of resolving the situation so we put our names to this petition to appeal for his royal benevolence in this matter.'[25]

The vast group of middle-class Thais of Chinese descent strongly sub-scribe to the aforementioned cultural thinking, and also want to ensure that the political leaders' power and influence are kept in check in relation to the excessive 'economic rent' imposed on them. A historical awareness that unites this group with the monarchy has emerged since the late 1960s. A large num-ber of literary works, family chronicles and memoirs have appeared under the theme of the 'one-pillow-one-mat migrant Chinese' prospering under the 'royal benevolence'. In the eyes of these middle-class Chinese, 'democracy' must be under royal protection (*pokklao pokkramon*) and with the King as Head of State,[26] so that they could continue to rely on *phrabarami*.

The middle class's culture of thinking and the meanings that they have ascribed to various institutions are closely related to the evolution of ideas regarding 'Thai-style government' and 'Thai-style democracy' that gave birth to the meaning of the Democracy with the King as Head of State. Detailed analyses of the construction of the ideas and meanings of different systems of government are crucial to understanding the reproduction and

---

23 *Ibid.,* 68–69.

24 Nidhi Eoseewong, มโนธรรมของชนชั้นนำทางอำนาจ [The Power Elite's Conscience], ผู้จัดการ รายวัน [Manager Daily], 27 November 1992; See also Kittisak, 'The Views of Newspapers and Public Intellectuals on the Status and Role of the Monarchy', 6.

25 *Ibid.,* 72.

26 Sittithep Eaksittipong, ลูกจีนรักชาติ: สำนึกประวัติศาสตร์และนิยามประชาธิปไตย [Patriotic 'luk-jin': Historical Awareness and Definitions of Democracy], วารสารมนุษยศาสตร์ [Manusayasat Journal], 16, 2, 2015, 112–156.

modification of the meanings of Thai politics and government. They will also shed some light on the dynamic influence of this culture of thinking on the emergence in 2006 of the 'judicialisation' movement, especially to its crucial role in the power contestation with major political business groups who are defined by the middle class as representing 'immoral and unethical capitalism' and who deceive the rural mass into becoming pawns in their quest for political power.

THE ESTABLISHMENT OF IDEAS ON 'THAI-STYLE GOVERNMENT' AND 'THAI-STYLE DEMOCRACY' IN THE DECADE AFTER 1957

The emergence and evolution of ideas about 'Thai-style government' and 'Thai-style democracy'[27] ran parallel to the reproduction of meanings surrounding the 'people', 'politician' and 'political party' to show that 'Western-style democracy is not suitable for Thai society', and therefore would have adverse impacts on Thailand. The meanings of these words which had been constructed since the time of the absolute monarchy were constantly reproduced from the late 1940s onwards. The emphases have shifted and modified to suit the changing political contexts of each period, and has become a political discourse that argues that 'Western democracy and electoral democracy are not suitable for Thai society' and 'Thailand should have its own Thai-style government, namely, Democracy with the King as Head of State'. This, in order that the people may rely on *phrabarami* in all matters especially in the regulating of rulers or in appointing 'a good person (*khondi*)' to be prime minister.

The origin of the notion of a suitable system of government for Siam, which later became the key foundation of the middle class's culture of political thinking, may be traced to the early Rattanakosin period when King Mongkut disseminated the words of the Stone Inscription No. 1. This inscription indicates a system of government under kings or 'Phor Khun'

---

27 The phrase 'Thai-style government' was used by M.R. Kukrit Pramoj to dispute the phrase 'Thai-style democracy' that the government used in the 1960s. It should also be noted that the post-World War II international movements together with the rapid expansion of the Thai middle class who demanded an election made it impossible for the government to reject 'democracy'. In addition, the demand to have the monarchy appoint a Prime Minister to give military leaders political legitimacy led to the use of the phrase 'Thai-style democracy' (See details in the previous section)

who kept their subjects happy and peaceful under the paternalistic system. Kings relied on Buddhist teachings in their administration and fair judgment in a trial. They sanctioned private ownership and made 'Sukhothai good' (or 'Thailand good').[28] The book *Nana Dharmawijanrini* (นานาธรรมวิจาริณี) composed by King Mongkut, outlined the desired qualities of a 'phramahasommutiraj' (elected monarch) as a person who 'possesses great intellect, industry, perseverance, compassion for equal happiness to all people and absolute dedication to justice'. The book also states that 'such justice, power, knowledge and intellect of a person of great integrity and compassion for all people will certainly bring righteous thoughts'.[29] These statements reflect the importance that King Mongkut gave to a ruler's intellect and morality in facilitating 'justice' (which means righteousness).

As an absolutist state arose during the reign of King Chulalongkorn, the notion of a suitable system of government for Thai society was distilled in 'the Royal Explanation on Unity'. An excerpt from this writing states that,

> The people are likely to believe more in a monarch than in members of the parliament because at present they generally trust a monarch to be a just person who, more than anyone else, loves his subjects and wants to bring them happiness ... to cheerfully adopt the ideas of those who work for the governments of European countries ... to Thailand is completely inappropriate since they come from a different background. This is like copying and applying a manual on wheat growing in Europe to rice growing in Thailand ... If political parties are to be formed ... there will be nine to ten members per party ... but there will be hundreds of other people who still cling to the old ways of doing things. Members of two or three political parties will be scornful of the hundreds of people stuck in the old ways ... because the latter have neither knowledge nor capital ... Within the political parties ... there will be opposition cliques ... These will only bring disputes and fighting which will be of no benefit at all.[30]

King Chulalongkorn also reiterated that, 'People in Thailand used to be united in thought which is to accept the ideas of the king ... This is be-

---

28 Corpus of the Sukhothai Stone Inscriptions.

29 See Thanet Arpornsuwan, กำเนิดการเมืองและความยุติธรรม [The Birth of Politics and Justice], in ไพร่กระฎุมพีแห่งกรุงรัตนโกสินทร์ [The Dependent Bourgeoisie of Rattanakosin], Bangkok: Matichon, 2006,106–8.

30 King Chulalongkorn, พระบรมราชาธิบายว่าด้วยความสามัคคี [The Royal Explanation on Unity], in ประวัติศาสตร์และการเมือง [History and Politics], Bangkok: Thammasat University Press, 1973,169–76.

cause the king's initiatives are generally justified as they are based on the royal compassion that the king has for his people. The people also gladly welcome the royal benevolence. The king is trusted by all.'[31] This remark of King Chulalongkorn has been reproduced in many forms including in the construction of meaning surrounding the title Somdet Phra Piyamaharat [the loved king] through a monument and a variety of rituals. When combined with the cultural heritage that has been passed down from ancient times, the monarchy is of such extreme importance in the Thai state that the revolutionary People's Party could not abolish it.

After the revolution of 1932, there have been constant arguments on whether Thailand should adopt the Western style of government or not, whether most Thais are ready for the electoral and parliamentary systems or not and arguments on the pros and cons of the parliamentary system for Thai society. Regarding the monarchy, in the first fifteen years after the revolution the political significance and role of the monarchy had greatly diminished, as seen from the debates and resolutions of the Constitutional Drafting Committees and the House of Representatives between 1932 and 1946 in which the mainstream view was to be steadfast to the principle of 'all sovereign power belongs to the people'. Even Phraya Monopakorn Nitithada [Thailand's first prime minister after the 1932 revolution] confirmed that 'sovereign power ... derives from the nation, which is a collection of people ... the king who is the head of state exercises such power ... he cannot use the sovereign power at will but has to use it as stipulated by provisions of the constitution.'[32] As for the argument about the use of royal power to veto the legislative drafts that have been approved by the parliament, parliament failed to approve such royal power in 1934 and again in 1946. Instead, parliament confirmed its adherence to the principle that the 'supreme power' is vested in a parliament elected by the people.[33]

After World War II, the monarchy's political power and status would rise with the People's Party loss of power following the 1947 military takeover. Thinkers, writers, journalists, civil servants and the middle class, who suffered during the aftermath of World War II and witnessed the power contestation among and the abuse of power by the elite in the new political system, were of the opinion that 'democracy' had degraded Thai society. At the

31 Ibid., 179.

32 Somchai, *Debates on the Monarchy*, 15–18.

33 Ibid., 90–97.

same time, the meaning of 'Thainess' in relation to government was hailed by the 'royalist' group who opposed the government established by the 1947 coup d'état. The royalists revived and advocated the existing concepts 'Dharmaraja' and 'paternal rule' with modified emphases and meanings to suit the changing political contexts. The idea of Thai 'democracy' with 'the king as the head of state' was eventually included in the 1949 constitution and the royal power in certain key issues, such as the power to appoint members of the Senate, was approved by the parliament. M.R. Seni Pramoj cited the reasons for these moves as follows: 'the constitutional monarchy is the most effective means that we can use to prevent dictatorship. As long as the supreme power remains with the monarchy we will be safe from the clutch of people with excessive political ambition, they will not have a desire to become a dictator'.[34] This notion had been forcefully expanded and reproduced through convincing arguments and concrete examples in conjunction with the construction of the meaning regarding 'Thainess' that centre around the monarchy and Buddhist teachings.[35] These ideas became prevalent and later had a profound impact on the cultural thinking of the Thai middle class. At the same time, the argument that 'Western democracy is not suitable for Thai society' had been strongly reiterated together with the argument that 'there are very few people with sufficient knowledge and preparedness for self-government'. This argument is in the same league as the argument that 'politicians are corrupt and political parties are low in quality and incompetent' which had been tenaciously constructed and reproduced from the decade of 1957 onwards. Even Kulab Saipradit [a progressive humanist] wrote in an article published on 16 May 1947 that,

> There are low levels of educational attainment and attention to the idea of self-government ... these are not promising signs for democracy ... We have witnessed increasing acts of dishonesty, mental decline, suspicion and distrust among the people. We will eventually see political instability, despicable and untrustworthy behaviour among larger number of politicians as well as serious breaches among political parties and indistinguishable party policies.[36]

---

34 Translated and cited in Kasian Tejapira, ระบอบประชาธิปไตยอันมีพระมหากษัตริย์ทรงเป็นประมุข [Democracy with the King as Head of State], in ฟ้าเดียวกัน [Same Sky] 9, 1, 2011, 97.

35 See Saichon, *Kukrit and the Invention of 'Thainess'* Vol. 2.

36 Kulab Saipradit, เสถียรภาพทางการเมือง [Political Stability], in Suchat Sawatsri (ed.), มนุษย์ไม่ได้กินแกลบ [Humans are not Stupid], Bangkok: The organizing committee of the centennial of Sriburapa, 2005, 171.

The reproduction of notions regarding the 'importance of having leaders who are a good person' and the 'naivety of the people' advanced the idea of bad politicians and incompetent political parties. M.R. Kukrit Pramoj asserted that 'when politicians have political power they will use it to enhance their status in every way'.[37] He also showed admiration for Field Marshal Sarit Thanarat by stating that 'there are still good people'[38] and emphasised that the general population 'are not aware of their duties ... naïve to the goings on in the world ... irresponsible ... live in remote areas ... poor ... have no interests to protect, no hope in life, no education, lack sophistication ... do not know what they want'.[39] Apart from showing the advantages of a dictator who is 'a good person', Kukrit also pointed out that a system of government based on the concept of 'the power belongs to the people' might lead to 'bloodshed' as in the case of 'Hitler's rise to power which undeniably happened through genuinely democratic means'.[40]

Several writers, journalists and intellectuals have been involved in the construction of the above-mentioned ideas and meanings through the genre of political and historical writing between 1946–50. Such works generally displayed a negative attitude toward the 1932 Revolution, and attacked politicians and praised dictatorial leaders.[41] One author said of Field Marshal Sarit Thanarat that, 'there is nothing strange if the goal of dictatorial rule is for the good of the people ... it is better than cronyism in the guise of democracy that is designed to deceive the fools'.[42] This writer went on to attack politicians by stating that '[Phibun's] Seri Manangkhasila Party used its massive influence and financial backup ... bought over three out of four elected representatives to switch to the government's party and to vote for the government on all issues ... They were nicknamed 'pea-pods' by the people, being representatives who raise their hands up to cast votes

---

37 Kukrit Pramoj, ยิว [Jews], 284 cited in Saichon, *Kukrit and the Invention of "Thainess"* Vol. 2, 69.

38 Kukrit Pramoj, ตอบปัญหาประจำวัน [Answers to Problems], สยามรัฐรายวัน [Siamrat Daily] 5 March 1957, cited in Saichon, *Kukrit and the Invention of "Thainess"*, 70–71.

39 cited in Saichon, *Kukrit and the Invention of "Thainess"* Vol. 2, 73.

40 Kukrit Pramoj, ประชาธิปไตยกับเสรีภาพ [Democracy and Freedom], cited in Saichon, *Kukrit and the Invention of "Thainess"* Vol. 2, 68.

41 Sombat Chantornvong, ภาษาทางการเมือง [Political Language], Bangkok: Institute of Thai Studies, Thammasat University, 1990, 97–230.

42 Sawang Lanluea, 37 ปี แห่งการปฏิวัติ [37 Years of the Revolution], Bangkok: np., 1969, 461, cited in Sombat, *Political Language*, 228–229.

as told'.[43] These ideas and meanings were repeatedly reproduced in the following period and are widely acknowledged and circulated to this day.

THE CONSTRUCTION OF THE MEANING OF 'THAI-STYLE GOVERNMENT'

The precise meaning of 'Democracy with the King as Head of State' is partly attributed to the construction of the meaning of the 'Thai-style government' by M. R. Kukrit Pramoj who constantly educated the public on this subject, and which he explicated from the time that he first wrote his famous novel, *Si Phaendin* (Four Reigns) in 1951 and 1952. This novel presented the absolute monarchy in Thailand as the period of peace, order, stability and progress. Kukrit subsequently went on to suggest that although the supreme power under this system is vested entirely in a single leader, a good society can exist with a monarch who strictly observed the ten virtues of righteous kingship, who takes good care of his subjects and makes sure that there is justice for all and 'enables the people to live together in happiness'. Towards the end of the 1960s when there was a political contest between the government of Field Marshal Thanom Kittikachorn (who had firm control power) and the conservative-royalist faction which was gaining strength, M.R. Kukrit Pramoj reiterated the fact that the king was the spiritual centre of the people and 'the throne is an obstacle to power'. He also suggested that 'Thailand has always used its 'social head' or the monarchy to restrain injustice and any mistakes that may occur ... This is the principle that Thais have always upheld'.[44] M.R. Kukrit Pramoj had also identified the people's rights that came from the fact that the king 'is one and the same with his people'. This allows 'people ... to have the right to petition the king on all matters. This right of the people has never left the people and is the most important'. The king has, therefore, become the genuine 'benefactor' that the people can rely upon at all times.[45] This idea provides the foundation for people's consent to the royal powers of the king in the monitoring and regulating of national leaders or government. It also allows the people to petition the king to rely on his *phrabarami* which occurs frequently in times of political struggle.

---

43 *Ibid.,* 227.

44 Kukrit Pramoj, ในหลวงของประชาชน [The People's King], cited in Sala Likhitkul, ในหลวงกับ คึกฤทธิ์ [The King and Kukrit], Bangkok: Sappasat, 2003, 103–4.

45 Saichon, *Kukrit and the Invention of "Thainess" Vol.2,* 39–52, 221, 306.

THE CONSTRUCTION OF THE MEANING OF 'THAI-STYLE DEMOCRACY'

The meaning of 'Thai-style Democracy' has been systematically disseminated through newspaper articles and reproduced on the 'Song Soon Radio Station Broadcasting' between 1964–65. The essence of these messages was that Thailand should be ruled under a 'Thai-style democracy'. These articles argued that by drawing on the ideational heritage, old ideas could be modified and revitalised and turned into the ideational basis that the middle class could always use to understand Thai politics.

Another explanation was taken from the idea that 'Western democracy is not suitable for Thai society'. Since its introduction in 1932 democracy had caused so many problems in connection with the parliament, political parties and elections; all of which had resulted in serious schisms within the country.[46] At the same time, the evil of politicians and political parties continue to be reiterated through descriptions of politicians as ' ... winning the election through vote buying, bribing voters with food and drink or using personal connection rather than winning by political knowledge or ideologies ... parliamentary power should be restricted to prevent them from becoming too powerful'.[47] While political parties are repeatedly blamed because 'they do not really have shared obligations or discipline under the party system. This allows the government ... to buy votes from parliamentary members, many of which exploited the government financially. These troublesome conducts resulted in the never-ending coups d'état'.[48] There was also an emphasis on the idea that 'the majority of the population do not have much interest in national matters. They lack the education and the discipline to come together as a political party'. It is, therefore, appropriate to 'restrict the parliamentary power'.[49]

Some articles reiterated that the failure of Thai democracy from 1932 onwards could be attributed to corrupt representatives who tended to

---

46 This explanation was used by Field Marshal Sarit Thanarat. ประมวลสุนทรพจน์ของจอมพล สฤษดิ์ ธนะรัชต์: พ.ศ. 2502–2504 Collection of Field Marshal Sarit Thanarat's Speeches 1959–61], Phranakhon: Office of the Prime Minister, 1964. See his 'National Day Speech Given on 24 June 1959 in this collection, 16.

47 Song Soon Radio Station Broadcasting, ประชาธิปไตยแบบไทยและข้อคิดเกี่ยวกับรัฐธรรมนูญ [Thai-style Democracy and Opinions on the Constitution], 1965, 228–30.

48 *Ibid.,* p. 217.

49 *Ibid.,* p. 212–19.

obtain benefits for themselves, and that the electoral system could result in a dictatorship.[50] These arguments concluded with 'it is fitting ... to give more power to the executive branch and make the election less important because the cabinet is not an elected one'.[51] On the issue of the head of the state, several articles stressed that 'Thai kings are put in their position under the principle of '*anakenikorn samosornsommut*' (by popular consent) and rule according to the ten virtues of righteous kingship, and the latent democratic characteristics of their royal attributes and royal conducts earn them the people's deep respect ... kings are the heart and soul of the national unity ... therefore, it is most essential for Thailand to have a king as the head of state and Thai democracy must keep the throne secure at all costs'.[52] And 'when we decide to establish a specifically Thai-style democracy we must take the monarchy into consideration. The European constitutional monarchy where kings sit on the throne but does not rule does not apply to our kind of democracy. The Thai-style democracy must glorify the monarchy and dedicate itself to the royal power to allow the king some part in ruling the country and the citizens'.[53] The objective in stressing the unique characteristics of the Thai monarchy is clearly indicated in an article which stated that the President of the Constitutional Drafting Committee revealed that 'the present draft of the constitution stipulates that the king shall appoint the prime minister'.[54]

In addition, the concept of 'Thai-style democracy' was linked to the country's economic development. For example, it asserted that 'the creation of economic democracy ... is not based on the old liberal model in which the economy was left to grow on its own. But it will be based on the new liberal model where there is planned progress according to proper academic principles and in keeping with the real circumstances.'. It also stressed that 'Thai-style democracy' in which the executive branch has more power than the parliament will create the political stability that allows for efficient economic development.[55] This notion is most appealing to the Thai middle class.

The ideas of 'Thai-style government' and 'Thai-style democracy' became highly influential at later periods (despite the differences of their fun-

---

50 *Ibid.*, pp. 29–33.
51 *Ibid.*, pp. 94–5.
52 *Ibid.*, pp. 91–3.
53 *Ibid.*, pp. 195–6.
54 *Ibid.*, pp. 221–2.
55 *Ibid.*, 86.

damental ideologies and political goals).[56] Both ideas provide legitimacy to the government leaders who did not come from an election. It also leads Thai society to recognise the importance of political stability and national unity while accepting certain restrictions on the rights and liberty of the people. More importantly, the justification and meanings provided by these ideas to confirm the need to adopt the 'Thai-style democracy' have become integral to minimizing the importance of electoral democracy.

The idea that the monarchy has the royal power to appoint a prime minister has never been stipulated in any version of the Thai constitution, and the Thai middle class wants a 'royally-appointed prime minister' in times of political crisis only. His Majesty the King has been very cautious in exercising the royal power in Thailand's increasingly complex political context. After the 14 October Event, it should be noted that a majority in the National Legislative Assembly supported increasing royal powers in the new constitution by allowing the President of the Privy Council to countersign the appointment of an unelected senate, but his Majesty the King objected to the idea. The royal objection was given on the basis that since it was the king who appointed the president of the king's privy council, the proposed royal power provisions conflicted with the principle that the king is above the politics. In approving such a provision, the status of the president of the king's privy council would be equivalent to a political organization, and this was clearly contradictory to Article 17 of the 1974 constitution.[57] Later on, His Majesty the King mentioned to M.R. Thongnoi Thongyai to 'keep in mind that the monarchy can fully participate in politics only when a genuine political vacuum has developed … once the vacuum is eliminated, the monarchy must return to be above politics as quickly as possible in order to be able to intervene again when another vacuum appears.'[58]

This royal perspective is consistent with the key principle that the Thai middle class has long observed. They always hope that when a political

---

56 The idea of the 'Thai-style government' was initiated to support the regime of Field Marshal Sarit Thanarat. Its meaning was subsequently expanded to oppose the power of Field Marshal Thanom Kittikachorn's government, while the idea of 'Thai-style of Democracy' aimed to provide political legitimacy to Thanom's government.

57 Thongthong Chansangsu, พระราชอำนาจของพระมหากษัตริย์ในทางกฎหมายรัฐธรรมนูญ [Royal Power in Constitutional Law], Bangkok: SC Print and Pack Co., Ltd., 1994, 110.

58 Cited in Nakharin Mektrairat, พระผู้ทรงปกเกล้าฯ ประชาธิปไตย: 60 ปี สิริราชสมบัติกับการเมืองการปกครองไทย [The Protector of Democracy: 60 Years on the Throne and Thai Politics] Bangkok: Thammasat University Press, 2006, 165, 183–186.

crisis erupts the sovereign would 'step down to solve it' and restore the national order, stability, peace and prosperity, after which 'electoral democracy' would return. At the next political crisis, the middle class will ask 'to rely on the king's *phrabarami* again. This means that if such hope prevails the middle class will forever support and safeguard 'Democracy with the King as Head of State'.

Furthermore, during the time when the student movement and the 'royalists' fought against Field Marshal Thanom Kittikachorn's government, the meaning of Democracy with the King as Head of State was reproduced by several academics who helped amplify the dynamic power of this concept. For example, in 1972 Kramol Thongthammachart asserted that royalism meant worshipping the monarchy as the centre of power in Thai society. It was the means to preserve social order and an ideology to keep Thai society safe from turmoil because it was an 'ism' that emerged locally and was not imported. Having 'a royal head of state as a secure symbol may be compared with having a constant propagator of the ideology'.[59] In his 1974 speech to the National Legislative Assembly, Niphon Sasithorn reiterated that 'pure royal power is of utmost importance … (His Majesty) is the focal point and the centre of morale for all people. He is the most important, the supreme and the last benefactor of all Thais'.[60]

From the late 1970s, 'royal hegemony'[61] and the royalist ideology of the 'National Father' was strong.[62] The reliance on the king's *phrabarami* during the May 1992 Event further increased the king's role in abating political conflict. Therefore, although in 1997 a constitution with an emphasis on sovereignty as well as the rights and liberty of the people was in place, ideologically the middle class continued to put their hope in the idea of relying on *phrabarami*. Apart from the deep shock that they experienced [in 1992], the middle class was still in deep shock from the economic crisis of that decade and were still

---

59 Kramol Thongthammachart, อุดมการกับสังคมไทยในปัจจุบัน [Ideology and Contemporary Thai Society] in Chatthip *Ideology and Thai Society*, 107–16.

60 Somchai, *Debates on the Monarchy*, 49.

61 See Chanida Chidbandit, โครงการอันเนื่องมาจากพระราชดำริ: การสถาปนาพระราชอำนาจนำใน พระบาทสมเด็จพระเจ้าอยู่หัว [The Royal-Initiated Projects: Establishment of His Majesty the King's Hegemony], Bangkok: Foundation for the Promotion of Social Sciences and Humanities Textbooks Projects, 2007.

62 See Attachak Sattayanurak, ประชาธิปไตย คนไทยไม่เท่ากัน [Democracy: Thais are not Equal] Bangkok: Matichon, 2014, and Saichon Sattayanurak, ประวัติศาสตร์รัฐไทยและสังคมไทย [History of the Thai State and Thai Society], Chiang Mai: Chiang Mai University Press, 2015, 255–84.

distrustful of politicians' morality. It could be seen that politicians of the period still relied on their political vote canvassers who were mostly people of influence such as *kamnan* (district leaders), *phuyaiban* (village leaders), teachers, landowners and ruffians. Politicians created networks of relationship with these people and resorted to buying allegiance of political canvassers, threatening or killing political opponents and their political canvassers.[63] The middle class was very weak politically at that time because historically they had been accustomed to and satisfied with the windfalls from previous national development policies. In earlier periods the middle class had to conduct their business and earn their living under the dictatorial rule that they had no control over. The lack of press freedom denied the middle class the rights and opportunity to access news and information that would have allowed them to check the government's power. Under such circumstances, the middle class was accustomed to solving their problems by 'relying' on people of influence in various circles. They had not accumulated much experience in organizing political movements or using political institutions as a bargaining power. Even under the electoral politics of subsequent periods, the middle class was unable to join forces into block votes, either as in their capacity as an interest group or as a political party.[64] The middle class was, at the same time, subject to the hegemony of the mainstream meanings surrounding the 'Thai nation' and 'Thainess'. Explanations of the middle class's problems and 'alternatives' had, therefore, been constructed under the forceful power of the mainstream ways of thinking, which have become the principal limitations for the middle class's search for novel ideas and alternatives. Consequently, the practice of relying on *phrabarami* as well as a reliance on royal initiatives and royal speeches had tacitly become the most important choice for the middle class.

THE REPRODUCTION OF IDEAS AND MEANINGS IN THE PERIOD 1997–2007

Beginning in the early 20th Century whenever a political conflict becomes critical the mass media and academics will actively revive and reproduce the older political concepts. For example, the *Manager Newspaper* and many key anti-Thaksin scholars such as Chai-anan Samudavanija, Thirayut Bunmi

---

63 Tamada, '"Influence" and "Power"', 329–30.
64 *Ibid.*, and Nidhi, 'The Thai Cultural Constitution', 125–55.

and Sombat Thamrongthanyawong were involved in intensifying particular ideas that were circulating in Thai society. The key ideas and meanings that these academics reproduced in their fight against the Thaksin regime, and which played a significant role in inducing the middle class to accept the concept of judicialisation, will now be discussed.

1. The Idea and Meaning of 'Western Democracy is not Suitable for Thai Society'

The idea that 'Western democracy is not suitable for Thai society' has been reproduced by many scholars. As for the claim that 'Thai politicians are corrupt', this conveys the notion that most politicians are immoral or unethical, and vote buy both directly and indirectly through the introduction of populist policies. Moreover, the claim of 'corrupt political parties' conveys the idea that politicians become the party bosses in order to seek infinite benefits for themselves and that they plan to have a 'long stay' in power to reap benefits. Emphasis is placed on the idea that politicians are of 'low quality and incompetent' while 'the majority of the people are not yet ready for democracy'. Moreover, scholars have analysed the negative impacts of electoral democracy on the 'Thai nation' and the Thai society, such as the rise of parliamentary dictatorship, disunity within the society, crisis of faith in the democratic system, corruption, and government legitimacy crisis, etc. Discussion of these topics constitutes a reproduction of the 'Western democracy is not suitable for Thai society' concept which later became the rationale behind the non-parliamentary political movements and 'judicialisation'.[65]

2. Ideas and Meanings of the 'Thaksin regime' that is dangerous to 'the Thai Nation' and 'the Monarchy'

Scholars who support 'judicialisation' have stoked fear of the 'Thaksin regime' as dangerous to both the Thai nation and the beloved king who is the people's 'last resort'. Academics such as Chai-Anan Samudavanija noted

---

65 Surmised from the draft of a research report on นักวิชาการไทยกับการต่อสู้ช่วงชิงความหมาย 'ประชาธิปไตย'ในภาวะวิกฤตทางการเมืองพ.ศ. 2548–2557 [Thai Academics and the Contest over the Meanings of 'Democracy' in a Time of Political Crisis (2005 – 2014)], project funded by The Office of Thailand Research Fund (ongoing research).

that 'protesters called for the establishment of 'a new Thai state'. Stickers with the words 'Thaksin – President of the new Thai state' were posted in public, which led to the understanding that a 'new Thai state' was likely to be a 'republic'. [66] He recounted how protestors in the name of The United Front for Democracy Against Dictatorship 'adopted urban guerrilla warfare tactics ... and spread negative rumours against the monarchy'.[67] He averred that the 'Palang Prachachon Party [a pro-Thaksin party]was likely to have received advice on such tactics' from 'those who were members of the Communist Party of Thailand' whose approach was 'to try to diminish the influence of this traditional institution to be a symbolic one only'.[68]

Chai-Anan Samudavanija also insinuated that some of the groups who 'burnt down the city and attacked soldiers' were citizens of Myanmar and Cambodia, the old enemies of Thailand. 'There were Burmese writings at the Democracy Monument stating that 'children of King Bayinnaung had come to take revenge on the Thai people.'[69] The former government's special economic zone initiatives were perceived as measures 'to create a state within a state whereby the unified sovereignty of the country will disappear'.[70] Thaksin's sale of his stocks to a Singaporean company was seen as affecting national security.[71] Since the ideas of national unity and unity among the people are the key ideas for the nationalistic ideologies, 'Thaksinomics' has been repeatedly said to have destroyed the previously longstanding settlement in society.[72]

Similarly, Thirayut Bunmi observed that 'some political business groups were into vote buying and provided certain benefits to politicians, civil servants and the grass roots in order to establish an integrated corrupt structure

---

66 Chai-Anan Samudavanija, รัฐไทยใหม่ [The New Thai state], 16 May 2010. Accessed 18 February 2015, www.manager.co.th/Daily/ViewNews.aspx?NewsID=9530000067459.

67 Chai-Anan Samudavanija, ยุติความรุนแรง [Stop the Violence], 10 May 2009. Accessed 18 February 2015, www.manager.co.th/Daily/ViewNews.aspx?NewsID=9520000051996.

68 Chai-Anan Samudavanija, ระบอบพรรคเดียวกับผู้นำมวลชน [The One-Party System and Leaders of the Mass], 20 April 2008). Accessed 18 February 2015, www.manager.co.th/Daily/ViewNews.aspx?NewsID=9510000045967.

69 Chai-Anan Samudavanija, ต้นทุนของประชาธิปไตย [The Costs of Democracy], 25 April 2010. Accessed 18 February 2015, www.manager.co.th/Daily/ViewNews.aspx?NewsID==9510000045967.

70 Chai-Anan Samudavanija, อันตรายแปดอย่างของทักษิณ [The Eight Dangers of Thaksin], 24 March 2006. Accessed 18 February 2015, www.manager.co.th/Daily/ViewNews.aspx?NewsID=9490000040162.

71 Chai-Anan Samudavanija, ราชประชาสมาสัย [King-People Mutuality], 19 March 2006. Accessed 18 February 2015, www.manager.co.th/Daily/ViewNews.aspx?NewsID=9490000037259.

72 Chai-Anan, 'The Eight Dangers of Thaksin'.

of power. Unlimited use of power by these groups has alarmingly threatened the status quo of several traditional institutions that the latter responded with such a forceful reaction that caused deep ruptures throughout the nation's social and political fabric … the rifts have been so severe that certain groups have lost their traditional standing and faith in the system, which may continue to intensify'.[73] He wrote in another article that the political business groups in the 'Thaksin regime' were ready to 'destroy the national interest' and 'sell the country to other countries' with 'no guarantee that they would not sell Thailand to any other country if they could gain sufficiently high benefits'.[74]

The idea of 'bad politicians' was robustly reproduced to instil fear that they used the cloak of electoral democracy for absolute power. For this reason, the middle class was ready to participate in or support political movements against the Thaksin regime. They also supported 'judicialisation' to abolish absolute dictatorship by unethical politicians. It should be noted that from March 2006 Chai-Anan Samudavanija started to talk about the construction of 'an absolute dictatorship' through 'a merging of financial and political power … enabling it to rally the people's support'.[75] He also stressed that the hold on such absolute power enabled these politicians to make unlawful conduct lawful, they also used such power to gain unlimited benefits.[76]

Chai-Anan Samudavanija analysed such development as 'leading to a privatization of the country'.[77] This form of dictatorship was possible for 'when a single party enjoys the majority of votes in the parliament, members of the House of Representatives have no role to play except rubber-stamping

---

73 Thirayuth Bunmi, บทเสนอแนะ การฝ่าวิกฤติการเมืองไทย ที่ตระหนักถึงรากเหง้าแท้จริงของปัญหา [A Suggestion on Getting Through the Thai Political Crisis by Recognizing the True Roots of the Problem], 28 November 2008. Accessed 17 February 2015, www.prachathai.com/journal/2008/11/19132.

74 Thirayut Bunmi, สุดท้ายของระบอบทักษิณ สร้างรากฐานใหม่ให้ประเทศไทย? [Does the End of Thaksinomics Provide a New Foundation for Thailand?], 15 January 2014. Accessed 17 February 2015, thaipublica.org/wp-content/uploads/2014/01/.

75 Chai-Anan, 'The Eight Dangers of Thaksin'.

76 Chai-Anan Samudavanija, การเมืองต้องช่วยแก้ปัญหาสังคม [Politics Must Help Solve Social Problems], 14 January 2007. www.manager.co.th/Daily/ViewNews.aspx?NewsID=9400000004736.

77 Chai-Anan Samudavanija, ทำให้รัฐเป็นกลาง [Make the State Neutral], 31 October 2010. Accessed 18 February.

legislation'.[78] Thus, he argued that eradication of the 'Thaksin Regime' had been increasingly difficult and should be expedited because apart from 'having dominated the legislative branch of power', it was claimed that the Thaksin regime was finding a way to dominate the judicial branch of power ... especially when they have learned that the judicial system is now beginning to take up political roles. It was clear that if Thaksin remained in power, he would definitely take over the judicial system'.[79] The grave concerns of the middle class in this matter drove them towards 'judicialisation'.

Thirayut Bunmi also played a part in inciting the middle class's fear that big capital groups would succeed in acquiring absolute power for a long time and use that power to further corruption. He warned that 'This group of influential capitalists has channelled their financial power into politics and would use nefarious capitalism to gain absolute power for a lengthy period ... corruption rates have reached record highs and many people have lost patience. Nefarious politico-capitalism ... has opportunistically and shamelessly benefitted from government policies, projects and national resources on all fronts'.[80] Sombat Thamrongthanyawong maintained that 'being an elected dictatorship means the leader of the majority political party can dominate the entire parliament'[81] and 'the legislative branch performs only clerical duties for the government ... the government can ultimately control the votes in the parliament. The mechanism of checks and balances by the opposition become meaningless'. Moreover, the 'leader of the majority political party' can 'have the ultimate and absolute control of power both over members of the Thai Rak Thai party and all permanent

---

78 Chai-Anan Samudavanija, ปฏิรูปการเมืองอีกครั้ง [Political Reform Again], 17 September 2006. Accessed 18 February 2015, www.manager.co.th/Daily/ViewNews.aspx?NewsID= 9490000117300.

79 Chai-Anan Samudavanija, จะเกิดอะไรขึ้นในเดือนกรกฎาคม [What Will Happen in July?], 4 June 2006. Accessed 18 February 2015, www.manager.co.th/Daily/ViewNews.aspx ?NewsID=9490000073233.

80 Thirayuth Bunmi, ทบทวนทิศทางประเทศไทย [Reconsidering Thailand's Direction]. A Special Lecture given on the 35th Anniversary of the 14 October, Democracy Commemoration Day, 26 July 2008), Kilawet Building, Bangkok (Thai-Japan) Youth Centre. Accessed 17 February 2015, www.14tula.com/activity/p-2008-teerayut.pdf.

81 สมบัติธำรงธัญวงศ์ ยันเจตนาแก้วงจรอุบาทว์การเมือง [Sombat Thamrongthanyawong Confirms his Intention to Correct the Vicious Political Cycle], 2 March 2011. Accessed 13 February 2015, www.khaosod.co.th/view_news.php?newsid=TUROd2lyd3dNVEF5TURNMU5BPTO%3D.

civilian, police and military officers … because all of them are subservient to the leader of the government.[82]

It should be noted that anti-Thaksin academics who supported 'judicial-isation' and analysed the impact of 'the Thaksin Regime' did so imbued with particular meaning of the 'Thai nation' and 'Thainess'. This allowed them to incite shared feelings among others and powerfully foment a political movement. It weakened the legitimacy of an elected government and paint-ed 'electoral democracy' as a critical national problem.

Academics who support 'judicialisation' also stressed that the normal mechanisms and channels of a democratic system could not effectively eradicate the 'Thaksin regime', and 'there are no alternative measures in accord with the principles of democracy' to achieve the same.' This was the opinion of Sombat Thamrongthanyawong when he argued that the prob-lem with vote buying was that it allowed politicians to seize absolute power and use it to 'retrieve their investment', while the 'weak checks and balances system' made it impossible to solve this problem through normal constitu-tional mechanisms.[83] It was therefore inevitable for the middle class to turn to 'Article 7 of the 1997 Constitution' or 'judicialisation' to unshackle Thai politics from the political 'impasse'. The key anti-Thaksin regime scholar who frequently reiterated the problem of 'an impasse in Thai politics' was Chai-Anan Samudavanija. He argued that 'Thai politics is faced with an im-passe … the crucial problem is the lack of confidence in the prime minister, the parliamentary system and the Election Commission of Thailand … it is not surprising that protestors have hoped to rely on the king's *phrabarami* and on the judicial system'.[84] Nine days prior to the 19 September 2006 coup d'état he wrote, 'in the monitoring and regulating of politicians we still have the justice courts as our last resort'.[85] This statement was consistent

82 Sombat Thamrongthanyawong, การเมืองการปกครองไทย: ยุคเผด็จการ-ยุคปฏิรูป [Thai Politics and Government: From the Age of Dictatorship to the Age of Political Reform], 4th edition, Bangkok: Sematham, 2011, 893.

83 Sombat Thamrongthanyawong, Prof. Sombat Thamrongthanyawong, Ph.D (6 May 2014). Accessed 16 February 2015, www.facebook.com/Prof.SombatThamrongthanyawong/posts/755740181133642.

84 Chai-Anan Samudavanija, บทบาทของสื่อในการเปลี่ยนแปลงทางการเมือง [Role of the Media in Political Change], 28 May 2006. Accessed 18 February 2015, www.manager.co.th/Daily/ViewNews.aspx?NewsID=9490000069878.

85 Chai-Anan Samudavanija ช่วยกันป้องกันไม่ให้คนชั่วและบ้ามีอำนาจ [Let's Prevent Bad and Mad People from Having Power], 10 September 2006. Accessed 18 February 2015, www.manager.co.th/Daily/ViewNews.aspx?NewsID=9490000114555.

with what he had proposed in June of the same year, noting that because 'the need of the court to step in to deal with political problems, because it is one of the three sovereign powers, confirms that Thai politics is truly faced with an impasse'.[86] Moreover, he argued that the coming election, which was the normal mechanism of a democratic system of government, was not the solution to this impasse because 'there is a lack of confidence that the new election will be clean and fair'.[87]

Chai-Anan Samudavanija strongly emphasised the problem of 'no checking mechanism is possible'. For example, he stated that 'because the government controls both the House of Representatives and the Senate ... the people do not trust that the electoral monitoring processes will be clean and fair'.[88] It was, therefore, essential to turn to 'the last resort'. In some articles, 'the last resort' refers to the court or the judicial system while in some articles it means the monarchy.[89] Thus, it may be said that 'judicialisation', arose from the judiciary taking 'the royal behest upon their heads' (*sai klao sai kramom*) to execute, and this had become the middle class's high hope. Chai-Anan summarised: 'when these politicians cannot be purged by the legislative mechanism and process, we will see an increase in the role of the judiciary'.[90]

3. Ideas and meanings on 'Thai society and culture have their own unique characteristics and should be governed by Democracy with the King as Head of State'. And the notion that 'judicialisation' initiated by His Majesty the King's Royal Address 'is a major alternative for the breaking of a political crisis of a political impasse'.

Evidently the meaning of 'Democracy with the King as Head of State' would go through another period of intense reproduction from 2005 on-

---

86 Chai-Anan Samudavanija, จะเกิดอะไรขึ้นในเดือนกรกฎาคม! [What Will Happen in July?], 4 June 2006. Accessed 18 February 2015, www.manager.co.th/Daily/ViewNews.aspx ?NewsID=9490000073233.

87 Chai-Anan, 'Role of the Media'.

88 Chai-Anan Samudavanija, การเมืองไทยหลังทักษิณ (ออกไปแล้ว) [Thai Politics after Thaksin (has gone)] 23 July 2006. Accessed 18 February 2015, www.manager.co.th/Daily/ ViewNews.aspx?NewsID=9490000094208.

89 Chai-Anan, 'What will Happen in July?'.

90 Chai-Anan Samudavanija, ความชอบธรรมที่มีเงื่อนไข [Conditional Legitimacy], 20 July 2008. Accessed 18 February 2015, www.manager.co.th/Daily/ViewNews.aspx?NewsID= 9510000085133.

wards. For example, Amon Chantharasombun stated that the key problem in Thai politics is corruption and that the constitution needed to be revised to allow the king to play an important role for the reason that the king's power is a pure force that is above politics. His royal conducts have been carried out with his goodwill towards the people and the country. Thus, a good government is possible if it is based on the knowledge and ability of 'a good person' under the king's guidance. This is particularly true when 'the Thai nation' faces a political crisis and has to rely on the king's virtues to establish good government.[91] Chai-Anan Samudavanija addressed this issue in one of his articles as follows: 'Thai politics is unique in that ... leadership requires persons with a high level of *barami* capable of becoming a leader of the masses. It is the monarch who can bring stability, unity and continuity to the country ... in times of serious problems we can rely on his *phrabarami*'.[92]

On many occasions, Chai-Anan Samudavanija chose to turn to the mechanism of submission of a petition to the king. For example, on 6 February 2006, he suggested that 'political reform cannot take place under the present circumstances ... there is only one method ... a petition must be submitted to the king once again to request him to exercise the royal power stipulated in Article 7 of the Constitution ... there must be no election until the constitutional amendment is completed.'[93] On 4 June 2006, Chai-anan Samudavanija stated that 'we have the monarchy institution which is close to the people ... the judiciary system's acceptance and application of His Majesty the King's suggestions to the solving of current political problems is a favourable development as it saves the monarchy from being directly involved in political conflicts himself'.[94] Chai-Anan also expressed his continuing support for judicialisation and stressed that the

---

91 Amon Chantrasombun, พระราชอำนาจกับการปฏิรูปการเมือง" ครั้งที่ 2 [Second Address on 'Royal Power and Political Reform'], held at the main auditorium of Thammasat University, 22 November 2005, reported in *Matichon Daily*, 24 November 2005, 2.

92 Chai-Anan Samudavanija, เปิดการเมืองให้กว้าง [Make Politics More Open], 6 November 2005. Accessed 18 February 2015, www.manager.co.th/Daily/ViewNews.aspx?NewsID=9480000153435.

93 Chai-Anan Samudavanija, การงดใช้รัฐธรรมนูญบางมาตรา [Suspending Certain Articles of the Constitution], 26 February 2006. Accessed 18 February 2015, www.manager.co.th/Daily/ViewNews.aspx?NewsID=9490000026368.

94 Chai-Anan, 'What will happen in July?'

judiciary [sitting in newly independent agencies such as the administrative and constitutional courts] was 'the fourth independent branch of power'.[95]

Thirayut Bunmi lent his opinion and knowledge in support of judicialisation on many occasions. He regularly cited the royal addresses in his writings. For example, '(His Majesty the King) suggested that the court uses its highly respected status to solve crisis and to use its 'highly extensive' powers and duties to solve national crises. This should be considered the most significant of His Majesty the King's ingenuity ... He recommended the use of existing social and cultural dimensions, which are the social and moral capitals embodied in the judiciary, which are the highest in society to solve problems'.[96]

Explanations and solutions offered by academics who champion judicialisation in their fight against the 'Thaksin regime' have been constructed under the influential culture of thinking and meanings that have long existed in the Thai society. They played a pivotal role in the formation of judicialisation in 2006. Nevertheless, the most influential writing in 2005 that paved a solid foundation for the rise of 'judicialisation' is none other than Pramuan Rujanaseri's book, *The Royal Power*. This widely publicised book went through nine printings during its first year of publication and has since been disseminated through numerous websites. It is a detailed compilation of the essence of the Thai political culture under the system of 'Democracy with the King as Head of State'. The book's discussion of the roots of the 'royal power' can be seen to have prepared people for the coming of 'judicialisation'. Older ideas are revived in the book to support the idea of relying on the king's *phrabarami* to solve political crises. The judiciary's roles and duties have also been extensively accentuated in the book. Its dedication page proclaims that 'At present, the Thai people are highly anxious ... most of them know well that in times of a national crisis which is beyond the ability of the government or the legal system to rectify by normal mechanism, their king will always be able to put things right'.[97]

95 Chai-Anan Samudavanija, อำนาจที่สี่ [The Fourth Power], 22 July 2006. Accessed 18 February 2015, www.manager.co.th/Daily/ViewNews.aspx?NewsID=9550000089909. Editors' note: Chai-Anan notes that the Thai judiciary enjoys a high degree of freedom, but his designation of a 'fourth power', joining the executive, the legislature and the judiciary, is specifically of the newly independent agencies that came into being under the 1997 constitution.

96 Thirayut Bunmi, อัดทักษิณ' นำการเมืองแบบบ้าอำนาจ [Attacking Thaksin, a Power Hungry Politician], 2 August 2006. Accessed 18 February 2015, www.parliament.go.th/news/news_detail.php?prid=22739.

97 Pramuan Rujanaseri, พระราชอำนาจ [The Royal Power], 5th edition, Bangkok: No publisher.

The book also recorded His Majesty the King's words about the book that were relayed to Pramuan Rujanaseri through Piya Malakul Na Ayutthaya: '[W]e have read it. We truly like it. It is well-written and accurate.'[98]

On the roles of the judiciary, Pramuan Rujanaseri emphasised that they must conduct themselves in accordance with 'the oath that they have pledged to the king', which means:

> All courts from the Constitutional Court to the Court of Justice and the Administrative Court ... need to keep in mind the oath that they have given to the king and the name of the king that they represent, and must not pass their judgment on the basis of the law alone ... As the head of the state who has relegated his judicial power to all of you to act on his behalf in the status of a righteous king ... whose noble ideas have always been for the good of his country and his people ... This is what all the judiciary must adopt as the principles for their judgment of any case.[99]

Amidst the abovementioned culture of thinking 'judicialisation' was initiated and perceived by the middle class as being legitimate and a last resort or refuge in a time of political crisis, especially when there was a growing and influential call for the king to maintain a status 'above politics' and when there was widening criticism of the monarchy.

CLASHES OF DIFFERENT CULTURES
OF IDEAS AND MEANINGS

After the emergence of the 'judicialisation' movement, the King Prajadhipok's Institute conducted an opinion survey and found people's trust in the judiciary had significantly decreased since 2006. Another survey in 2009 found that 'although people's trust in the judiciary had slightly increased after a dip to its lowest point in 2008, ... the level of trust remains very low compared to the 2003–04 levels'.[100] The survey findings reflected that a large number of people still do not accept the 'judicialisation' movement. 'The United Front for Democracy Against Dictatorship (UDD)' gave a special meaning to 'judicialisation' as a 'double standard' as it has come into existence as a means to protect and preserve the power of the elite bureaucratic and military establishment (*ammart*) who have tried in every possible way to obstruct

---

98 *Ibid.*
99 *Ibid.,* 149–50.
100 Patama, 'The Thai Judiciary'.

and reject the principle that sovereign power belongs to the people. These new ideas have been received and believed by the [provincial] lower middle class as a consequence of a new culture of thinking among this group.

Up to now, the Thai middle class's political culture is still closely associated with the mainstream meanings of the 'Thai nation' and 'Thainess' or the 'national culture'.[101]The anti-Thaksin regime movement has led to an energetic reproduction of these original ideas that resulted in a culture of thinking that is potent and more extreme. The existing culture of knowledge has also familiarised the middle class with the framework of 'Thainess' and the explanation of problems from the perspective of morality. The middle class shows no inclination to follow new developments that may equip them with new knowledge to better understand the diversity and complexity of the Thai society. They do not always follow recent changes in the livelihood and outlook of the rural 'villagers'. This makes the middle class more susceptible to the explanations and meanings constructed by the anti-Thaksin regime academics and to accept them without critical thinking (which is not much different from the provincial lower middle class who similarly uncritically accepts the explanations and meanings constructed by the UDD leaders). Since the middle class does not have sufficient understanding of the legal culture of the Thai judiciary system, they fail to consider the consequences of the judiciary's involvement in the exercising of political power and, therefore, give their full support to the 'judicialisation' movement.

CONCLUSION

The 'judicialisation' process was enabled by the accumulated culture of thinking regarding Thai politics and government. Since the middle class lacks the proper mechanism to challenge and negotiate with military leaders or politicians who have a monopoly on the power of the state, they want to have 'good persons' in authority and hope to rely on their 'virtue' to control the exercise of power by dictatorial leaders. This is influenced by the notion of 'having a good person as a ruler'. Whenever a ruler violates virtue, they will forfeit their legitimacy. This will lead to the middle class pressuring immoral leaders to relinquish their political power or political posts, based on depending on the power of the idea of Democracy with

---

101 See Saichon, *10 Siamese Intellectuals vols. 1 and 2*

the King as Head of State. Such movements have rested on the foundation of the ideologies of *rachaprachasamasai* (king–people mutuality) and 'royalist paternalism'.[102] Thai political leaders are expected to be righteous and, importantly, to be loyal to the monarch. They must accept the king's advice and 'bear these upon their head' when taking action, while the people can always rely on the king's *phrabarami* for the resolution of political crises.

By the mid-2000s, Thai politics was more complex leading to concerns that the monarchy has been pulled into direct involvement with political conflicts. Reliance on the political role of the judiciary who are independent from the executive branch and perform their duties on behalf of the king has become the middle class's preferred alternative. To retain the legitimacy of their political roles, the judiciary still need to rely on the king's *phrabarami* in keeping with the Thai tradition of 'Democracy with the King as Head of State'. However, since there have been many significant changes in the current political situations, adjustments to the culture of thinking and meaning is 'an alternative' and 'a means for survival' that the middle class can no longer refuse.

---

102 See Saichon, *History of the Thai Nation and Thai Society.*

Bibliography

(Please note that details for most newspaper articles are available in the footnotes and do not appear here).

Anek Laothamatas 1995. *Song nakara prachathipathai: naew thang patirup kan muang sethakit pua prachathipathai* [Two Cities of Democracy: Directions for Reform in Politics and Economy for Democracy], Bangkok: Matichon.

Anut Arphaphirom. 1972. อุดมการและค่านิยมในสังคมไทยดั้งเดิม [Ideology and Values in Traditional Thai Society] in Chatthip Nartsupha (compiler) อุดมการกับสังคมไทย [Ideology and Thai Society], Bangkok: Social Sciences Association of Thailand.

Appadurai, A. 1996. *Modernity at Large,* Minneapolis: University of Minnesota Press.

Aswapahu [King Vajiravudh]. 1915. ทรัพยศาสตร์ เล่ม 1 ตามความเห็นเอกชน ผู้ได้อ่านหนังสือนั้น [Sappayasart (Vol. 1) According to An Individual Who Has Read It] สมุทรสาร [Samutthasarn] 2, 9 September.

Attachak Sattayanurak. 2014. ประชาธิปไตย คนไทยไม่เท่ากัน [Democracy: Thais are not Equal] Bangkok: Matichon.

Baker, C. 2016. 'The 2014 Thai Coup and Some Roots of Authoritarianism', *Journal of Contemporary Asia,* 46, 3.

Baradat, L. P. 1979. *Political Ideologies: Their Origins and Impact,* Englewood Cliffs, N.J.: Prentice-Hall.

Bell, D. A., Brown, D., Jayasuriya, K. and Jones D.M. 1995. *Towards Illiberal Democracy in Pacific Asia,* New York: St Martins.

Bowie K. 1997. *Rituals of National Loyalty: An Anthropology of the State and the Village Scout Movement in Thailand,* New York: Columbia University Press.

Bull, H. 1977. *The Anarchical Society: A Study of Order in World Politics,* New York: Columbia University Press.

Chai-Anan Samudavanija. 1973. อุดมการณ์ทางการเมือง [Political Ideology], Bangkok: Kled Thai Press.

Chai-Anan Samudavanija. 1974. 14 ตุลา: คณะราษฎรกับกบฏบวรเดช [14 October: The People's Party and the Boworadet Rebellion], Bangkok: History Club, the Academic Aksonsat Group, Chulalongkorn University.

Chai-Anan Samudavanija. 1975. ร่างรัฐธรรมนูญของพระปกเกล้าฯ [Drafts of King Rama VII's Constitution] Mimeographed document.

Chai-Anan Samudavanija. 1977. ประชาธิปไตยสังคมนิยมคอมมิวนิสต์กับการเมือง ไทย [Democracy, Socialism, Communism, and Thai Politics], Bangkok: Rongphim piganet, 2nd ed.

Chai-Anan Samudavanija. 1980. การเมือง การเปลี่ยนแปลงทางการเมืองไทย 2411–2475 [Politics and Thai Political Change 1868–1932], Bangkok: Bannakit.

Chai-Anan Samudavanija. 1986. ปัญหาอุดมการณ์ทางการเมือง [Problems in Political Ideologies], inในปัญหาทางการเมืองไทยปัจจุบัน, เอกสารการสอน ชุดวิชาสาขาวิชารัฐศาสตร์, เล่มที่ 1 หน่วยที่ 2, [Current Problems in Thai Politics, Teaching Materials in Political Science Volume 1, Unit 2], Bangkok, Samnakphim sukhothai thammatirat.

Chai-Anan Samudavanija. 1987. ปัญหาการพัฒนาทางการเมืองไทย, [Problems in Thai Political Development], Bangkok, Chulalongkorn University Press.

Chai-Anan Samudavanija. 1997. 'Old Soldiers Never Die, They Are Just Bypassed: The Military, Bureaucracy and Globalisation', in Kevin Hewison (ed.), *Political Change in Thailand: Democracy and Participation*, London: Routledge.

Chairat Charoensin-olarn. 1995. 'Kanmuang baep mai, khabuankan khloen-wai thang sangkhom rup baep mai, lae wathakam kan phatthana chut mai' [New Politics, New Social Movements and New Alternative Discourses on Development], *Warasan Thammasat*, 21,1.

Chalermkiat Phiu-nuan. 1983. ความคิดทางการเมืองของปรีดีพนมยงค์ [The Political Thought of Pridi Banomyong], Thai Studies Institute.

Chalermkiat Phiu-nuan. 1986. ทางสายกลาง [The Middle Path], in บานไม่รู้ โรยนิตยสารรายเดือน [Baan Mai Ru Roi Monthly Magazine], December.

Chalermkiat Phiu-nuan. 1991. ประชาธิปไตยแบบไทย ความคิดทางการเมือง ของทหารไทย 2519–2529 [Thai-style Democracy: The Political Ideas of the Thai Military] a report submitted to the Thai Studies Institute, Thammasat University.

Chalermkiat Phiu-nuan. 1992. ความคิดทางการเมืองของทหารไทย 2519–2535 [The Political Thought of the Thai Military, 1976–1992], Bangkok: Samnakphim phujatkan, 1992

Chanida Chidbandit, 2007. โครงการอันเนื่องมาจากพระราชดำริ: การสถาปนาพระราชอำนาจนำในพระบาทสมเด็จพระเจ้าอยู่หัว [The Royal-Initiated Projects: Establishment of His Majesty the King's Hegemony], Bangkok: Foundation for the Promotion of Social Sciences and Humanities Textbooks Projects.

Chatthip Nartsupha. 1974. "ความคิดทางเศรษฐกิจของพระยาสุริยานุวัตร [The Economic Ideas of Phraya Suriyanuwat] สังคมศาสตร์ ปริทัศน์ [Social Science Review] 12, 9.

Chuchai Suphawong and Yuwadi Katganglai (eds). 1997. *Pracha sangkhom: tatsuna nak kit nai sangkhom thai* [Civil society: a Thinker's View in Thai society], Bangkok: Matichon.

Chulalongkorn, King. 1970. พระบรมราโชวาทในพระบาทสมเด็จพระจุลจอมเกล้าเจ้าอยู่หัว ทรงพระราชนิพนธ์ เมื่อ พ.ศ. 2428 [The 1885 Royal Guidance of King Chulalongkorn] in พระบรมราโชวาท ในรัชกาลที่ 5 พระราชทานพระเจ้าลูกยาเธอ [King Chulalongkorn's Royal Guidance to His Sons] in the cremation book distributed at the royally-bestowed cremation of Rong Ammart Tho Khun Samaksukhakarn, Bangkok: Rungruengtham Press.

Chulalongkorn, King. 1973. พระบรมราชาธิบายว่าด้วยความสามัคคี [The Royal Explanation on Unity], in ประวัติศาสตร์และการเมือง [History and Politics], Bangkok: Thammasat University Press.

Chulalongkorn, King. 1975. พระราชดำรัสในพระบาทสมเด็จพระจุลจอมเกล้าเจ้าอยู่หัวทรงแถลงพระบรมราชาธิบาย แก้ไขการปกครองแผ่นดิน [The Royal Speeches of King Chulalongkorn on the Explanation of the Administrative Reform], in Chai-Anan Samudavanija and Khattiya Karnasuta (compliers) เอกสารการเมือง-การปกครองไทย พ.ศ. 2417–2477 [Documents on Thai Politics-Administration, 1874–1934], Bangkok: The Textbook Projects, The Social Sciences Association of Thailand.

Connors, M.K. 2003. 'Goodbye to the Security State: Thailand and Ideological Change', *Journal of Contemporary Asia*, 33, 4.

Connors, M.K. 2007. *Democracy and National Identity in Thailand*, Copenhagen: Nordic Institute of Asian Studies Press, (originally published Routledge, 2003).

Connors, M.K. 2008. 'Article of Faith: The Failure of Royal Liberalism in Thailand', *Journal of Contemporary Asia*, 38, 1, 2008.

Connors, M. K. 2009. 'Liberalism, Authoritarianism and the Politics of Decisionism in Thailand', *Pacific Review*, 22, 3.

Connors, M. K. 2011. 'When the Walls Come Crumbling Down: Monarchy and Thai-style Democracy', *Journal of Contemporary Asia*, 41, 4, 2011.

Connors, M.K. forthcoming. 'Towards a History of Conservative Liberalism after the Siamese Revolution: an Ideological Analysis', *Asian Studies Review*.

Cox, R.W. 1995. 'Critical Political Economy' in B Hettne (ed.), *International Political Economy: Understanding Global Disorder*, London: Zed Books.

Damrong Rajanubhab, Prince. 1971. ลักษณะการปกครองประเทศสยาม แต่โบราณ ปาฐกถาที่สามัคคยาจารย์สมาคม 8 ตุลาคม 2470 [The Character of Siamese Administration since Antiquity, a Speech Given to Samakyajan Samakhom October 8, 1927] in อ่านประกอบคำบรรยายวิชาพื้นฐานอารยธรรมไทย [Introductory Lectures on Thai Civilization] Bangkok, Thammasat University Press.

Department of Broadcasting. 1939. ไทยในสมัยรัฐธรรมนูญ: ที่ระลึกในงานฉลองวันชาติและสนธิสัญญา 24 มิถุนายน 2582 [Thailand in the Constitutional Period: In Remembrance for the National Day Celebration and the 24 June 1939 Treaty], Phranakhon: Department of Broadcasting.

Duan Bunnag and Phairot Chaiyanam. 1934. คำอธิบายกฎหมายรัฐธรรมนูญ [Commentary on Constitutional Law], 2 volumes, Phranakhon: Rongphim nithisan.

Ebenstein, W. 1973. *Today's Isms*, Englewood Cliffs, N.J.: Prentice-Hall, 7th ed.

Eiji Murashima. 1988. 'The Origin of Modern Official State Ideology in Thailand', *Journal of Southeast Asian Studies*, 19, 1.

Foucault, M. 1972. *The Archaeology of Knowledge*, translated by A.M. Sheridan Smith, New York: Pantheon/Random House.

Foucault, M. 1980. *Power/Knowledge: Selected Interviews and Other Writings, 1972–1977*, in Colin Gordon (ed.), New York: Pantheon/Random House.

Freeden, M. 1996. *Ideologies and Political Theory: A Conceptual Approach*, Oxford: Oxford University Press.

Galyani Vadhana Krom Luang Naradhiwas Rajanagarindra, Princess. 1987. เจ้านายเล็กๆ – ยุวกษัตริย์: พระราชประวัติพระบาทสมเด็จพระเจ้าอยู่หัวอานันท มหิดลและพระบาทสมเด็จพระเจ้าอยู่หัวภูมิพลอดุลยเดช เมื่อทรงพระเยาว์ 2468–2489 [From Little Princes to Young Kings: The Royal Biography of Their Majesties King Ananda Mahidol and King Bhumibol Adulyadej at Young Ages, 1925–1946,. Bangkok: The Royal Thai Army and the Siam Commercial Bank.

Gamble, A. 1996. 'The Limits of Democracy', in Paul Hirst and Dunil Khilnani (eds), *Reinventing Democracy,* Oxford: Blackwell.

Gray, C. 1986. 'Thailand: The Soteriological State in the 1970s', Ph.D. dissertation, University of Chicago.

Gray, C. 1991. 'Hegemonic Images: Language and Silence in the Royal Thai Polity', *Man* (n.s.) 26, 1.

Handley, P.M. 2006. *The King Never Smiles: a Biography of Thailand's Bhumibol Adulyadej,* New Haven: Yale University Press.

Hewison, K. 1997. 'The Monarchy and Democratization', in K. Hewison (ed.), *Political Change in Thailand: Democracy and Participation,* London: Routledge.

Interim National Executive. 1951. คำแถลงการณ์ฉบับที่ 1 ของคณะบริหาร ประเทศชั่วคราว ลงวันที่ 29 พฤศจิกายน 2494 [Declaration 1 of the Interim National Executive 29 November 1951].

Ivarsson, S. and Isager L. (eds). 2010. *Saying the Unsayable: Monarchy and Democracy in Thailand,* Copenhagen: NIAS Press.

Jackson, P. A. 1993. 'Re-interpreting the Traiphuum Phra Ruang: Political Functions of Buddhist Symbolism in Contemporary Thailand', in T. Ling (ed.) *Buddhist Trends in Southeast Asia,* Singapore: ISEAS.

Jackson, P. A. 2009. 'Markets, Media, Magic: Thailand's Monarch as a Virtual Deity', *Inter-Asia Cultural Studies,* 10, 3.

Jakraphop Penkair. 2009. รัฐบาลภายในรัฐบาล [Government within a Government], ไทยเรดนิวส์ [Thai Red News], September 18–24.

Jayasuriya, K. 1998. 'Authoritarian Liberalism, Governance and the Emergence of the Regulatory State in Post-Crisis East Asia', paper for the conference on 'From Miracle to Meltdown: The End of Asian Capitalism?', Murdoch University, 20–22 August.

Jayasuriya, K. 1998. 'Rule of Law and Capitalism in East Asia', *Pacific Review*, 9, 3.

Jory, P. 2016. *Thailand's Theory of Monarchy: The Vessantara Jakata and the Idea of the Perfect Man*, Albany, SUNY Press. E-book edition.

Kamol Somwichian. 1972. อุดมการกับสังคมไทย. [Ideology and Thai Society] in Chatthip Nartsupha (compiler) อุดมการกับสังคมไทย [Ideology and Thai Society], Bangkok: Social Sciences Association of Thailand.

Kanok Wongtrangan. 1984. การเมืองในระบอบประชาธิปไตยไทย [Politics in Thai Democratic System], Bangkok, Research Publication Program, Chulalongkorn University.

Kanokrat Lertchoosakul. 2016. *The Rise of the Octoberists in Contemporary Thailand*, New Haven, CT: Yale Southeast Asia Studies.

Kasian Tejapira. 1991. ประชาธิปไตยของประชาชนต้องเป็นอิสระจากรัฐและทุน [People's Democracy must be Free from the State and Capital] บานไม่รู้โรย [Ban Mairuroei], 4, 8 September.

Kasian Tejapira. 2008. รัฐประหาร 19 กันยายน พ.ศ. 2549 กับการเมืองไทย [The 19 September 2006 Coup d'état and Thai Politics] รัฐศาสตร์สาร [Ratthasatsan], 29, 3.

Kasian Tejapira. 2009. 'The Misbehaving Jeks: The Evolving Regime of Thainess and Sino-Thai Challenges', *Asian Ethnicity*, 10, 3.

Kasian Tejapira. 2011. ระบอบประชาธิปไตยอันมีพระมหากษัตริย์ทรงเป็นประมุข [Democracy with the King as Head of State], in ฟ้าเดียวกัน [Same Sky] 9, 1.

Kasian Tejapira. 2016. 'The Irony of Democratization and the Decline of Royal Hegemony in Thailand', *Southeast Asian Studies*, 5.

Kasian Tejapira. 2018. รัฐพันลึก, the First Chinese Coup และ the Bhumibol Consensus' [The Deep State, the First Chinese Coup และ the Bhumibol Consensus], *Prachatai*, 4 July prachatai.com/journal/2018/07/77684.

Kengkij Kitirianglarp and Hewison, K. 2009. 'Social Movements and Political Opposition in Contemporary Thailand', *The Pacific Review*, 22, 4.

Kittisak Sujittarom. 2014. ทัศนะของสื่อหนังสือพิมพ์และปัญญาชนสาธารณะที่มีต่อสถานะและบทบาทของสถาบันกษัตริย์ ระหว่าง พ.ศ. 2535–2540 [The Views of Newspapers and Public Intellectuals on the Status and Role of the Monarchy between 1992 and 1997] M.A. thesis in History, Faculty of Liberal Arts, Thammasat University.

Kramol Thongthammachart and Sippanon Ketutat. 1983. อุดมการณ์ของ ชาติแนวความคิดและแนวทางการดำเนินงาน [National Ideology, Concepts and Operationalization]', in Office of the Prime Minister อุดมการณ์ของ ชาติ [National Ideology], Bangkok: Office of the Prime Minister.

Kramol Thongthammachart. 1972. อุดมการกับสังคมไทยในปัจจุบัน [Ideology and Contemporary Thai Society] in Chatthip Nartsupha (compiler) อุดมการกับสังคมไทย [Ideology and Thai Society], Bangkok: Social Sciences Association of Thailand.

Kramol Thongthammachart. 1981. วิวัฒนาการของระบอบการเองไทย [The Evolution of the Thai Constitutional System], Bangkok: Bannakit.

Kramol Thongthammachart. 1983. อุดมการณ์ของชาติกับการพัฒนาชาติไทย [National Ideology and the Development of the Thai Nation], in Office of the Prime Minister อุดมการณ์ของชาติ [National Ideology], Bangkok: Office of the Prime Minister.

Kramol Thongthammachart. 1986. ปัญหาการใช้รัฐธรรมนูญ [Problems in Applying the Constitution], in ในปัญหาทางการเมืองไทยปัจจุบัน, เอกสาร การสอนชุดวิชาสาขาวิชารัฐศาสตร์, เล่มที่ 1 หน่วยที่ 4, [Current Problems in Thai Politics, Teaching Materials in Political Science Volume 1, Unit 4], Bangkok, Samnakphim sukhothai thammatirat.

Krikkiat Phipatseritham. 1987. การเปลี่ยนแปลงทางเศรษฐกิจกับปัญหาสิทธิ มนุษยชนในประเทศไทย [Economic Changes and Human Rights Issues in Thailand], Bangkok: Thai Studies Institute, Thammasat University; and Chalermkiat Phiu-nuan, ปรัชญาสิทธิมนุษยชนและพันธกรณีในสังคม ไทย [Philosophy of Human Rights and Obligation in Thai Society], Bangkok: Religion For Society Coordinating Group.

Kritpatchara Somanawat. 2014. อำนาจแห่ง อัตลักษณ์' ตุลาการ [Power of the Judiciary's Identity] นิติสังคมศาสตร์ [Nithisangkhomsat], 7, 1.

Kromamun Bidayalabh Brdihyakorn. 1974. อัตชีวประวัติ [Autobiography] Bangkok: Rongphim tiranasan.

Krommun Naradhip Bongsprabandh. 1971. วิทยา สารานุกรม [Encyclopaedia] Phranakhon: Phrae phittaya.

Kukrit Pramoj, M.R. 2005. การปรับตัวของระบบราชการไทยหลังการเปลี่ยนแปลง การปกครอง [Adjustment of the Thai Bureaucracy after the Change of Government] in Woradej Chandrason and Wanit Songprathum (eds), ระบบราชการไทย: สภาพปัญหาและข้อเสนอจากฝ่ายการเมือง ข้าราชการ นัก

วิชาการ และธุรกิจเอกชน [Thai Bureaucracy: Problems and Proposals from the Political, Bureaucratic, Academic and Private Sectors], Bangkok: Faculty of Public Administration, NIDA.

Kulab Saipradit. 1944. ความหมายของประชาธิปไตย [The Meaning of Democracy], นิติสาส์น [Nithiisan] June–September.

Kulab Saipradit. 2005. เสถียรภาพทางการเมือง [Political Stability], in Suchat Sawatsri (ed.), มนุษย์ไม่ได้กินแกลบ [Humans are not Stupid], Bangkok: The organizing committee of the centennial of Sriburapa.

Likhit Dhiravegin. 1987. วิวัฒนาการการเมืองการปกครองไทย [Evolution of the Thai Political and Administrative System] Bangkok: Chulalongkorn University.

Luang Prajert Aksonlak. 1934. กฎหมายรัฐธรรมนูญ [Constitutional Law] Phranakhon: Thammasat and Politics University Press.

Macdonell, D. 1986. *Theories of Discourse: An Introduction,* Oxford: Basil Blackwell.

Malaengwi [Seni Pramoj]. 1947. เบื้องหลังประวัติศาสตร์ [History Behind the Scene] Phranakhon: Rongphim sahauppakorn.

Malini Khumsupha. 2005. อนุสาวรีย์ประชาธิปไตยกับความหมายที่มองไม่เห็น (The Democracy Monument and Hidden Meanings], Bangkok: Samnakphim wiphasa.

McCargo, D. 2005. 'Network Monarchy and Legitimacy Crises in Thailand', *The Pacific Review,* 18, 4.

McCargo, D. 2019. *Fighting for Virtue: Justice and Politics in Thailand,* Ithaca and London: Cornell University Press.

McCargo, D. and Ukrist Pathmanand. 2004. *The Thaksinization of Thailand,* Copenhagen: NIAS Press, 2004.

Mérieau, E. 2016. 'Thailand's Deep State: Royal Power and the Constitutional Court (1997–2015)', *Journal of Contemporary Asia,* 46, 3.

Ministry of Education. 1984. แนวพระราชดำริเก้ารัชกาล [The Royal Ideas of Nine Monarchs] Bangkok: Academic Department, Ministry of Education.

Morell D., and Chai-Anan Samudavanija. 1981. *Political Conflict in Thailand, Reform, Reaction, Revolution,* Cambridge: Oelgeschlager, Gunn and Hain.

Nakharin Mektrairat and Thanet Arpornsuwan. 1987. สเน่ห์ จามริก กับสังคม ราชูปถัมภ์ [Saneh Chamarik and the Royal Patronage Society], วารสาร ธรรมศาสตร์ [Thammasat Journal], 15, 4.

Nakharin Mektrairat. 2003. ความคิดความอำนาจการเมืองในการปฏิวัติสยาม 2475 [Ideas, Knowledge and Political Power in the Siamese Revolution of 1932], Bangkok: Fa Diaokan.

Nakharin Mektrairat. 2006. พระผู้ทรงปกเกล้าฯ ประชาธิปไตย: 60 ปี สิริราช สมบัติกับการเมืองการปกครองไทย [The Protector of Democracy: 60 Years on the Throne and Thai Politics], Bangkok: Thammasat University Press.

Nakharin Mektrairat. 2010. การปฏิวัติสยาม 2475 [The 1932 Revolution in Siam], Bangkok: Fa Diaokan.

Naruemon Teerawat. 1982. พระราชดำริทางการเมืองของพระบาทสมเด็จ พระจอมเกล้าเจ้าอยู่หัว [The Political Ideas of King Mongkut], M.A. thesis in History, Department of History, Graduate School, Chulalongkorn University.

Naruemon Thabchumpon. 2016. 'Contending Political Networks: A Study of the "Yellow Shirts" and "Red Shirts" in Thailand's Politics', Southeast Asian Studies, 5, 1.

Nidhi Eoseewong. 1991. ป๋วย อึ๊งภากรณ์: สิทธิมนุษยชนแบบไทย [Puey Ungphakorn: Thai-style Human Rights] จดหมายข่าวสังคมศาสตร์ [Social Sciences Newsletter] February-April.

Nidhi Eoseewong. 1992. มโนธรรมของชนชั้นนำทางอำนาจ [The Power Elite's Conscience], ผู้จัดการรายวัน [Manager Daily], 27 November.

Nidhi Eoseewong. 1995. รัฐธรรมนูญฉบับวัฒนธรรมไทย. The Thai Cultural Constitution] in Nidhi Eoseewong, ชาติไทย, เมืองไทย, แบบเรียนและ อนุสาวรีย์ [Thai Nation, Thailand, School Texts, and Monuments] Bang-kok: Matichon.

Nidhi Eoseewong. 2011. วัฒนธรรมทางการเมืองไทย, [Thai Political Culture], วารสารสถาบันวัฒนธรรมและศิลปะ [Culture and Art Institute Journal, Srinakharinwirot University], 12, 2.

Pasuk Phongpaichit. 1999. Civilising the State: state, civil society and politics in Thailand, Amsterdam: Centre for Asian Studies, Wertheim Memorial Lecture, Amsterdam.

Pasuk Phongpaichit and Baker, C. (eds). 2016. Unequal Thailand Aspects of Income, Wealth and Power, Singapore: NUS press, 2016.

Pasuk Phongpaichit and Baker, C. 1996. *Thailand, Economy and Politics,* Oxford: Oxford University Press.

Pasuk Phongpaichit and Baker, C. 1998. *Thailand's Boom and Bust,* Chiang Mai: Silkworm Books.

Pasuk Phongpaichit and Baker, C. 2009. *Thaksin,* 2nd ed. Chiang Mai: Silkworm. Books.

Pasuk Phongpaichit and Sungsidh Piriyarangsan. 1996. *Corruption and Democracy in Thailand,* Chiang Mai: Silkworm Books.

Pinkaew Laungaramsri. 2016. 'Mass Surveillance and the Militarization of Cyberspace in Post-coup Thailand', *ASEAS – Austrian Journal of South-East Asian Studies,* 9, 2.

Pitaya Wongkun. 1998. 'Thit thang khabuankan prachachon miti mai: naew santitham lae sang khwam mankhong haeng chiwit' [The Direction of New People's Movements: Peace and Building Life Security], in *Prachaphiwat: botrian 25 pi 14 tula* [People's Revolution: Lessons from 25 Years of 14 October], Bangkok: Withithat, Globalisation Series 7.

Polanyi, K. 1957. *The Great Transformation,* Boston: Beacon.

Pramuan Rujanaseri. 2004. การใช้อำนาจเป็นธรรมชาติของมนุษย์ [The Use of Power is Human Nature], Bangkok: Munithi phathana phalang phaendin.

Pramuan Rujanaseri. 2005. พระราชอำนาจ [Royal Powers], Bangkok: Sumet rujanaseri.

Pranot Nanthiyakul (ed.). 1983. จิตวิทยาความมั่นคง [Security Psychology], Bangkok: Institute of Security Psychology.

Praphat Pintobtaeng. 1998. *Kan muang bon thong thanon: 99 wan samatcha khon jon* [Politics on the Street: 99 days of the Assembly of the Poor], Bangkok: Krirk University.

Prasert Pathamasukon (complier). 1974. รัฐสภาไทยในรอบสี่สิบสองปี (2475–2517) [Thai Parliament over Forty-two Years (1932–1974)], Bangkok: Chor. Chumnum Chang.

Prasong Soonsiri, Sqn. Ldr. 1985. การเสริมสร้างเอกลักษณ์ของชาติกับการพัฒนาชาติไทย [Promoting National Identity and the Development of the Thai Nation], in รายงานการสัมมนาเรื่องเอกลักษณ์ของชาติกับการพัฒนาชาติไทย [Report on Seminar on National Identity and the Development of the Thai Nation], Bangkok: National Ideology Subcommittee of National Identity Committee, the Secretariat of Prime Minister.

Preecha Uitrakun and Kanok Tosurat. 1987. *Chaobon: sangkhom lae watthanatham* [Chao Bon: Society and Culture], Bangkok: Social Science Association of Thailand.

Prem Tinsulanonda, General. 1985. ประมวลสุนทรพจน์ ฯพณฯ พลเอกเปรม ติณสูลานนท์นายกรัฐมนตรีพุทธศักราช [Collected Speeches: His Excellency, Prime Minister General. Prem Tinsulanonda,1985], Bangkok: Rongphim aksonthai.

Pridi Banomyong [Pridi Banomyong and Thai Society], Bangkok: Thammasat University Press, 1983, 391.

Pridi Banomyong. 1972. บางเรื่องเกี่ยวกับการก่อตั้งคณะราษฎรและระบบ ประชาธิปไตยไทย [Certain Issues Related to the Founding of the People's Party and Democracy] Bangkok: Rongphim nitiwet.

Pridi Banomyong. 1975. รวบรวมบทความบางเรื่องของนายปรีดี พนมยงค์ เกี่ยวกับระบอบประชาธิปไตยไทยและการร่างรัฐธรรมนูญ [A Collection of Miscellaneous Articles on Democracy and Constitutional Drafting by Pridi Banomyong], Bangkok: Santitham.

Pridi Banomyong. 1983. ประชุมกฎหมายมหาชนและเอกชน [Compilation of Public and Private Law], Bangkok: Thammasat University, 1983 [1931], 150.

Prince Dhani Nivat. 1954, 'The Old Siamese Concept of the Monarchy', in *Selected Articles from the Siamese Society Journal, 1929–53,* Bangkok: Siam Society.

Prudhisan Jumbala and Maneerat Mitprasat. 1997. 'Non-Governmental Development Organisations: Empowerment and Environment' in Kevin Hewison (ed.), *Political Change in Thailand: Democracy and Participation,* London: Routledge.

Prudhisan Jumbala. 1998. 'Constitutional Reform Amidst Economic Crisis', in *Southeast Asian Affairs 1998,* Singapore: ISEAS.

Rangsan Thanaphonpan. 2007. จารีตรัฐธรรมนูญไทยกับสันติประชาธรรม การ แสดงปาฐกถาพิเศษป๋วย อึ๊งภากรณ์ 9 มีนาคม 2550 [Special Lecture – the Traditional Thai Constitution and Santiprachatham], Bangkok: Openbooks.

Revolutionary Council. 1958. คณะปฏิวัติ ฉบับที่ 9 ลงวันที่ 20 ตุลาคม 2501 [Announcement 9 of the Revolutionary Council, October 20, 1958].

Revolutionary Council. 1958. ประกาศของคณะปฏิวัติ ฉบับ ที่ 2 ลงวันที่ 20 ตุลาคม 2501 [Announcement 2 of the Revolutionary Council, October 20, 1958].

Revolutionary Council. 1958. ประกาศของคณะปฏิวัติ ฉบับที่ 3 ลงวันที่ 20 ตุลาคม 2501 [Declaration of the Revolutionary Council 3, 20 October 1958].

Revolutionary Council. 1958. ประกาศของคณะปฏิวัติฉบับที่ 10 ลงวันที่ 21 ตุลาคม 2501 [Announcement 10 of the Revolutionary Council, October 21, 1958].

Revolutionary Council. 1971. ประกาศของคณะปฏิวัติ ฉบับที่ 3 ลงวันที่ 17 พฤศจิกายน พ.ศ.2514 [Announcement 3 of the Revolutionary Council 3 17 November 1971].

Reynolds, C. J. 1987. *Thai Radical Discourse: The Real Face of Thai Feudalism Today* Ithaca: Southeast Asia Program, Cornell University, 1987.

Rong Sayamanond. 1977. ประวัติศาสตร์ไทยในระบอบรัฐธรรมนุญ [Thai History in the Constitutional System], Bangkok: Thai Wattana Panich.

Saichon Sattayanurak. 2002. มติมหาชน: ฐานทางความคิดของระบอบประชาธิปไตยในยุคเชื่อผู้นำชาติพ้นภัยสายชล สัตยานุรักษ์), [Public Opinion: The ideational Basis of the Thai Democracy in the Age of 'Believe the Leader, Keep the Nation Safe'in Sirilack Sampatchalit, Siripon Yotkamolsat (eds), คือความภูมิใจ: รวมบทความวิชาการในวาระครบรอบ 60 ปี ศาสตราจารย์ ดร. ฉัตรทิพย์ นาถสุภา เกษียณอายุราชการ [With Pride: Collected Articles to Commemorate Professor Chatthip Nartsupa's Retirement], Bangkok: Sarngsan.

Saichon Sattayanurak. 2007. คึกฤทธิ์กับประดิษฐกรรม 'ความเป็นไทย' เล่ม 2 [Kukrit and the Invention of 'Thainess' Vol. 2], Bangkok: Matichon.

Saichon Sattayanurak. 2014. 10 ปัญญาชนสยาม เล่ม 1 ปัญญาชนแห่งรัฐสมบูรณาญาสิทธิราชย์ [10 Siamese Intellectuals Volume I: The Absolute Monarchy Era], Bangkok: Openbook Press.

Saichon Sattayanurak. 2014. 10 ปัญญาชนสยาม เล่ม 2 ปัญญาชนหลังการปฏิวัติ 2475 [10 Siamese Intellectuals Volume II: After the 1932 Revolution], Bangkok: Openbook Press.

Saichon Sattayanurak. 2016. มรดกทางประวัติศาสตร์และการบังเกิด"ตุลาการภิวัฒน์"ในรัฐไทย, [Historical Legacy and the Emergence of Judicialisation in the Thai State] วารสารนิติสังคมศาสตร์มหาวิทยาลัยเชียงใหม่, [Journal of Law and Social Sciences Chiang Mai University, 9, 1, 2016 pp. 8–58.

Saiyut Kerdpol, General. 1986. ปัญหาความมั่นคงแห่งชาติ [Problems in National Security], in ปัญหาการเมืองไทยปัจจุบัน, เอกสารการสอนชุดวิชาสาขาวิชารัฐศาสตร์, เล่มที่ 3 หน่วยที่ 12 [Current Problems in Thai Politics, Teaching Materials in Political Science Volume 3, Unit 12], Bangkok, Samnakphim sukhothai thammatirat.

Saneh Chamarik. 1980. พุทธศาสนากับสิทธิมนุษยชน [Buddhism and Human Rights], in รวมบทความก้าวต่อไปของสังคมไทย [Collected Articles: The Next Steps for Thai Society], Bangkok: Political Science Student Committee, Thammasat University.

Saneh Chamarik. 1986. การเมืองไทยกับพัฒนาการรัฐธรรมนูญ [Thai Politics and Development of the Constitution] Bangkok: Institute of Thai Studies, Thammasat University and the Foundation for the Promotion of Social Sciences and Humanities Textbooks Projects.

Saneh Chamarik. 1989. การเมืองไทยกับพัฒนาการรัฐธรรมนูญ [Thai Politics and Development of the Constitution], Bangkok: Thai Studies Institute.

Sarit Thanarat, Field Marshal. 1964. คำกล่าวเปิดการประชุมปลัดจังหวัดและนายอำเภอทั่วราชอาณาจักร 27 เมษายน 2502 [Opening Remarks for the National Conference of Deputy Governors and District Chiefs on April 27, 1959], in ประมวลสุนทพจน์ของจอมพลสฤษดิ์ ธ นะรัชต์, เล่มที่ 1 พ.ศ. 2502–2504 [Collected Addresses of Field Marshal Sarit Thanarat Volume 1, 1959–1961], published by the Cabinet Council on the occasion of Field Marshal Sarit's funeral ceremony on March 17, 1964.

Sarit Thanarat, Field Marshal. 1964. ประมวลสุนทรพจน์ของจอมพลสฤษดิ์ ธนะรัชต์: พ.ศ. 2502–2504 Collection of Field Marshal Sarit Thanarat's Speeches 1959–1961], Phranakhon: Office of the Prime Minister.

Sarun Krittikarn. 2010. 'Entertainment Nationalism: The Royal Gaze and the Gaze of the Royals', in S. Ivarsson and L. Isager (eds), *Saying the Unsayable: Monarchy and Democracy in Thailand,* Copenhagen: NIAS Press.

Sawaeng Senanarong. 1977. รวมคำบรรยายของพลเอกแสวง เสนาณรงค์, [A Collection of General Sawaeng Senanarong's Lectures] in อนุสรณ์งานพระราชทานเพลิงศพพลเอกแสวง เสนาณรงค์ [Cremation Volume of General Sawaeng Senanarong], Bangkok: The Royal Thai Survey Department Press.

Schultz, E.B. 1966. *Democracy,* New York: Barron's Educational Series.

Seksan Prasertkul. 1974. เอียงข้างประชาชน [Leaning toward the People] Bangkok: Chumrom nangsue saengchan.

Sitthithan Rakprathet. 1976. สู่สังคมใหม่ [Toward a New Society] Bangkok: Amnuayrak kanphim.

Sittithep Eaksittipong. 2015. ลูกจีนรักชาติ: สำนึกประวัติศาสตร์และนิยาม ประชาธิปไตย [Patriotic 'lukjin': Historical Awareness and Definitions of Democracy], วารสารมนุษยศาสตร์ [Manusayasat Journal], 16, 2.

Sittithep Eaksittipong. 2017. 'From Chinese "in" to Chinese "of" Thailand: The Politics of Knowledge Production during the Cold War', *Rian Thai: International Journal of Thai Studies,* 10,1.

Smith, E. 2011. 'Old and Protected? On the "Supra-Constitutional" Clause in the Constitution of Norway', *Israel Law Review,* 44, 3.

Sombat Chantornvong. 1990. ภาษาทางการเมือง [Political Language], Bangkok: Institute of Thai Studies, Thammasat University.

Sombat Chantornvong. 1991. ภาษาทางการเมือง: พัฒนาการของแนวอธิบาย การเมือง และศัพท์การเมืองในงานเขียนประเภทสารคดีทางการเมืองของไทย พ.ศ. 2475–2525 [Political Language: Development of Political Explanations and Political Vocabulary in Thai Political Documentary Writings 1932–1982], Mimeographed document.

Somchai Preechasilpakul and Team. 2014 เสรีภาพในการชุมนุมโดยสงบและปราศจาก อาวุธตามบทบัญญัติของกฎหมาย [Peaceful Assembly According to Legislated Law], Research supported by the Secretariat of the Constitutional Court.

Somchai Preechasilpakul. 2006. อภิรัฐธรรมนูญไทย [The Supra-constitution of Thailand]. Bangkok: Pridi Banomyong Institute.

Somchai Preechasilpakul. 2017. ข้อถกเถียงว่าด้วยสถาบันพระมหากษัตริย์ในองค์กร จัดทำรัฐธรรมนูญของไทยตั้งแต่ พ.ศ. 2475–2550 [Debates on the Monarchy in Thai Constitution Making Organs from 1932–2007]. Chiang Mai: Keant Press.

Somchai Rakwichit and General Saiyut Kerdpol. 1976. ยุทธศาสตร์เพื่อความ อยู่รอดของชาติ [Strategies for National Survival] Bangkok: Pitakpracha.

Somkiat Wanthana. 1982. รัฐสมบูรณาญาสิทธิราชย์สยาม 2435–2475, [The Siamese Absolute Monarchy 1892–1932], Bangkok: Social Sciences Association of Thailand.

Somkiat Wathana. 1993. ชนชั้นนำกับประชาธิปไตยไทย [Elites and Thai Democracy], in Suthachai Yimprasert (ed.), 60 ปี ประชาธิปไตยไทย [Sixty Years of Democracy], Bangkok: Creative Publishing.

Song Soon Radio Station Broadcasting. 1965. ประชาธิปไตยแบบไทยและข้อคิดเกี่ยวกับรัฐธรรมนูญ [Thai-style Democracy and Opinions on the Constitution], Bangkok: Samnakphim chokchaitewet.

Srisupon Chuangsakul. 1987. ความเปลี่ยนแปลงของคณะสงฆ์: ศึกษากรณีธรรมยุติกนิกาย พ.ศ. 2368 – พ.ศ. 2464 [Changes in the Sangha: A Case Study of Dhammayuttika Nikaya, B.E. 1825–1921], M.A. thesis in History, Graduate School, Chulalongkorn University.

Strange, S. 1996. *The Retreat of the State: The Diffusion of Power in the World Economy*, Cambridge: Cambridge University Press.

Streckfuss, D. 2011. *Truth on Trial in Thailand: Defamation, Treason, and Lèse-majesté*, New York: Routledge.

Sulak Sivaraksa 1986. ความคิดที่ขัดขวางและส่งเสริมประชาธิปไตยของไทย [Ideas that Obstruct and Ideas that Promote Thai Democracy] Bangkok: Aksornsarn.

Sumin Chuthangkon. 1986. การกล่อมเกลาทางการเมือง โดยใช้แบบเรียนหลวงเป็นสื่อในสมัยรัชกาลที่ 5 [Political Socialisation through Royal Textbooks in the Reign of King Rama V], M.A. thesis in Political Science, Department of Administration, Chulalongkorn University.

Surichai Wun'Gao. 1985. 'Non-Governmental Development Movement in Thailand', in *Transnationalisation, the State and the People: The Case of Thailand*, Tokyo: United Nations University.

Surin Pitsuwan. 1980. 'The Next Step for Thailand Must be a Step into a New Direction', in ก้าวต่อไปของสังคมไทย: รวมบทความ [The Next Steps of Thai Society: Collected Articles], Bangkok: Student Committee, Faculty of Political Science, Thammasat University.

Suwanna Wongwaisayawan. 1987. บุญกับอำนาจ: ไตรลักษณ์กับลักษณะไทย [Merit and Power: Trilaksana and the Characteristics of the Thai], in Sombat Chantornvong and Chaiwat Satha-anand (eds) ในอยู่เมืองไทย รวมบทความทางสังคมการเมืองเพื่อเป็นเกียรติแด่ศาสตราจารย์เสน่ห์จามริกในโอกาสอายุครบ 60 ปี [Living in Thailand: A Collection of Socio-political essays in Commemoration of Professor Saneh Chamarik's 60th Birthday], Bangkok, Thammasat University Press.

231

Tamada, Y. 1991. '*Itthiphon* and *Amnat*: an Informal Aspect of Thai Politics' in *Southeast Asian Studies*, 28, 4.

Tamada, Y. 2000. อิทธิพล และ อำนาจ การเมืองไทยเต้านที่ไม่เป็นทางการ ['Influence' and 'Power': The Informal Dimension of Thai Politics] in Amara Phongsapich and Preecha Kuwinpant (eds) ระบบอุปถัมภ์ [The Patronage System], Bangkok: Chulalongkorn University Press.

Thaemsuk Numnonda. 1978. รวมปาฐกถา [Lectures 1977–1978], Bangkok, Social Sciences Association of Thailand.

Thai NGO Support Project. 1995. *Thai NGOs: The Continuing Struggle for Democracy*, Bangkok.

Thak Chaloemtiarana. 1983. การเมืองระบบพ่อขุนอุปถัมภ์แบบเผด็จการ [The Politics of Despotic Paternalism], translated by Phanni Chatrapollarak and M.R. Prakaithong Sirisuk, Bangkok: Thammasat University.

Thanaphol Ewsakul. 2006. เสาหลักทางจริยธรรมชื่อเปรม [The Pillar of Ethics Called Prem], ฟ้าเดียวกัน [Same Sky] 4, 1.

Thanet Arpornsuwan. 2006. กำเนิดการเมืองและความยุติธรรม [The Birth of Politics and Justice], in ไพร่กระฎุมพีแห่งกรุงรัตนโกสินทร์ [The Dependent Bourgeoisie of Rattanakosin], Bangkok: Matichon.

Thanet Wongyannawa. 1985. อ่านงานฟูโก้ [Reading the Work of Foucault], วารสารธรรมศาสตร์ [Thammasat Journal], 14, 3.

Thanin Kraivichien. 1977. ระบอบประชาธิปไตย [Democracy], Bangkok: Ministry of Education, 4th ed.

Thirayut Bunmi. 1987. ทางสองแพร่งของประชาธิปไตยไทยในทัศนะสังคมวิทยาการเมือง [Thai Democracy at the Crossroads: a Politico-sociological Perspective), วารสารสังคมศาสตร์ [Social Science Review], 24, 1.

Thirayuth Boonmee. 1993. *Jut plian haeng yuk samai* [The Turning Point of the Era), Bangkok; Winyuchon.

Thirayuth Boonmee. 1998. *Thammarat haeng chat: yutthasat ku haiyana prathet thai* [National Good Governance: Strategy to Rescue Thailand from Disaster], Bangkok: Saithan.

Thongchai Winichakul. 2008. 'Toppling Democracy', *Journal of Contemporary Asia*, 38, 1.

Thongchai Winichakul. 2016. *Thailand's Hyper-royalism: Its Past Success and Present Predicament*, Singapore: ISEAS, 2016.

Thongthong Chansangsu. 1994. พระราชอำนาจของพระมหากษัตริย์ในทางกฎหมายรัฐธรรมนูญ [Royal Power in Constitutional Law], Bangkok: SC Print and Pack Co., Ltd.

Tomkins, A. 2003. *Public Law*, Oxford: Oxford University Press.

Ukrist Pathmanand and Connors, M. K. 2019. 'Thailand's Public Secret: Military Wealth and the State', *Journal of Contemporary Asia*, Published online first.

Ukrist Pathmanand. 2001. 'Globalization and Democratic Development in Thailand: The New Path of the Military, Private Sector, and Civil Society', *Contemporary Southeast Asia*, 23,1.

Ünaldi, S. 2014. 'Working Towards the Monarchy and its Discontents: Anti-royal Graffiti in Downtown Bangkok', *Journal of Contemporary Asia*, 44, 3.

Vajiravudh, King. 1963. ปลุกใจเสือป่า [Instilling the Wild Tiger Ethos], Phranakhon: Maha Makutratchawittayalai.

Wanwaithayakorn Worawan, M.C. 1932. ปาฐกถาพิเศษเรื่องสยามพากษ์ [Special Lecture on the Thai Language] วิทยาจารย์ [Withiyajan] 33, 1.

Wisut Phothithaen. 1981. ประชาธิปไตย: แนวความคิดและตัวแบบประเทศประชาธิปไตยในอุดมคติ [Ideal Democracy: Ideas and Models of Democratic Countries], Bangkok: Thammasat University.

Index

bold=extended discussion or key reference; n=footnote